WALKING
NORTHERN
RAILWAYS

VOL.II WEST

Baxenden Bank, near Accrington

WALKING NORTHERN RAILWAYS
VOL.II WEST

Charlie Emett

© Charlie Emett 1989
ISBN 1 85284 006 4

For
My Darling Wife
BET
with all my love

Front Cover:
La-al Ratty at Dalegarth, Eskdale.
Photo: Walt Unsworth

Back Cover:
Old railway arch, Sedbergh.
Photo: Walt Unsworth

CONTENTS

The Country Code

Guard against all risk of fire
Fasten all gates
Keep dogs under proper control
Keep to the paths across farmland
Avoid damaging fences, hedges and walls
Leave no litter, take it home
Safeguard water supplies
Protect wildlife, plants and trees
Go carefully on country roads
Respect the life of the countryside

ACKNOWLEDGEMENTS

A book of this scope would not have been possible without the help of a great number of people and my grateful thanks go to them, all of whom have been unstinting in providing a gread deal of information, much of which I have been able to use in building up this network of walks. As with Vol.I, David Bell, whose maps and photographs grace this book, heads the list.

He joins me in thanking the following people for their help and encouragement because without their help Vol.II might not have been written. Dave Mathias of Staffordshire District Council; Margaret Hughes of Wirral County Park, Thurstaston; Monty Burton, head of the Marple Railway Publishing Venture; St. Helens Metropolitan Borough Council; Sheila Richardson of the Information Centre, Bakewell; Catherine Pearson and Robin Green, Keeper of the Textile Industry, Helmshore; David Isherwood and Deborah Grey of the Rossendale Groundwork Trust; Debbie of the Lancashire Trust for Nature Conservation; Mr. Hyde, Merchandising Director, East Lancashire Railway Preservation Society, Bury; Frank Watson, teacher and railway enthusiast of Accrington; Carl Pollitt of the North West Railway Ramblers; The East Lancashire Preservation Society, Bury; David Tattersall BA.MCD.FRTPI., Lancashire County Planning Officer, Preston; Carol Mitchell, Project Development Manager, The West Cumbria Groundwork Trust; Ann Riddell of the Nature Conservancy Council, Workington; Diana Bagge of the Cumbria Trust for Nature Conservation, Barrow-in-Furness; Steve Barker, West Cumbrian Wildlife Officer, Cleator Moor; all gave their time and specialised knowledge enthusiastically and in so doing lightened my task.

Thanks also, to the helpful staff of the Harris Library, Preston and those at Carlisle, Chester and Darlington.

Thank you, Mrs. Yorke of Formby for making my visit to the Haskayne Railway Cutting Nature Reserve such a memorable one.

The verse from the evocative poem *This Time Remembered* is quoted with the kind permission of Michael Ffinch, the author.

For sharing with me their unrivalled knowledge of the Kelton iron workings my sincere thanks go to Donald Hayton of Kirkland and his lovely wife. For serving even more information along with some fine ale I thank Mr. & Mrs. C.Edwards of The Wheatsheaf Inn, Kirkland.

For going to considerable trouble on our account and making a thumping success of your 'public relations job' special thanks must go to P.C. Peter Lewis of Clapham. You are a credit to the uniform you so proudly wear and I'm privileged to call you friend.

Thank you, Ken Hudson, for always being available with back-up transport when needed and for putting your photographic skills to good use time and time again.

Extra special thanks must go to Stephen Barker and Ron Dodsworth, both of whom have walked through several books with me and shared a height or two. If there are more convivial walking companions I have yet to meet them.

For translating my handwriting into type I am deeply endebted to Barbara Barker, to whom I give my grateful thanks.

I've saved the most important 'till last. Bet, my delightful wife, who let me out to do the field work and kept out of the way while I wrote the M.S. Thanks, love.

If anyone has been omitted, it is unintentional and David and I apologise.

KEY TO MAPS

┼┼┼┼┼┼┼┼┼┼┼┼	Double Track - Open
▬▬▬▬▬▬▬	Double Track - Closed
┼┼┼┼┼┼ ┼┼┼┼┼	Single Track - Open
─────────	Single Track - Closed
▬ ▬ ▬ ─ ─ ─	Trackbed Disappeared
∙∙∙∙∙∙∙∙▬▬∙∙∙∙∙∙∙	Sections Walked
──□──────⊠──	Station - Open/closed

Notes on Maps

To draw a map for every walk in this book would have required a separate book of maps. It was, therefore, necessary to edit these in some some way and I have limited the maps to those lines with more than the usual number of railway features and to those where detours are needed.

The maps are only intended to be used as guides and it is recommended that they be read in conjunction with the text and a detailed map such as the 1" or 1:50,000 Ordnance Survey maps.

David Bell

INTRODUCTION

North West England is a land of contrasts, a curious and exasperating mixture of rural and industrial England where town and country live cheek by jowl in a paradox of friction and harmony.

It embraces the magnificent Derbyshire Peak, the butt end of the Pennines, which is made on the same three tier pattern as the rest of the range, a great thickness of white limestone on top of which lie the alternating sandstone and shales of the Yoredale Series which, in turn, are capped with tough layers of millstone grit.

The limestone scenery of the Peak is a windswept, gently sloping plateau wrinkled with dales that are so abrupt and narrow they are not seen until you are on top of them. Dovedale, with its wanton luxuriance contrasts strongly with austere Wolfscote Dale. Deep Dale, a two miles long gorge near Buxton, is mostly dry, the stream running deep underground. The entrance to Chee Dale is so narrow you can touch both sides. In Lathkil Dale thick woods cluster round the best trout stream in Derbyshire. The variety is infinite.

In the High Peak the tops are flat, not rounded, and the highest of them, Kinder Scout, is a triangular wedge of gritstone three miles long and one hundred feet thick. The flat gritstone holds water so the surface of Kinder summit is mostly peat bog which has about it a savage, primeval beauty.

The western side of the Peak overflows into Cheshire bringing a little of Derbyshire's great beauty into an agricultural county best known for its cat, its cheese and its diverse scenery.

East of Macclesfield the gentle lowlands end, the hills begin and the scenery becomes rugged. Above the hills the moorlands roll, 200 square miles of them many over 1,000ft. high. Up there, on the 1,659ft. contour, north east of the hamlet of Wildboarclough and 800ft. above it, is the top of Shutlings Low, the loneliest height in eastern Cheshire. Not far away, near the source of the Dane, the most beautiful of Cheshire's rivers, are the heights of Bosley Minn and Bosley Cloud, from where are obtained the finest panoramic views of the county. Within this small compass, at 1,690ft. above sea level, is to be found The Cat and Fiddle, the second highest inn in the country.

Much maligned Lancashire contains within its borders scenery any other county would be proud to possess. Whilst it is true that drab towns do exist there and that some of the countryside is sadly despoiled, Lancashire is far from being a dreary industrial conglomeration of mills, mines, workshops and smoke blackened fields, which is the widely accepted and completely erroneous notion of it. The concept of back to back terraced houses, overhung with perpetual, smoky pall dies hard. Yet most of these terraces were bulldozed into rubble years ago. Large tracts of Lancashire are, in fact, free from the murk of industrialisation. Today's Lancashire contains broad expanses of cornfields, gentle meadows, pleasant vales and bare moorlands. Its northern extremity shares with Cumbria some of the finest scenery in Britain.

Even in its most densely populated parts, traces of former loveliness linger and it is often possible to look beyond the factory chimney to 'the frayed Pennine edge of urban Lancashire where the factory hooter wakes the grouse and you hear the clogs before dawn tapping a dotted line of sound through peat and bracken'. Yes, the grouse are still there: only the clogs have gone.

Oldham is not one of Lancashire's prettiest towns, yet there are moors on its doorstep. Blackstone Edge, which once left Daniel Defoe awestruck, is within easy reach of the conurbation of Greater Manchester. Bolton, sitting as it is on the western edge of a great moorland tract, offers easy access to extensive, heathery heights over Winter Hill to the Anglezarke, Turton and Darwen moors or to the tower of Rivington Pike from where there is a wide prospect across west Lancashire, a sagging and spreading flatland which runs into the sea along the Blackpool and Southport shores, northwards, beyond the Ribble, the Fylde and over Morecambe Bay to the Furness Fells, and southwards to the mouth of the Mersey and, beyond, North Wales.

Clitheroe's Norman Keep crowns a limestone crag high above the town. East of this former stronghold of the de Lacy's rises one of Lancashire's most famous landmarks, Pendle Hill, home of the Pendle witches. This great mass, which sweeps upwards from the Calder Valley, gives fine views, including Bowland's wild fells and the whole of Ribblesdale from the Yorkshire heights of Ingleborough and Penyghent to the coast.

Lancaster Castle, built on a hill by the Lune by Roger de Poictou 800 years ago, was once the stronghold of John of Gaunt. Lancashire, originally Lancastershire, derives its name from Lancaster, its county town. It is a County Palatine, an honour bestowed upon the Duke of Lancaster by Edward III.

From the castle to westwards lie Morecambe Bay with its shimmering sands and its breathtaking sunsets and, beyond, to the north west, the Cumbrian fells. To the north the Lune can be seen winding seawards from what was Westmorland. Turning from north to east the Bowland Fells can be seen, as can Gragareth where, before the boundary changes of 1974, Lancashire, Westmorland and Yorkshire met at 2,250ft. Similarly at the top of Wrynose Pass the Three Shires Stone used to mark the meeting of Lancashire, Cumberland and Westmorland. Now Cumberland and Westmorland have become Cumbria and swallowed all of Lancashire north of the sands.

Cumbria is simply beyond compare. No other English county is endowed with such breathtaking beauty; and its greatest asset is the Lake District, an area of craggy high ground fringed by plains. The Lake District is Britain's largest National Park comprising some 866 square miles of high mountains and lonely fells, large lakes and small tarns, rushing becks and clear, fast flowing rivers, narrow valleys and broad vistas. It stretches from north to south for 30 miles and has a maximum width of 25 miles. To the north the land gradually flattens to become the Solway Plain. To westward a narrow coastal plain separates the lakeland heights from the sea. The industrialised part of the county is to be found on this plain. In the east the broad and fertile vale of Eden separates the Lake District from the Pennines. To the south, the rivers drain into Morecambe Bay, an estuary of great natural splendour dominated by treacherous tides and shifting quicksands.

The Lake District is not planned on the grand scale. Scafell Pike, its highest mountain, only attains 3,210ft. Windermere, its largest lake, is only 10½ miles long. But for all its modest dimensions, Lakeland gives the impression of being a mountainous area. Through some magical alchemy it contrives to exaggerate its proportions so that often when confronted with a full sweep of hillside from its crest to the margin of a lake you have the illusion of seeing a mighty peak larger than reality.

Lakeland makes the most of its materials: and what superb resources it has! Buttermere with Haystacks in the background, the crests of Crinkle Crags and Bow Fell, Great Gable, Pillar Rock, the twin buttresses of the Langdale Pikes, Red Screes, Fairfield, Saddleback, serene little Rydal Water, Dove Cottage, Striding Edge, Sharp Edge, the lovely green vale of Grasmere, Helvellyn, Silver How and St. Sunday Crag. Any one of these would be a credit to another county yet all of them and oh so many more besides are an integral part of Lakeland's charm and combine to make it unique.

However, not all the beauty of Cumbria lies within the girdle of Lakeland: not by any means. Outside that ring there is an abundance of prospects so varied and interesting they demand attention. Merrie

11

Carlisle with its stirring past; windswept Alston, England's highest market town, perched high on the Pennines; desolate Cross Fell; High Cup with its Nick, that great bite into England's backbone; the fertile vale of Eden; peaceful, olde-worlde Appleby-in-Westmorland; mellow Kirkby Stephen, eastern gateway to the Lakes; and Mallerstang, morass of the wild duck, with Pendragon Castle, home of Uther, father of King Arthur.

But where exactly *is* the North West? For the purpose of this book it is all the land west of the Pennines to the Scottish border north of a line from Ashbourne north west to Macclesfield, then due west across northern Cheshire through Northwich to the river Dee estuary on the Welsh border. All the walks along the abandoned railways presented here lie within this area.

I have divided the North West into four areas:-

No.I The Derbyshire Peak
That portion of the Peak District bounded by Ashbourne, Wirksworth, Matlock, Bakewell and Buxton.

No.II Northern Cheshire
Cheshire north of an imaginary line westwards from the Derbyshire border east of Macclesfield through Northwich to the Dee estuary.

No.III Lancashire
The whole of this County Palatine.

No.IV Cumbria
The whole of Cumbria.

The railways came to the north west on 15th September 1830, with the opening of the Liverpool and Manchester Railway. Within ten years passengers could travel from Liverpool and Manchester to Birmingham and London. By the late 1850s there were rail connections between almost all the industrial towns west of the Pennines and with places as far away as Edinburgh, Glasgow, Leeds, York, Newcastle and Hull. In fact so dense a network of lines was laid that it proved to be its own undoing. By 1874 four routes connected Liverpool and Manchester and many other places were linked by the lines of competing companies. This duplication of lines caused serious problems and many lines built by small companies were later sold as loss making concerns to the main railway companies who probably had been operating them from the start and who, for this reason, obtained them for less than they would have cost to build.

In 1923, as a direct consequence of the Railways Act of 1921, the 120 companies then in operation were compulsorily merged into four group companies, L.M.S., L.N.E.R., G.W.R. and S.R. Twenty of these small companies were operating in the north west, of which the

L.N.W.R. and the Midland were the top leaders.

Although made part of the huge, centralised and autocratic L.M.S., which was claimed to be the largest private enterprise business in the world, the L.N.W.R. and the Midland remained separated for a long time by commercial rivalry and differences in managerial outlook.

The L.N.W.R. which proudly called itself 'The Premier Line', prided itself on a gentlemanly, conservative outlook. Its chairman from 1861 to 1891, Sir Richard Moon, used to deliver the following homily to all newly appointed officers:-

'Remember, first, that you are a gentleman; remember, next, that you are a North Western officer and that whatever you promise you must perform - therefore be careful what you promise, but having promised it, be careful that you perform it.'

The L.N.W.R. had management trainees or 'Cadets' which originally had been called 'runners'.

The Midland, on the other hand, which got most of its income from freight, always believed in treating its passengers well. It was the Midland that pioneered third class carriages with upholstered seats on all trains and Pullman sleeping cars.

Where the L.N.W.R.'s policy was slow growth through amalgamations, the Midland was more aggressive and down to earth.

The four great companies existed for twenty five years until, on 1st January 1948, they were nationalised. Throughout their lifetime, which was one of enterprise and struggle, they saw many changes, which inevitably continued with British Rail. Basic industries went into decline. The great Lancashire coalfield contracted. Road transport was expanding and taking away both passenger and freight traffic. This trend increased tremendously following the 1955 rail strike. In 1963 the Beeching Report was published. It recommended the closure of many of the smaller or less profitable lines and that duplication of routes be phased out. In 1975 soaring fares and charges resulted in a further decline.

British Rail has already had a substantially longer life than the four great railway companies it succeeded. During this time so many branch lines have been closed that today in most of our schools there are whole classes of teenagers of whom not one has travelled in a train.

In the north west the coming of the railways brought tourists to remote areas like the Lake District and in so doing helped to establish tourism as a major industry. Those gleaming parallel lines became an umbilical cord binding rural communities to the teeming life and thoughts of the sprawlng urban centres.

Since railways catered for man's movement they needed mass markets. Responding to this need, enterprising railway companies, whose finance and vision had built the lines, promoted the growing fashion for seaside and country trips. They produced guidebooks extolling their lines by pointing out the sights to be seen from the carriage window and what interests lay within a short distance of a wayside station or a halt.

Before the advent of the railways, travel, for the most part, was the prerogative of the rich and the privileged, who would come to the country by carriage or on horseback. Train travel changed all that. Enticed by publishers of guides keen to exploit the railways, tourists from all levels of society would alight at a station, spend the day walking in the country and return home from a station miles away from where they had set off. For a great many people these hiking excursions became a popular escape from their humdrum workaday worlds.

Today the north west, in common with the rest of Britain, is strewn with closed lines, many of which are a paradise for naturalists. However, in the same way that you do not have to be an engine driver to enjoy a train ride, you do not have to be a naturalist to enjoy walking along disused lines. Many miles of disused track have been sold to private buyers but experience has shown that the courteous walker will seldom, if ever, be refused permission to walk a particular stretch. Many more lines have been purchased by enlightened authorities with the prime objective of making them as attractive as possible for public use. In this they have been successful beyond their wildest dreams and the general public is reaping rich rewards thanks to the forsight of these go-ahead authorities.

Walking these lines has its responsibilities. They are common sense, really, and are there to help not to hinder: follow the country code: if tackling privately owned lengths of track, first seek permission from the owner: preserve nature - and this does not mean pickling a squirrel!

So go to it: best foot forward and have a lot of fun.

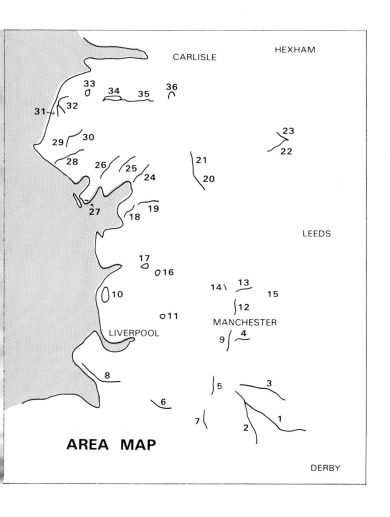

AREA MAP

I. The Derbyshire Peak

The Peak District applies to the upland area of Derbyshire as a whole and not to any particular district. It contains no single mountain or summit named The Peak and in fact, the word 'peak' comes from the old English *peac*, meaning hill. The people who settled there in the seventh century were called *pecsaetans* or hill dwellers. Two flat-topped moors, Kinderscout and Bleaklow, both of which are over 2,000 feet high, form the highest parts, Kinderscout summit, at 2,088 feet, being the highest point of all. A distinction is sometimes made between the northern and southern uplands, one being called High Peak and the other Low Peak, or the Dark Peak and White Peak, reflecting the gritstone and limestone respectively.

The Peak was designated the country's first National Park in December 1950. This distinction was irrefutable on the grounds of quality and variety of scenery alone. Within its boundaries vast open moorlands spread from Kinderscout summit. Glistening streams like the Derwent, the Dove and the Wye flow swiftly through green dales, their exceptionally pure waters, 'the clear waters of Derbyshire', as Isaak Walton called them, teeming with brown trout and, except near their head waters, grayling. Scenery of an altogether different kind can be found in the Peak's many caves, the majority of which are sited around the edge of the limestone area close to streams which flow onto it from the surrounding higher gritstone tracts.

Nearly half the population of England lives within fifty miles of the Peak National Park boundary. Of the country's ten National Parks, it is the closest to London. It can be approached from all directions and people from the nearby industrial centres frequent it throughout the year. It is part of highland Britain yet is readily accessible from the lowlands. Because of this it exhibits elements of both environments.

Covering 542 square miles, it is smaller than both the Lake District and Snowdonia but larger than all the other National Parks. It is forty miles long, north to south, and about twenty-four miles wide. Roughly oval, it has a long, narrow wedge of lowland reaching into it from New Mills to a point some five miles south-east of Buxton.

If Nature had been left to herself unhampered by man, the Peak would have been covered with mixed forest - oak, ash and other deciduous trees with a few conifers. But man has been very much involved down the years and his exploitation is all too evident. Forests

16

have been removed from some areas and created in others. Mining and quarrying have left their scars. Yet in some respects the effects of man's long-term occupation have been gainful rather than otherwise for they have given the region an individuality it did not have before.

The Peak, despite its elevation and broken surface, is predominantly an agriculural region. Most people living there depend on farming for their livelihood. Dairy farming predominates, even on rough grazing, Friesians and Shorthorn Crossbreeds being deemed more important than store cattle.

Successful cattle grazing depends on the quality of the pasture. To maintain grassland on the acid soils of the gritstone country, heavy applications of lime are needed. In limestone country conditions are much better. In the Peak the commonest grass is poor quality agrostis. However, on the higher, north-western parts of the limestone plateau mountain fescue pastures are found.

Sheep are essentially the product of moorland grazing. There are hill sheep on all the moors, mainly Blackface and Swaledale while Gritstones, which are indigenous to Millstone Grit country, and Lonks remain important on the northern moors.

It rains a lot in the Derbyshire Peak, partly because of its elevation and in part because it lies directly in the path of depressions moving eastwards from the Atlantic. Low cloud, fog and mist combine to reduce sunshine to small amounts, especially in winter.

An astounding 29 per cent of the Peak National Park, some 160 square miles in extent, is comprised of reservoirs, thus making the region a lakeland, albeit an artificial one. All the reservoirs are confined to the Millstone Grit country, the carboniferous limestone being too permeable. These reservoirs are too numerous to mention; but the Upper Derwent Valley scheme, one of the largest in the country, deserves special mention.

An Act of Parliament in 1899 authorised the formation of the Derwent Valley Water Board representing a joint-project to supply Sheffield, Derby, Nottingham and Leicester with water from the hitherto untapped sources of the Upper Derwent and its tributaries. The first and uppermost reservoir, Howden, was completed in 1912, Derwent, the middle one, was completed in 1916 and in 1943 the lower one, Ladybower, was finished.

In 1943 Derwent became one of a few reservoirs used by 617 Squadron for low-level night flights over water in preparation for their attack on the Mohne and Eder dams in the Ruhr Valley. In 1955 much of the filming of *The Dam Busters* was done at Derwent Reservoir and in 1977 five survivors of the raid went back to Derwent to celebrate the thirty-fourth anniversary by watching the last operational Lancaster buzz the dam.

In a lonely hollow a little over a mile north-west of Flash, the highest village in England, two streams and three counties meet at Three Shire Heads. Hemmed in by bracken-clad slopes, heather and rocks, this difficult to find spot has a notorious past for it was to there, that highwaymen, coiners and other law-breakers fled to escape justice. At Three Shire Heads they could simply step between Cheshire, Derbyshire and Staffordshire knowing that the pursuing police, restricted to their own patches, could not follow.

Many shady characters lived rough on the moors close to Three Shire Heads and used Flash as a base. They became known as 'Flash men' and the money they forged became 'Flash money'. They gave the English language the word 'flashy' meaning not as good as it looks. Today the characters living rough on those same moors are not so much shady as unusual. They are wild wallabies and can be seen roaming around the craggy climbing area of the Roaches, Five Clouds and, a little apart, Hen Cloud. Should their numbers fall too low help is always to hand. At ruinous, mock-medieval Riber Castle, now a sixty acre reserve and the world's main breeding centre for lynxes, wallabies are also bred. When the need arises, reinforcements are released to join the wild ones roaming the Peak's south-western heights.

Some nine miles N.N.E. of the Roaches, at the head of the Wye Valley, sitting in a hollow on the border between limestone and gritstone country is Buxton where, although it is not England's highest market town, the country's highest market place is to be found. Buxton is really two towns with separate identities and the market place is in the older settlement. Modern Buxton has developed on lower ground. Hence the paradox.

It was the Duke of Devonshire, who in 1780, began the transformation of Buxton into what he hoped would be another Bath; a task which took almost four years to complete, and was a hopeless cause anyway.

The country seat of the Dukes of Devonshire is Chatsworth House, a palatial pile; wherein are exquisitely decorated and furnished state apartments as splendid as any in Europe. 'Capability' Brown landscaped the park and the garden, which contains a fantastic 200 yards long water staircase of consummate excellence and a fountain, the Emperor Fountain. It is the highest in Europe and at full blast can throw up a jet 290 feet into the air.

Leaving things temporal at Chatsworth House for matters spiritual

THE DERBYSHIRE PEAK: ROUTE 1

at Cliff College, headquarters of the Methodist ministry, the River Derwent is crossed at Calver. There a former cotton mill that was built in 1786 can be seen. This building became well known throughout Britain when it was used as Colditz Castle in the T.V. series about that infamous prison.

Cliff College has its own farm and gardens. Theology students spend part of each day working on the farm and in the gardens and the rest of it in study. Billy Graham frequently preaches at Cliff.

The Derbyshire Peak is transitional for it is there that England passes from the Midlands to the North. Ashbourne just outside the southern limit of the National Park boundary is a small Midland town pushed as far north as it will go. Some fifteen miles away to the N.W. lies Leek which, with its old, cobbled market place, its chimneys and its dark mills, is one of the most southerly of northern towns; and the alterant is the Peak.

The area makes a fine, romantic start for anyone seeking out and exploring the disused railways of the north-west, for it has about it a wild beauty and a fascinating past.

1. THE HIGH PEAK TRAIL

Length   :   17½ miles
Opened   :   From Cromford Canal to Hurdlow Incline Foot -
               29th May, 1830
               From Hurdlow Incline Foot to Whaley Bridge -
               6th July, 1831
Closed   :   In sections from 2nd January, 1869
               Final stretch from Friden to Parsley Hay -
               21st November 1967
O/S   :   Sheet No.119; Series 1:50,000

> *Did you ever? - No, you never - dreamt of such absurdities -*
> *Enough to make your noddle ache - it is, upon my word it is;*
> *A handy thing for travelling I've pretty often heard it is,*
> *And so I've been investing in a 'Bradshaw's Guide'.*
> > *Henry S. Leigh.*

It should have been a canal; and had the terrain been suitable it would have been.

To the south-east of the Peak the Cromford Canal, opened in February, 1793, connected Richard Arkwright's cotton mills at

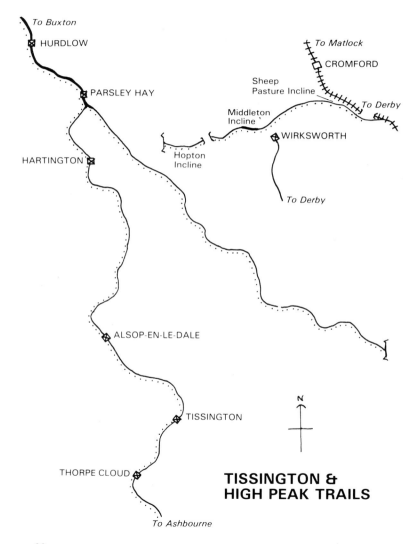

To Buxton

HURDLOW

To Matlock

CROMFORD

PARSLEY HAY

Sheep
Pasture Incline

To Derby

Middleton
Incline

HARTINGTON

Hopton
Incline

WIRKSWORTH

To Derby

N

ALSOP-EN-LE-DALE

TISSINGTON

THORPE CLOUD

**TISSINGTON &
HIGH PEAK TRAILS**

To Ashbourne

Cromford with the Erewash Canal and the Trent. On its north-west side the Peak Forest Canal was opened to basins at Buxworth and Whaley Bridge on 1st May, 1800, giving access from Manchester to the limestone of the Peak District.

The high land between these two canals, much of it over 1,200ft. above sea level, formed a barrier between the coalfields and agricultural areas of Derbyshire, Nottinghamshire and Leicestershire and the textile mills of Lancashire.

In 1810 it was proposed to construct a canal to be called the High Peak Junction Canal across this high limestone country to join the Cromford and High Peak Canals. A survey was carried out and an estimate of its cost came to £650,000, a prohibitive figure. Numerous tunnels and locks would have had to have been built and, since the canal would cut through limestone country, maintaining water in it would have been a major problem. So the idea was abandoned.

A canal being out of the question, the obvious alternative was a railway. Accordingly, on 16th June, 1824, a meeting was held at Matlock to consider building one linking the two canals and with a branch to Macclesfield. No one from Macclesfield attended the meeting so it was resolved that 'the consideration of forming a branch railway to that place be deferred'. Another resolution was that no expense should be incurred until £50,000 had been subscribed.

At the next meeting, in Manchester on 28th July, 1824, it was reported that the required cash had been raised and that the Macclesfield branch would not be built.

Josias Jessop, 2nd son of William Jessop, the Cromford canal builder, was chosen as the engineer in 1824. An Act of Parliament dated 2nd May, 1825 for 'a Railway or Tramroad for the passage of Waggons and other Carriages to be propelled by Stationary or Locomotive steam engines or other sufficient power' was granted. Parliament also authorised share capital of £164,000 with £32,880 in loans. It was all systems go.

Work began immediately on the 33 miles 70 chains long line. It was constructed on canal building principles with long level stretches connected not by flights of locks but by steep inclines. These lifted the railway 1,000 feet to its highest point at Ladmanlow, 1,264 feet above sea level some two miles south-west of Buxton. In all there were nine inclines and the wagons, which horses pulled along the level sections, were hauled up them by stationary steam engines using the endless rope system. It took two days for goods to travel the line, called the Cromford and High Peak Railway, from end to end. As though to stress its strong association with the canal age all the C.H.P.R.

station's were called wharves. The whole line, in fact, marked a transition from the age of canals to that of the railways.

The line, which cost about £180,000 to build, proved a useful link between Lancashire and the East Midlands. The main freight carried along it was limestone with coal, in tonnage terms, coming second. Corn, malt, flour and manufactured goods were also carried in both directions. Yet despite the volume of freight and goods moved the line was always in financial difficulties.

A limited passenger service was introduced but it was a failure. Actually it was nothing more than a modified guards van known as 'The Fly' which accommodated sixteen people inside and fourteen outside. It was drawn by a horse which moved along all the level sections at a good, sharp trot making the motion of the fly exceedingly pleasant for the passengers. At the bottom of each incline the horse was removed and led to the top while the fly was attached to the chain of a stationary engine. This pulled the chain over a series of fixed pullies which steadied the fly while it was pulled up at a very respectable speed. The same principle applied on the descents. The horses were changed at certain stations along the line.

In an article about the passenger service published in the *Derby Mercury* on 20th September, 1854, the public is assured that riding up the steep inclines in the fly is perfectly safe because 'the conductor told us he could stop the carriage on the steepest part of these inclines, by his brakes, in about one minute - consequently no one could feel the slightest fear'. With some of the inclines having a gradient of 1 in 8 or steeper I should have thought that there was great cause for alarm if the guard took up to a minute to operate the brake!

By a further Act of Parliament in 1855 the C.H.P.R. was allowed to modernise the railway by using steam locomotives. The fly was attached to the rear of goods trains and company rules forbade the carrying of passengers up and down the inclines. Guards of the fly trains were known as 'Flymen' and those of other trains as 'Slowmen'. At every one of the nine inclined planes the locomotives, wagons and fly had to be hauled up and down by ropes making the journey between Cromford and Whaley Bridge tedious. With passenger receipts ridiculously low, only 14 shillings and 9 pence for the whole of May, 1862, the C.H.P.R. used a fatal accident in 1877 - not connected to the passenger service - for it to be discontinued. Perhaps this was just as well, for passenger travel on the C.H.P.R. was at best uncertain. This was due, in part, to the weight of goods carried and the difficult terrain which slowed the trains. Then there was the occasional need to clear sheep from the line, added to which the crews enjoyed relaxing in pubs along the way.

In 1862 the London and North Western Railway leased the C.H.P.R. and in 1877 the two were amalgamated. During the period of the lease further modernisation was carried out and two inclines were removed.

By 1890 the London and North Western Railway Company, fully aware of the growth of Buxton as a major spa town, decided to use part of the C.H.P.R. to form a line from Buxton to Ashbourne to make a direct link with London. The necessary permission was granted and the first section, the five miles from Buxton to Dowlow, was opened on 17th June, 1892. The original line of the railway from Dowlow to Whaley Bridge was abandoned and the track removed.

As road transport increased and the limestone quarries along the line ceased production, so much of the C.H.P.R. became abandoned.

The southern section of the line, between Parsley Hay and Cromford Wharf remained pretty much as built until its final closure in April, 1967, with the exception of the 1 in 14 Hopton incline which ceased to be cable-hauled when more powerful locomotives could make the ascent under their own power. This made Hopton incline the steepest gradient climbed by adhesion on the British Rail network.

The C.H.P.R. supplied drinking water for several of the villages it passed close to or through. Large water tenders being hauled up the inclines to be shunted into sidings along the line were a common sight.

Now the track is gone, the inclines have been grassed over and the 17½ miles from Cromford to Dowlow purchased by the Peak Park Planning Board and converted into a footpath and bridle way, leaving the original ash bed surface.

The High Peak Wharf, where this fine walk begins, stands almost intact at the foot of the Sheep Pasture incline alongside the old Manchester main line and the canal. There, barges, which carried a maximum weight of 22 tons instead of the usual 35 tons because of the shallow water, exchanged cargoes with the wagons of the C.H.P.R. The wharf shed in which the goods were transferred is now a hostel for self-catering parties.

The workshop buildings, where the haulage chains and the locomotives used to be maintained, are open to the public and well worth a visit. For there, lining either side of an inspection pit, is a unique set of three foot long fish-bellied rails bearing the initials 'C. & H.P.R. Co.' The workshop also houses some of the pulleys that were used on the rope worked inclines.

An old signal post stands beside the end of the workshop. It was from a large water tank opposite this post that old tenders were filled with water for carrying to various sites along the line.

Originally two inclines were used to lift the C.H.P.R. up to the limestone plateau, a lower one, the Cromford incline, 580 yards long with a gradient of 1 in 9, and a higher one, Sheep Pasture, 711 yards long and with a 1 in 8 gradient. On 16th October, 1857, the two inclines were joined together and the intermediate engine house abandoned.

Wagons were hauled and lowered by means of a one inch diameter wire rope, 2,880 yards long. The maximum load permitted to be hauled was either two loaded or five empty wagons. Since the line was double it was possible to have a balanced load of three empty wagons ascending and either two loaded or five empty wagons descending, thus easing the strain on the engine at the top. Tapered chains, plaited round the wire and secured with leather straps held the wagons to the rope.

The catch pit near the bottom of the incline, just above a bridge with a skew, elliptical arch carrying the A6 road over it, was built as a direct consequence of a near fatal accident on 1st March, 1888.

Snow lay deep on the ground that dark winter night, which was just as well because it probably saved the lives of the guard and a labourer. It was about 7.00p.m. and a wagon full of lime and brake van loaded with two hundredweight of gunpowder were just beginning the descent of the incline when the connecting chain broke. As the vehicle shot forward the guard and the labourer leaped from the van into a snowdrift. The vehicles thundered down the incline reaching a calculated speed of 120m.p.h. at the curve at the bottom. They sailed through the air across the canal, damaging its banks and bounced over a stone wall. Then one of the canisters of gunpowder exploded throwing fragments of the vehicles in all directions. Some of their remains sailed across the Midland line shortly before a train was due and came to rest in a field opposite.

The empty shell of the stationary engine shed stands at the incline top as a monument and a shelter. Close to it is the reservoir for the engine water supply.

Between Sheep Pasture top and Middleton Foot there are magnificent views across the Derwent Valley with Cromford immediately below and, in the distance, High Tor towering above Matlock and, on the hill beyond, Riber Castle.

High Tor is a broad 390 foot high limestone cliff, often garlanded with intrepid rock climbers, that rises sheer from the eastern bank of the River Derwent as it flows through a ravine at Matlock Bath. On its western side, on Masson Hill, are the Heights of Abraham. General

Wolfe, whose victory over the French on the Plains of Abraham at the cost of his life secured Canada, in 1759, for Britain, has associations with the area. His mother was born in Marsden, further north in the Peak District.

There are 30 acres of wooded hillside with zig-zag walks and superb views on Masson Hill. Dizzy cable-car rides in 'bubble cars' that journey steeply up and down it provide thrills in plenty. The show mines which burrow into it, Nestus, once mined for lead and possibly silver, and the more winding Great Masson Cavern, inform in a most interesting way. The grounds of the High Tor offer woodland walks, picnic areas and two caves that are actually worked out lead mines. There is a famous, annual, Venetian Festival on the river from August to October with fireworks and illuminated boats. All this and much more is on offer at Matlock Bath which, added to its proximity to Cromford, makes it an ideal centre from which to walk the High Peak Trail.

Fine as they are, the views to the right over the Derwent Valley cannot compare with those the left-hand side of the Trail has to offer. For thereabouts the course of the old line passes the foot of Black Rocks, a gritstone escarpment at the northern end of Cromford Moor. It is a favourite climbing ground, up to 80 feet high in parts and with overhanging buttresses. Weathered into strange shapes, it contains many top grade climbs. The rocks, set in 430 acres of forest and moorland, provide an enjoyable scramble with, at the end of it one of the very best panoramic views of Derbyshire and the Trail obtainable.

Nearby are a picnic area, car park and the remains of a smelt mill.

Between the Sheep Pasture and Middleton inclines the going is easy and progress is fast along a stone-faced embankment. Two roads are crossed on arched bridges and, beyond them, can be seen where branch lines once led to some of the larger quarries which are so much a feature in this neck of the woods.

The second of the two roads, the B5036 goes in a southerly direction to the nearby historic market town of Wirksworth, once the centre of the Low Peak lead mining industry. Situated at the top end of the Ecclesbourne Valley whose river flows into the Derwent, this 'homestead' of Weorc is first recorded in 835, but its heyday was in the 18th century when lead mining was flourishing. Its steeply sloping market place contains many old houses with late 18th and early 19th century fronts that conceal older structures. More fine old houses decorate the main street of this interesting place, which is generally agreed to be the 'Snowfield' of George Eliot's novel *Adam Bede*.

Every Whitsuntide Wirksworth keeps up the old custom of well-

Middleton Incline from the bottom

dressing although there are no longer any wells there, all the water being pumped into the town.

Wirksworth has strong associations with Sir Richard Arkwright. The older part of Haarlem Mill was built by him as a cotton spinning mill. When spinning ceased, circa 1814, during the cotton depression, the mill was converted to tape weaving which is still carried on there. Wirksworth is well and truely bound up in red tape, being the largest manufacturer of tape, both red and white, in the country.

The town won a Europa Nostra award in 1983.

The level stretch ends abruptly at Middleton Incline which is 908 yards long and rises 253 feet in that distance on a gradient of 1 in 8½. At the foot of the incline is the pit containing the tensioning pulley. Originally there was just a single line up the incline but on 2nd April, 1894, another line was added.

Passengers on the C.H.P.R. had to walk up the incline, at the top of which a notice warned staff to 'exercise great care when walking up and down and keep a sharp lookout for movement of the wire rope. When the rope starts to move staff must stop and stand clear of approaching wagons. No one must remain within the 'Danger Zone' notice boards in the centre of the incline when wagons are moving.'

The warning might have been extended to include the long suffering passengers: after all, they had paid to walk up the incline.

Standing at the top of the incline is the engine house, inside which is the winding engine, sole survivor of eight supplied to the C.H.P.R. between 1825 and 1829. The beam engine was built by the Butterley Company and worked at the very low pressure of five pounds per square inch. The boiler house outside housed two Lancashire boilers.

The 'run' of wagons to be hauled up the incline would be matched by a slightly heavier number of loaded wagons descending. The function of the engine was to balance the load on the steel cable and act as a steadying brake when necessary.

Middleton locomotive shed has been demolished but looking down the incline little imagination is required to picture a Kitson 0-4-0 ST. Dock Tank, so common on the C.H.P.R. in its latter years, making the ascent by being chained to the continuous wire rope.

Middleton Top provides a car park, a picnic area in a drained reservoir, toilet facilities and an information office and shop. Cycles may be hired there.

Now comes another fairly level section along an embankment with stone sides. Beyond Intake Quarry on the right is Hopton tunnel, 113 yards long, 20 feet wide, partly unlined and with deep rock cuttings at each end. The immediate area around the tunnel is a Nature Reserve managed by the Derbyshire Naturalists' Trust. The tunnel is one of only four on the C.H.P.R.

Soon Hopton incline is reached. With, at its steepest, a gradient of 1 in 14, it was the steepest incline in Britain on which there were moving engines. Its summit is 1,100 feet above sea level.

The locomotive ascending Hopton incline could pull only five loaded wagons or seven empties and in order to reach the top it would charge it in a mad dash. The incline's original length of 457 yards was reduced by an embankment to 200 yards to make the pull up easier. Even so, a too enthusiastic approach to it was the cause of a fatal accident in October, 1937, when excessive speed caused the locomotive to spread the track, derail itself and plummet to the bottom of the high embankment, killing the driver. Thereafter a top speed of 40m.p.h. was introduced. Descending Hopton incline was hair raising because of its steepness and sometimes runaways were experienced.

The official closure of this section of the C.H.P.R. in April, 1967, drew large crowds to see the final train ascend this remarkable incline. The train, composed entirely of brake vans, approached at a good speed, paused briefly at the bottom, then stormed to the top in spectacular style.

Now high on the limestone plateau, the Trail runs below terraces of weathered magnesium limestone known as the Harborough Rocks. A path from the Trail leads to this popular rock climbing ground where many of the routes were first climbed in the early 1930s.

Near the west end of the rocks, behind a disused refractory brick works, there is a cave which was first occupied by man during the Early Iron Age and again during Roman times.

Thousands of years ago the sabre-toothed tiger, hyena, bison, brown bear, elk, lynx and wolf occupied the Harborough caves as their bones testify.

Winter snows frequently interfered with operation on this upland section of the C.H.P.R. and snowdrifts often blocked the big, rocky cutting near Peak Quarry. In the last century gangs of up to 300 men were employed to clear the C.H.P.R. and Buxton to Ashbourne lines of snow.

Beyond Peak Quarry a sharp curve to the right leads past Longcliffe Quarry and past a ramp on which two water tenders used to supply locomotives.

At Longcliffe the Trail bridges two roads, the first being of well-tooled stonework, like so many on this line: the other is partly of iron. About a mile further on, where it crosses an underbridge consisting of two tall arches through a stone-faced embankment, the Trail enters the National Park and takes a circuitous course around Minninglow, the most prominent hill thereabouts. The hill wears a top knot of dying trees surrounding the remains of two Neolithic or New Stone Age 'long barrows'. In 1843 and again in 1849 Thomas Bateman, an authority on prehistoric Peakland, dug into these chambered tombs only to find that they had apparently been robbed as long ago as Roman times. Despite this, Minninglow is the best Neolithic discovery of its kind in the Peak District. Unfortunately there is no public access to it.

Minninglow embankment, some 300 yards long, is one of the line's principal features. From it the southwards view to the Minningglow tumuli is one of the best the Trail has to offer.

The car park and picnic area at Minninglow used to be the goods yard.

Now the Trail, in order to avoid dropping into valley heads, manoeuvres round some sharp bends, the most notorious being Gotham which has a radius of only 55 yards. Long wheel base rolling stock and locomotives were unable to work east of it; but to short wheel based rolling stock pulled by locomotives like the Allan 2-4-0 it presented no difficulties.

The refractory brick works at Friden stands on the site of the original station. Heat resistant bricks are made there from sand containing silica which is dug from pits in the neighbourhood.

Friden was the most important goods station on the C.H.P.R. It was there that goods from the small wheel based wagons which had negotiated Gotham curve were transferred to large wheel based ones pulled by larger and more powerful locomotives for the relatively trouble-free run to Buxton, for north of Friden the only curves to be encountered were gentle ones.

The long line of trees on the right of Friden marks the route of the Roman road to Buxton.

In less than a mile Newhaven tunnel is reached. As tunnels go this one is a tot, a mere 51 yards long; but what it lacks in length it gains in interest. The main A515 Ashbourne-Buxton road runs across it; but roads often run over tunnels. Newhaven tunnel's most interesting features are the inscriptions on both its southern and northern portals. The plaque at the southern end shows a wagon surrounded by the words 'Cromford & High Peak Railway, 1825'. The letters 'P', 'H', '&', 'Co', one in each corner, are thought to be the initials of the contractor but the only contractor known on this length of the line was Porteous & Co. The letters don't fit so a mystery presents itself. The plaque at the northern end is altogether more elaborate. It shows a wagon with, beneath it, the Latin motto *Devina Palladis Arte*, meaning 'by the devine skill of Pallas', who was the Greek goddess of engineering. Around it a circular inscription says 'Cromford & High Peak Railway Company'. Curved around the base of this inscription is the name 'Wm. Brittlebank', who was clerk to the C.H.P.R. In large lettering on a rectangular stone above the plaque are inscribed the words 'Joss Jessop Esq., Engineer'.

Once past the tunnel and out of the cutting the Tissington Trail comes into view on the left. Parsley Hay station is almost due north of the junction, a quarter of a mile further on. There you will find a car park and a picnic area. In getting there don't forget to shut the gates you have to go through on this part of the Trail.

Now the Trail runs more or less parallel to the Buxton road, skirting several large and still growing quarries.

Hurdlow station, opened in 1894 when the new London and North Western Railway line from Buxton to Ashbourne was being constructed, is now a car park. The station was closed on 15th August, 1949, and the buildings were demolished some ten years later.

In 1831 the Hurdlow incline, to the north of the station, was built. It was 850 yards long and had a gradient of 1 in 16. On 2nd January,

The junction of the High Peak Trail with the Tissington Trail

1869, it was abandoned when a more gentle gradient of 1 in 60, the Hurdlow Deviation Line, was built as part of a straightening out of the line between Hurdlow and Hindlow. It is along this more gentle embankment that the High Peak Trail goes, to end just beyond the National Park boundary with a fenced road bridge at Dowlow.

This fine walk is well but incorrectly named for no part of it goes anywhere near the High Peak which is the name given to the gritstone moorland around Kinder Scout. The railway from which it gets its name is equally misleading for the C.H.P.R. did not start at Cromford but further down the Derwent Valley at High Peak Junction. But do not let that put you off. Once you have found the Trail do walk it because it has so much to offer.

2. THE TISSINGTON TRAIL

Length : 13 miles from Mapleton Lane to Parsley Hay
Opened : 1899
Closed : Ashbourne, Mapleton Lane to Hartington - 1963
          Hartington to Parsley Hay - 1967

O/S   :   Sheet No.119; Series 1:50,000

> *Singing through the forests,*
> *Rattling over ridges,*
> *Shooting under arches,*
> *Rumbling over bridges,*
> *Whizzing through the mountains,*
> *Buzzing o'er the vale, -*
> *Bless me! this is pleasant,*
> *Riding on the Rail!*
> *John G. Saxe.*

The London and North Western, in its day the second largest railway company in Great Britain, had the shortest route between Manchester and London but it had to run part of the way, from Macclesfield to Colwich Junction, over a section of the North Staffordshire Railway. This was inconvenient for both train movements and financial reasons. The Company therefore decided to bypass this section of the line.

On 4th August, 1880, an Act of Parliament was passed permitting the construction of a line from Ashbourne to Buxton. At Parsley Hay it would join the C. and H.P.R., which the L. and N.W.R. already owned, and assume the route of the C. and H.P.R. to Buxton.

The engineer in charge of construction was Francis Stephenson and the railway was opened in 1899.

The line, although not as steep as the High Peak Railway, climbed from Ashbourne along an average gradient of 1 in 60, steepening to 1 in 41 as it approached Hindlow summit, which, at 1,200ft. made it one of the highest lines in England. From Hindlow to Buxton the average gradient was 1 in 60 throughout. It was because of these steep gradients that the route never became a main line.

From Ashbourne to Hartington the line was designed to double track standards but only built as a single track line with passing loops at the stations. The only section actually built as double track was from Parsley Hay to Hindlow.

Coldeaton cutting, ¾ mile long and 60 feet deep, is one of the line's major engineering features. The 378 yards long Ashbourne tunnel, now blocked, is another, as is the seven arched, 200 feet long viaduct which crosses Bentley Brook.

With the exception of Tissington station, which was built in dressed stone to conform with other buildings on the neighbouring estate, all the station buildings were built of wood to an austere design.

31

Despite initial high hopes the Ashbourne-Buxton line was never more than a branch line, although at one time milk from the Hartington creameries and cheese factory was carried along it daily en route for London's doorsteps. Transportation of cattle was an important source of revenue, but the principal traffic was limestone.

In 1923, when the L. and N.W.R. was absorbed into the L.M.S., passenger services were cut back and limited to purely local link services with Uttoxeter and Buxton, serving intermediate stations. Since the area served by the line was rural, devoid of large centres of population and susceptible to harsh winters, it is remarkable that the line lasted as long as it did.

Since the stations were often sited quite some distance from the communities they were intended to serve, an ambience of the countryside enveloped them and seeped into the bones of the Company's employees. The infrequency of the trains helped, for with time on their hands, station staff were able to do justice to their allotments and smallholdings; and the whistles of approaching trains gave them time enough to race back to their official duties, replacing cap and waistcoat as they did so.

It was just as well that these perks were available for the L. and N.W.R. Company was not renowned for its financial generosity to its employees. As a lengthman who, in the 1950s, walked the stretch of line between Tissington and Hartington most days between 7.30a.m. and 5.00p.m. for £5 per week put it, 'the railway life was keen: they wouldn't give you a penny where a halfpenny would do'.

Life on the line could be particularly hard in winter. Yet, paradoxically, when driven snow blocked cuttings many railwaymen welcomed it, for snow meant overtime.

Strong winds blowing across the exposed sections of the line were detested, particularly by lengthmen who had to battle against them. So strong were they that on one occasion they wrapped signal arms around their posts. But perhaps the most bizarre instance was when a brake van's complete roof was blown away leaving a startled guard staring at the stars! I wonder how he explained that away when he got back to his depot.

Regular passenger services ceased in November 1954, but excursions continued until October 1963, when the line was closed from Ashbourne to Hartington. The section from Hartington to Buxton remained open until 1967, possibly because of an undertaking to provide an emergency service in winter if road links between villages were severed because of drifting snow.

Towards the end of its life the level of traffic on the line dropped to virtually nothing. In some cases engine and guards van only were despatched to Parsley Hay solely to pick up the wages.

Further rationalisation of railway services meant that in 1967 the truncated line from Parsley Hay to Hindlow was closed and the track lifted.

Ashbourne, at the southern end of the Tissington Trail, is a town of exceptional interest. Situated where the old red sandstone of the Midland Plain meets the limestone hills above Dovedale and with its main street running east and west along the narrow valley floor, it exudes all the atmosphere of a frontier town. For it is there that the lowlands end and the uplands begin; and their different cultures meet and mingle.

There was a settlement in Ashbourne in Saxon times but it was not until the middle of the thirteenth century that it was laid out as a planned market town. Because of its strategic position Ashbourne prospered as an agricultural centre. In its sloping, triangular market place the sheep, wool and lead of the Peak were exchanged for the corn, horses and timber of the Midland Plain.

Ashbourne's long main street, St. John Street, and its westward continuation, Church Street, is thought by many to be the finest street in Derbyshire. Towards its eastern end is stretched a wooden beam supporting the unusual sign of the Green Man and Black's Head Royal Hotel. On one side of the sign the Black's Head is sad on the other he smiles. The inn is of Georgian origin and has associations with Boswell who, along with Dr. Johnson once stayed in the town. Formerly there were two inns but the trade of Blackamoor's Head was taken over by the Green Man.

To the western end of the thoroughfare, that part of it called Church Street, stands St. Oswald's Church, affectionately referred to as the 'pride of the Peak' and called by George Eliot 'the most beautiful mere church in England'. It's spire of 212 feet high, is the tallest in the country. In spring countless daffodils turn the churchyard into a golden carpet.

Between the inn sign and the church 16th, 17th and 18th century buildings grace both sides of the street. Gingerbread can be purchased at the Gingerbread Shop, a timber-framed building, thought to have been built in the fifteenth century.

Ashbourne's football pitch must be the longest in Britain for the goals, the wall of Sturstone Mill and a commemorative stone on the site of Clifton Mill, are three miles apart. Two famous matches between the Up'ards, those born north of Henmore Brook, and the Down'ards, those born south of it, are played every Shrove Tuesday and Ash Wednesday. The playing area is through streets of closed shops with shuttered windows. The rules are minimal and any number can play. Skill accounts for nothing in this game of strength and stamina which is played with a leather ball filled with cork. The ball is thrown up at Shaw Croft car park at 2.00p.m. and the game continues until darkness falls. It can be kicked, carried or moved by any other kind of human agency. There are no boundaries and the play continues without a halt until a goal is scored, after which a new ball is called for, the scorer keeping the one with which he scored. The game is slow moving and it is rare for more than one goal to be scored in one day.

Although the Tissington Trail cannot match the High Peak Trail for engineering and industrial interest it is by far the more charming of the two. Because quarrying has not inflicted upon it the same messy scars, the Tissington Trail scenery is better and this slants the interest more towards nature study.

The Trail does not begin in Ashbourne. Its southern terminus is at Mapleton Lane car park, less than half a mile north of Ashbourne, because the tunnel which penetrated a hill to the south of this spot is now blocked.

On leaving the car park the Trail soon crosses Bentley Brook on a seven-arched viaduct 200 feet long, and a mile or so further on and, surrounded by fine, pastoral scenery, enters the Peak National Park.

When the Peak Park Planning Board bought the track from British Rail in 1968 all the station properties were in a derelict and unsightly condition. So they were demolished and converted into car parks with toilets and picnic sites; and Hartington signal box was restored for use as a warden's briefing centre. When the track was removed the limestone ballast on which it lay looked decidedly uninviting, so the Trail, except that part of it north of Hartington station, was covered with 12,000 tons of soil and seeded. Now not only does it look good, the grass makes for easier walking and riding. North of Hartington the original bed, which between there and Parsley Hay was ash, has been retained.

Just beyond the third cutting from Mapleton Lane and within sight of the site of Thorpe station, a mile inside the National Park boundary, there are kissing gates on each side of the Trail. The one on your right leads very pleasantly over fields to Fenny Bentley. However, by going through the one on your left and following a faint trod you will reach Thorpe village which sprawls across a hillside east of the confluence of the Dove and Manifold rivers.

There, in this cul-de-sac of limestone houses, is an interesting small church with a squat Norman tower, St. Leonard's. Inside is a tub font, one of only three in Derbyshire.

The lane passing the church leads down to Coldwall Bridge which was built in 1726 and once carried the Ashbourne to Cheadle coachroad over the Dove. Now it carries a grassy track.

A little downstream of Coldwall Bridge, the confluence of the Manifold and Dove rivers marks the lower end of Dovedale, by far the best known and most photographed of the Peakland dales. Milldale, three miles away upstream, is its northern limit.

For the whole of its length from Axe Edge to where it flows into the Trent, the Dove forms the boundary between Derbyshire and Staffordshire. Across Coldwall Bridge a short road runs up the west or Staffordshire bank of the Dove to a car park, beyond which is a footbridge crosses the river to a path which goes along its east bank to those famous stepping stones that mark the southern end of the dale's two miles long most interesting bit.

The stepping stones are fun to cross and re-cross to savour the flavour in both directions. Then those wishing to do so can turn right and follow the path up Lin Dale around the base of Thorpe Cloud, back to Thorpe Village and so rejoin the Trail. Aeons ago the 942 feet high Thorpe Cloud - old English *clud* meaning a rock or hill - was a coral reef: today its ancient green flanks are lined with the paths worn by a large proportion of the estimated half a million annual visitors to Dovedale.

Even more people walk along the track alongside the river on the Derbyshire side above the stepping stones and in places the erosion has become so pronounced that the authorities have had to lay duckboards. On a fine bank holiday weekend there could be all of 4,000 people in the dale. The sheer scale of these holiday weekend invasions is alarming. Yet these people are not vandals. They are ordinary friendly folk who bring with them a good humoured camaraderie of the kind usually seen at the last night of the proms. Fortunately most never stray far from the stepping stones, leaving the manifold delights of this lovely dale to the walkers.

Going upstream from the stepping stones the river bends to the left around the height of Dovedale Castle beyond which lie the outcrops of the Twelve Apostles. These are best seen from the top of Sharplow Point, sometimes called Lover's Leap, a grassy spur on the east bank which offers a grand view of Dovedale's strange limestone outcrops. The path leaves the riverside to climb this spur and descends again close to the foot of the jagged Tissington Spires. A little further on the path passes a great limestone arch, the original mouth of Reynard's

Cave. The rest of it collapsed millions of years ago. Vestiges remain, further back, but the uphill climb to them and the exploration of the collapsed cave itself can be hazardous. However the views across the dale to Jacob's Ladder are terrific.

Upstream of Reynard's Cave the dale becomes very narrow and the path passes under Lion's Head Rock along a raised wooden structure. Beyond is a great fortress-like bastion of limestone known as Pickering Tor which, with its five distinct projections, is as spectacular as anything in the dale. Facing it is Ilam Rock, which rises sheer from the water's edge.

The gorge ends where the river flows between Raven's Tor crag and the Dove Holes, two arched recesses in the rocky hillside. From the Dove Holes a steep track climbs in a north-eastern direction past Hanson Grange and on, across a minor road and the A515, to Alsop station car park.

The Dove reaches the hamlet of Milldale by flowing through, first, Beresford Dale then Wolfscote Dale and Mill Dale, providing some 5 miles of glorious walking, only a short stretch of which, between Milldale Hamlet and Lodge Mill, is on a road. Even here the sparkling river runs alongside it. The walk ends at Hartington.

Dovedale has many historical and literary associations, among them Byron, Jean Jacques Rousseau and Mark Twain, whose shrewd observation that nothing helps scenery like ham and eggs is as true today as ever it was. But one man above all other has placed his imprint on this beautiful dale. That man is Izaac Walton whose *Complete Angler* assured him of lasting fame. He used to stay at Beresford Hall with his close friend, later to become his adopted son, Charles Cotton. The fishing house built in 1674 by Cotton where the Dove flowed through his land remains today and trout and grayling still abound in the sparkling waters.

Yes, indeed! Dovedale is worth a detour. It is a place not to be missed especially when wearing a sparkling coverlet of new fallen snow. But if you value its charms and acknowledge that it has an erosion problem please do not hang around like Banquo's ghost.

Just as Dovedale is acknowledged by many to be the prettiest of the Peak District dales, so Tissington is said to be its prettiest village. It has a broad green, a pond, an old village school and a church that is even older, most of it being Norman. Tissington Hall, set back behind a walled garden, was built in 1609 from which date it has been owned by the Fitzherbert family. It is an unusual manor house in that instead of gables it has a battlemented parapet.

Tissington is celebrated for its old custom of well dressing which some say originated in the mid-fourteenth century when pure water from the limestone saved the village from the Black Death. Others opt for the version that well dressing began in 1615 as a thanksgiving for the never failing supply of water from the wells during a great drought. The ceremony, which takes place on Ascension Day, is the culmination of about three day's work. Usually the pictures have a relgious theme and the designs and Biblical texts are picked out in petals, flowers, mosses, grasses, stones and other natural materials on smooth clay keyed by hundreds of nails and moistened with salt water. Materials that are not natural are seldom used. Many of the displays are upwards of twenty feet high and frequently edged with alder cones, known locally as 'black knobs'. Five wells are dressed in Tissington. Wells are also dresssed in around twenty other Derbyshire villages.

From Tissington the Trail runs parallel to the road for three miles to the site of Alsop station. It passes through a pleasing landscape patchworked with omnipresent limestone walls. The views are good, particularly eastwards where in a shallow valley set among delightful wooded uplands Alsop-en-le-Dale slumbers peacefully.

The Trail north of Alsop is particularly good. Soon after passing under the Buxton road it runs within half a mile of Dovedale then passes through Coldeaton cutting, three quarters of a mile long and some sixty feet deep. Beyond the cutting, on the left, is the tiny village of Biggin. Less than two grand walking miles to go to Hartington.

All that remains of Hartington station is its signal box, now an information centre. Today willows grow in profusion where the station used to be. Now it is one of the dozen access point to the Trail and the car park is the starting point for at least three excellent walks, all circular and varying in length between two and seven miles.

The National Park Ranger in charge of the High Peak and Tissington Trails lives in one of the original station cottages which have been modernised. He will be only too pleased to advise on how to get the most out of your visit to this lovely part of Derbyshire. He will most certainly suggest that you have a look at Hartington village. It lies about one and a half miles away to westward along the B5054, which the Trail crosses just north of the cottages.

The road runs down a typical dry limestone valley, Hand Dale, passing, on the left, Hand Dale Farm and, on the right, a dewpond made by the old method of stone and clay without concrete.

Hartington, gateway to Beresford, Wolfscote and Dove Dales, is a haunt of tourists in general and fishermen in particular. Although its seventeenth century Jacobean Hall is now a youth hostel and hotel

Hartington Signal Box, Tissington Trail

accommodation is available, Hartington caters mainly for day visitors. Built around a large open space and sporting a pond and ducks, this little village is one of the oldest market centres in the dales but, like Peter Pan, it never grew up, never expanded, and has now lost its market. It has not, however, lost its charm. The various forms of architecture displayed on the limestone buildings edging the square are particularly attractive.

Stilton cheese is made at the Hartington factory and exported around the world. (It is also made in Leicestershire and Nottinghamshire but not in the Huntingdonshire village whose name it carries!) The Nuttalls, a Leicestershire family, began making cheese in Hartington and now the Milk Marketing Board owns their factory. An incredible 1,600 tons of cheese are made there annually, 88 per cent Blue Stilton, 10 per cent Stilton and 2 per cent - dare I mention it? - Wensleydale!

Superb walks radiate from Hartington like the spokes of a wheel and this makes it an ideal base from which to explore this part of the Peak.

When the viaduct, which crosses the B5054, was being built workmen preparing the foundations broke through into an old mine and found some human skeletons, possibly those of trapped miners.

The long line of trees seen on the right as the Trail goes through a cutting and out onto a slight embankment was planted to shelter the line.

The next cutting, a larger one, is also very broad. It was built that way because the track was originally planned as a double line.

Beyond the cutting a typical limestone plateau farm, Hartington Moor Farm, appears on your left.

Now, on the left, the view opens out to Long Dale. The gashes in the hills between Long Dale and the Trail and the extensive workings ahead are old silica pits. A disused silica pit, close to the Trail as it goes along a high, curving embankment, has been used as a dump for tyres. In an attempt to screen this eyesore young trees have been planted.

Another cutting, this one very deep, is approached from under a bridge. Emerging from it a farm with a silage tower is seen on the left, the High Peak Trail closes in on the right and the hamlet of Parsley Hay lies ahead, its former station a cycle hire centre.

So ends a most memorable walk.

3. THE MONSAL TRAIL

Length   :   9 miles (4 separate lengths and 3 detours around closed tunnels)
Opened :   1863
Closed :   1968
O/S   :   Sheet No.119; Series 1:50,000 or 2 ½ ″ White Peak Tourist Map

> *It rushes on, the embodiment of Force,*
> *Devouring Distance and defeating Time,*
> *With power resistless moving on its course*
> *A common sight indeed, yet how sublime!*
> *Bertram Dobell.*

Screeching like banshees, swaying expresses thundered from the confining darkness of a tunnel straight onto airy Monsal viaduct, high above the River Wye. For more than a century this spectacular crossing of the lovely valley in the heart of England's 'Little Switzerland' thrilled passengers travelling from St. Pancras to Manchester. The viaduct's virtues were extolled by railway publicity and it was spoken of with admiration by successive generations of railway enthusiasts. Yet its construction was bitterly opposed by many

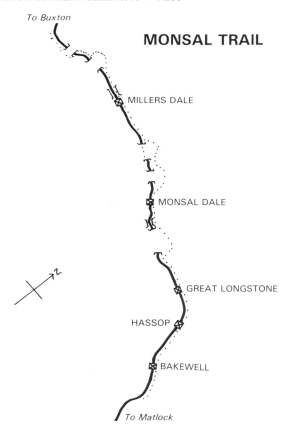

MONSAL TRAIL

who saw it as being detrimental to the dale. In 1867 Ruskin eloquently expressed these feelings when he wrote about the viaduct in *Fors Clavigera*.

'There was a rocky valley between Buxton and Bakewell, once upon a time, divine as the Vale of Tempe: you might have seen the Gods there morning and evening - Apollo and all the sweet Muses of the light - walking in fair procession on the lawns of it, and to and fro among the pinnacles of its crags. You cared neither for Gods nor grass, but for cash (which you did not know the way to get): you thought you could get it by what The Times calls 'Railroad Enterprise'. You Enterprised a Railroad through the valley - you blasted its rocks away, heaped thousands of tons of shale into its lovely stream. The valley is gone, and the Gods with it; and now every fool in Buxton can be at Bakewell in half-an-hour, and every fool in Bakewell at Buxton; which you think a lucrative process of exchange - you Fools Everywhere'.

When the line was closed and the suggestion made that the viaduct be demolished there was such an outburst of opposition that it was left standing and has now become part of the landscape.

For twelve years the National Park Board negotiated with British Rail to purchase that part of the line between Coomb's Road viaduct, south of Bakewell and the top of Chee Dale. They had two reasons for doing this: to prevent dereliction and to put the track to a new use. When, at long last, British Rail agreed to hand over the land they also donated £154,000 towards the cost of repairing the viaducts and tunnels. However, even with the welcome donation there were insufficient funds to cover the high cost of making safe and lighting the four longer tunnels and these had to be sealed. That is why the Monsal Trail has four distinct sections linked by footpaths and, at one point, along roads.

Bakewell, near the eastern end of the Monsal Trail and the only town in the Peak National Park, is its administrative centre. From there the Peak District National Park Joint Board controls a vast area comprising 542 square miles that stretches into six counties, Cheshire, Derbyshire, Greater Manchester, Staffordshire, South and West Yorkshire. Established in 1951, it was the first National Park Authority and is one of only two entirely responsible for running a National Park. The other is the Lake District Board. All the other parks in the country are administered by county council committees.

It is a pleasant little town lying mainly on the west bank of the Wye and is renowned for its agricultural and horticultural show, probably the largest one-day show in England. It was first granted a charter in 1254 but was a busy trading centre long before then. Monday is market day.

Bakewell's origins are Saxon, as a huge collection of Saxon coffin stones and crosses in the church of All Saints will testify. The first half of the name is a corruption of either *Badeca* meaning a Saxon or *bad*, a bath or spring. Bakewell does not qualify as a spa but it used to have about a dozen wells. Now most are dry or filled in.

Many people visit Bakewell in search of its tarts and frequently leave the place disappointed. For the truth of the matter is that there are few, if any, tarts to be found there. It is Bakewell *puddings* that are the attraction; and it all came about by accident. They were first created in the kitchens of the Rutland Arms, in the town centre, about 1859 when a servant, instead of using her egg mixture to make the pastry for a strawberry jam tart, as instructed, poured it over the jam. Thus another mouth-watering addition to England's culinary traditions was born.

Several shops sell Bakewell puddings: others sell provisions, souvenirs and books, maps and pamphlets on the Peak District. The information centre has so much to offer that the visitor tends to be spoiled for choice. Although Rutland Square now has a roundabout, Bakewell has not changed all that much in almost 400 years. It is still an agreeable place to saunter in.

North of the town Holme Bridge, a 17th century pack horse bridge, now a footbridge, crosses the river. Near the town centre a much older bridge carries the Baslow road over the Wye. This fine structure of five Gothic arches was built about 1300 and was widened on the north side a century ago. It was built on the site of a ford. In 924 Edward the Elder built a castle on the eastern side of this ford but all that remains is a mound. It stands close to the disused railway station, our first contact with the Monsal Trail.

From a very popular riverside walk, a little downstream of the Baslow road bridge, walkers and picnickers habitually toss fish food to the rainbow trout that congregate close to the riverside in large numbers eager to be fed. These fish were introduced to the Wye from North America in the 19th century and now breed there naturally.

Bakewell station, which has a car park, is a mile distant from the Monsal Trail's eastern end, but Stephen and I chose it as our starting point. We had spent more time in that fair town than we had intended but did not want to rush the walk. So we decided to split it into two sections, one east and one west of Bakewell station. The eastern section was a very short one but it passed within shouting distance of Haddon Hall, possibly England's finest medieval mansion. This was too good an opportunity to miss and, if we were to do justice to our visit, we needed time for viewing that would otherwise be used for walking. So, resolving to do the much longer section the next day, we set off along a reasonably firm and level surface to one mile distant Coomb's Road viaduct, the eastern end of the Monsal Trail. From there we dropped to the Coomb's road and took a track to the A6. We turned left along it and soon reached Haddon Hall, hidden by trees and a beech hedge.

Much older than Chatsworth House, Haddon Hall, believed by many to be the perfect fortified medieval house, is not to be missed. For this rambling mellow mansion, this absolute riot of towers, turrets and crenellated walls, all of which are purely decorative, simply oozes romance. It smacks of the Middle Ages, not as they were but as they should have been, when chivalry and valour were *de rigueur* and gallant knights with their gracious ladies spent halcyon days jousting, roistering, feasting and making love in this idyllic spot.

Haddon Hall straddles a limestone bluff overlooking the Wye where an old pack-horse bridge spans it. Built around two flagged court-yards, its oldest part is a chapel built, in part, by William Peveril between 1080 and 1090. In the ancient kitchen you can still see bowls carved in the wooden bench tops. Beyond the kitchen is the bake-house and butcher's shop which provided the food for the house. Just inside the entrance hall a 14th century banqueting hall complete with oak panelling and minstrel's gallery still contains a 400 year old long table. It was from this table and others like it, extending down the length of the hall, on either side of the hearth that members of the household ate.

This history of Haddon Hall is as peaceful as its setting. Its first owners, the Peverils, dabbled in politics and lost their estate. Their successors, the Avenels, the Vernons and the Manners stuck to affairs of estate, ignored affairs of State and thrived. Ownership changes came in a civilised way, through marriage.

In true Mills and Boon style Dorothy Vernon, wife of John Vernon, eloped with John Manners in 1563 and this was immortalised by Sir Walter Scott. Just off the Long Gallery are the steps down which the lovers are supposed to have fled. Ah!

Today Haddon Hall is a microcosm of life in a country house more than 400 years ago.

Somewhat reluctantly we departed this picturesque mansion, Horace Walpole's 'abandoned old castle', and in so doing stepped from the gentler ages it symbolised, where good manners and breeding counted for something, into a modern world of different, often lower, standards. We felt that, down the years something worth keeping had been left behind.

Haddon Hall is not open throughout the year; and when it is you have to pay to get in. But, oh! it is so worthwhile: it really is.

We retrace our steps to Bakewell station well satisfied with our most pleasant divertisement.

★　★　★

Not only is the Monsal Trail a lovely walk: because of its interesting geology much of the route has been designated an area of special scientific interest. Furthermore nature reserves cover much of the neighbouring land so it behoves the walker to treat the trail and its surroundings with respect.

The first few miles westward from Bakewell station are on a shale bedrock. The track surface is firm and the cuttings and embankments are covered with coarse grasses. Trees there are in plenty - ash, birch, elm, oak, thorn and sycamore - and the going is easy.

After about three miles, where a path from Ashford to Little Long-stone bisects the trail, go right along it for half a mile to this charming hamlet, which is proud of its limestone dwellings and its eighteenth century manor house.

Special permission is needed to continue along the line to the cutting east of Headstone Tunnel where the shale gives way to limestone. This is because the cutting is unsafe and the tunnel is closed.

From Little Longstone a short road walk will bring you to Monsal Head, perhaps the most exciting part of the whole walk.

Monsal Head, sometimes called Headstone Head, is one of the finest viewpoints in the Peak District. For this reason it attracts great numbers of people throughout the summer months, particularly at weekends. The views both up and down the River Wye are particularly fine and just below, where the Wye swings around Putwell Hill and Fin Cop, the famous Monsal Viaduct carries the Monsal Trail over it.

There are the remains of a large hill fort, probably built B.C., on Fin Cop; but this fact pales against the splendid landscape that holds the eye so firmly. It is all so beautiful and so English, this harmony of hill and dale, woods and rocks and lush pastures. When set against a chorus of bird song it is almost too much.

We moved on, across controversial Monsal Viaduct and in so doing left that part of the Wye Valley called Monsal Dale which ends at Monsal Head and entered Millers Dale which continues westward to the hamlet of Millers Dale at the junction with Monks Dale. West of Millers Dale hamlet lies Chee Dale where the lovely Wye is at its most delightful.

After only a mile of track walking Cressbrook Mill is reached where, because of closed tunnels ahead, a detour is indicated. But, like the other detours along the Monsal Trail, this one leads to enchantment. It comes in the form of a mill that looks for all the world like a small Georgian manor house.

Cressbrook Mill dates from 1815 and replaces an earlier mill built by

William Newton for Joseph Arkwright in 1779. Arkwright was one of the first to mechanise on a large scale. He built mills in the upper reaches of isolated valleys using fast flowing water for power. Cressbrook Mill was powered by the Cressbrook stream, a feeder of the Wye. The original mill was destroyed by fire. Newton probably rebuilt it after the fire: at any rate he became manager and part owner in 1810.

A remarkable man, William Newton was born at five miles distant Cockey Farm, Abney, in 1750. He learned carpentry, attained some mechanical skills and read widely, especially poetry, to compensate for a limited education. He also wrote poetry and his verse caught the attention of Anna Seward who gave him her patronage and dubbed him 'The Derbyshire Minstrel'.

William Newton had another very important facet to his character - his unusual humanity towards the mill's boy apprentices. According to a Factory Inspector's report of 1811 the Cressbrook Mill apprentices 'looked well and appeared perfectly satisfied with their situation'. Their lot was a happy one compared with that of the Litton Mill apprentices, two miles upstream, where life under Ellice Needham was 'one continued round of cruel and arbitrary punishments'. William Newton was able to change Litton Mill's harsh conditions for the better when, sometime before his death of 1830, he acquired it. He is buried in Tideswell churchyard.

An unusual feature of the present building is a cupola which once contained a bell used to summon the workers. Its central pediment below a hipped roof is more in keeping with a manor house than a mill.

Cressbrook Dale itself is renowned for its fine woods, its varied flora, its mosses and its tufa deposits. What is has to offer is enough to make a botanist drool; and it caters for the archaeologist too. A child's skeleton has been unearthed from a tumulus on Hay Top, above the dale, and Ravenscliffe cave has given up the bones of bear, reindeer and rhinoceros, probably discarded by Stone Age hunters.

The winding detour from Cressbrook Mill took us upstream along the northern bank of the Wye to Litton Milll, where we recrossed the river on a footbridge to rejoin the Trail; and what a splendid walk it is! For about a mile the river makes a great S-bend under fine limestone crags, flowing through a gorge rich in woods which in season are carpeted with flowers. This delightful stretch of water is known locally as Water-cum-Jolly. Climbers spend happy days suspended from these cliffs and botanists rapturise about the rich flora in the more accessible places.

The original mill at Litton Mill was built in 1782 and rebuilt in 1874 after a fire. It was a textile mill making cotton and worsted yarns for hosiery making in the local cottage industry. The mill, built and owned by Ellis Needham, one of the most notorious of the early mill owners, or factory masters as they were frequently called, had a very bad reputation. In the late 18th century pauper children over the age of nine were taken from the Poor House and indentured to the mill owners as apprentices. Needham got most of his apprentices from the London area. He worked them fifteen hours a day for 8/- a week from which 4/- was deducted for food and lodging. They lived in crowded conditions behind the mill and existed on a diet so poor that many died in epidemics. Corporal punishment, which included the pillory and the use of a cage suspended from the ceiling, was frequently used. When the children became too old to remain apprentices they were returned to the Poor House.

Today a man-made fibre is processed there and conditions are much improved.

North of Litton Mill, at Litton Slack, there is a dry valley, a typical feature of limestone scenery.

We walked on rough ballast for almost two miles to Millers Dale viaduct from where the track surface was firm and level, through Millers Dale station to the viaduct half a mile to the west.

Much of the limestone along this section of the walk is mottled and contrasts greatly with that further upstream in Chee Dale, which is much lighter and unstained. The Wye Valley limestone is Carboniferous which is quite different from the oolitic limestone of the Cotswolds and the magnesium limestone belt that extends from the Derbyshire-Nottinghamshire border northwards through Yorkshire. It is composed largely of carbonate of lime which originated in a sheltered sea and to which was added the remains of countless millions of tiny invertebrates which floated in the water. That the Wye Valley was once the bed of a shallow sea is clearly shown by the fossil shells and corals the limestone contains. Further, the sea must have been relatively calm and clear because there is very little inorganic material in the limestone except where sand and mud were carried into the sea as in Millers Dale to produce today's mottled effect.

The uniformity of limestone is broken here and there by dark outcrops of basalt. This was formed as the limestone beds were building up by periodic volcanic eruptions. The lava poured across the sea bed, spreading over a large area before it solidified. Further deposits of limestone were then laid down above it. The basalt beds are thin compared to the limestone so the effect on the landscape is slight. It

Miller's Dale

can best be seen on the smooth limestone crags in Millers Dale.

At the aforementioned viaduct we descend to the river and continued upstream for almost a mile along its northern bank. The path was poor but the detour was very exciting through a pleasant, sylvan landscape where, beneath the trees anemones and celandines carpet the springtime slopes.

For a while the course of the river was straight. Then we came to where, in a great sweep, it almost completed a circle as it rounded Chee Tor, a 200ft. pale limestone precipice well favoured by rock climbers. There are faint traces on its top of a prehistoric settlement, best seen when the sun is setting and the shadows are sharp. It was a most impressive sight, its clean, perpendicular face topped with shrubs and slender trees. An horizontal ledge, a natural crack in the limestone set about two thirds of the way up it looked for all the world like one I used to crawl along at home during the halcyon days of my long lost youth. The similarity made me shudder. Heck! The madcap things we used to do when we were young and daft!

Where the Monsal Trail crossed our path we climbed to the track and kept with it for the final mile to Blackwell Mill cottages, the top end of Chee Dale and the end of another excellent walk. Well, almost the end. We returned to the Wye and took the path, now on the south bank, upstream. Soon it took us away from the river to Wydale car park, off the A6, where transport awaited our arrival.

4. THE SETT VALLEY TRAIL

Length :   3 miles
Opened :   for passenger traffic - 1st March, 1868
             for goods traffic - 1872
Closed :   3rd January, 1970
O/S   :   Sheet No.110; Series 1:50,000

> *Come lasses and lads, take leave of your dads*
> *And away to the Fair let's hie;*
> *For every lad has gotten his lass*
> *And a fiddler standing by.*
> *For Jenny has gotten her Jack*
> *And Nancy has gotten her Joe.*
> *With Dolly and Tommy, good lack,*
> *How they jig it to and fro!*

The song 'Come Lasses and Lads' has become more famous than Hayfield's renowned annual fair which inspired it. The Sett Valley Trail, from Hayfield to three miles distant New Mills may one day become more famous than the railway line it has superseded.

Built for the Midland and Great Central Joint Railway Company by Rennie and Co. at a cost of £27,040, the line was opened for passenger traffic on 1st March 1868. The first locomotives used on it were 0-6-0 Tank Engines but these were replaced in the early 1900s by 4-4-2 Tank Engines, later called Class C13 and 14.

The line was a busy one carrying considerable goods and passenger traffic. Goods trains brought coals and raw materials to all the mills in the Sett Valley and took away finished products. Passenger trains, which ran regularly to Manchester, were well patronised. In the 1920s, on any summer Sunday, it was not unusual for between 4,000 and 5,000 passengers to pass through the ticket barrier at Hayfield.

Hayfield is to be found in a hollow to the west of Derbyshire's bog-trotting country. It sits astride the River Sett, a fast flowing stream which drains much of the Kinder moors and consequently floods frequently, hence its sombre appearance.

Hayfield's church, built in 1818 to replace an earlier one which had been swept away in a flood, houses the marble bust of a local pedlar, Joseph Hague, who made good in a big way. Born in the village of Chunal, some three mile north of Hayfield, in 1695 he began life as an itinerant boy pedlar, carrying his wares on his back until he could afford a donkey with a pack saddle: and as he moved about the hills selling his goods he learned about trade in general and textiles in particular. In 1716 he went to London where he gradually amassed a fortune dealing in imported cotton and fustian.

Circa 1775 he purchased Park Hall, a mile north of Hayfield and became a country gentleman and local benefactor. When he died in 1786, he was buried in Glossop and a marble bust and a memorial were erected in his honour against a wall of the chancel in Glossop parish church. Between 1826 and 1831 while the church was being repaired these items were stored in a Glossop lock-up where, one night, a drunk vandalised the bust. This so upset one Captain John White, who had succeeded Joseph Hague at Park Hall, that he had it removed to Hayfield church. Years later, in 1874, an old man called at Hayfield church and made enquiries about Hague's bust. It transpired that he was the drunk who had vandalised it all those years ago and had returned to the church to appease his conscience.

In the 17th and 18th century several pack horse trails met at Hayfield, giving it a measure of importance. The Industrial Revolution brought a calico printing works to the small town where today textiles and paper are manufactured.

Hayfield makes a good departure point for treks to Edale over Kinder Scout or to the Snake Inn on the A57; but our way was westwards along the Sett Valley to New Mills.

The Derbyshire County Council purchased the former Hayfield to New Mills railway line from British Rail as derelict land in 1973 and, following reclamation work at an estimated cost of £137,173, transformed it into a footpath bridleway with car parks and toilets at each end. In addition Hayfield station has an information centre and a picnic area.

The Trail is never far away from the River Sett which tumbles along the valley bottom between confining gritstone hills to join the Goyt spectacularly in the Torrs gorge at New Mills. The gradients are gentle, the countryside through which it passes is pleasing and in it are to be found the remains of a textile industry once so prominent in the Sett Valley. The Trail is a fine, broad one because although only a single track was ever laid, the line was made double width.

We left Hayfield in warming sunshine, two adults and two small children, along the old rail bed which swathed through young trees lush with summer greenery in a most inviting way. Within a mile we spotted, to the north, the two dams of a calico print works and a curving row of workmen's cottages; and soon a level crossing with, beyond, Birch Vale station house came into view.

Birch Vale used to be a small station with a goods yard built to serve Birch Vale Print Works whose mill chimney can be seen on the hillside north of the Trail. The station house was a hive of activity as we passed. The activity was centred on a horse box into which a frisky mare was being directed much against her wishes.

With Birch Vale behind us the lovely sylvan surroundings began to thin and a widening vista opened before us. The Trail narrowed to a slim path and dipped to cross the Thornsett road, the bridge having been demolished long since. Crossing this road was the only dangerous part of the whole walk for it took place half-way down a steep hill down which what traffic there was travelled at speed. On the far side of the road the path climbed to gain the height it had lost on the near side and immediately reverted to its original broad width. Back as it were, to normal it continued in a gentle downhill curve through more open country.

Two Rangers were checking the content of an interesting trailside pond. It was situated near a raised piece of ground thoughtfully topped with a seat on which sat two ladies totally engrossed in animated banter.

The Trail is patrolled by Rangers who provide information about it and the surrounding areas and see to it that the enjoyment of the general public is not marred by the thoughtless behaviour of others. When I asked about vandalism they told me that it did occur on converted lines, especially where they came close to urban areas, but that they hoped their regular presence would act as a deterrent. I sincerely hope so.

The footpath at Wilde's Crossing leads down to Thornsett on the north bank of the Sett. In the latter part of the 18th century, with the development of water-powered spinning equipment, swift and clear streams like the Sett and its feeders made ideal locations for water-powered spinning mills. Garrison Mill, now demolished, at Thornsett was probably one of these. The introduction of water-powered looms after 1820 encouraged further mill building along the Sett Valley and hand loom weaving as a cottage industry declined.

The Trail, now on a level gradient as it passes pastures dotted with grazing sheep and cattle, crosses High Hill Road and then begins its long ascent to New Mills, the outskirts of which are visible ahead. As the outer houses of the town are passed the summit of the ascent is reached and the Trail begins its descent into the middle of the town.

Having reached the end of the line we climbed out of Torrs gorge to find ourselves in a town that is pure L.S.Lowry Lancashire.

Beard: that was its name when it was a hamlet. It became New Mills in about 1500 when new cotton mills were built there. Its prosperity came from the much larger and grimmer 19th century cotton mills with their tall chimneys and poor working conditions. The textile industry lives on in New Mills, hence the Lowry matchstick men appearance of the place. But diversification has arrived. Today there is competition from the metal and engineering industries and the confectionery trade. Industrial archaeologist will love New Mills for, on the surface at any rate, it is more in keeping with the 19th century than the 20th.

5. THE MANIFOLD TRAIL

Length :   8½ miles
Opened :   27th June, 1904
Closed :   12th March, 1934
O/S   :   Sheet No. 1″ The Peak Tourist Map
            2½″ SK 05 and SK 15

'There is neither road nor footpath down the whole length of Manifold Valley, though these occur here and there. But the little railway threads it inmost recesses in a delightfully casual way, playing hide and seek with the cliffs and the waters, and the cars are built to make the best of the views in all directions'.

Thomas L. Tudor. 1926

Until the 1930s the Manifold Valley, for all its scenic grandeur, was well off the beaten track. No road ran along its full length, it was sparsely populated and its economic prospects were poor. A little quarrying was carried out but the land was poor agriculturally except for raising cattle and milk production. It was this dairy farming that prompted the idea of a railway freight service along the full length of the valley with day trippers providing the reason for a passenger service. It was a bold idea; but, unlike so many similar concepts, this one was dreamed up by men of vision and backed with hard cash.

The line was to be narrow gauge so that an Act of Parliament was not needed to authorise its construction. In 1896 the Light Railways Act was passed under which a standard or narrow gauge line could be authorised by the Government's Light Railway Commissioners. The standards required were far less stringent than those for other railways and there were certain speed and working restrictions to be observed. Nevertheless, it was a good way of opening up rural areas not already served by branch lines.

In May 1897, application was made to the Light Railway Commission jointly by Mr. Charles Bill, the local M.P., and the North Staffordshire Railway for a railway in two sections, one of standard 4ft.8½ins. gauge and the other to 3ft.6ins. gauge, totalling 17¼ miles at an estimated cost of £144,300. The promoters then altered the 3ft.6ins. gauge proposed to 2ft.6ins. and on 12th October, 1897, at a public enquiry at Leek, the L.R.C. approved the project. The Draft Order was submitted to the Board of Trade on 21st July 1898, and was approved on 6th March 1899.

The Manifold railway itself was to run from Waterhouses to Hulme End, a distance of eight miles eight chains. It was to be steam operated on a gauge of 2ft.6ins. The work had to be completed within five years. Among the specific provisions relating to the construction of the line were the following: 'No turntables need be provided': platforms were not needed if the carriages 'are constructed with proper and convenient means of access' from the ground: 'There shall be no obligation on the Company to provide shelter or conveniences at any station or stopping place'. The Company referred to was the Leek and Manifold Valley Light Railway Co., familiarly known as the Manifold.

That portion of the prospectus which concerned the narrow gauge section of the line stated that £15,000 of share capital would be raised in £1 shares, a grant of £10,000 would come from the Treasury and that £10,000 would be secured as a loan from the Staffordshire County Council to finance its construction. The N.S.R. agreed to work the line for 55% of the gross receipts. On 3rd October, 1899, with the Light Railway Order secured and the L. and M.V.R. Co. established, the Duke of Devonshire cut the first sod. The promoters were in business.

However, one of the Light Railway Commissioners, Col. Boughley, thought that the specifications for the construction of the line were unsatisfactory. He expressed his dissatisfaction in a letter to the company directors on 17th October 1900, recommended that an independent expert be called in to investigate and suggested E.A.Calthrop. Mr. Calthrop had spent many years on the Indian railways and his speciality was light railways. It was this background that had prompted Col. Boughley to suggest him for the Manifold project. The position of Engineer to the railway was offered to Calthrop and he accepted. It was a fateful decision which subsequently produced a masterpiece of British narrow gauge engineering.

All his design ideas depended on a very substantial permanent way and his 2ft.6ins. tracks rested on 5ft. long timber sleepers into which

Manifold Way

35lb. per yard flat-bottomed rails were spiked and screwed. He used bearing plates on each sleeper which tilted inwards just less than 3° from vertical so that the top surface of the line made as good a match as possible with the wheel tyre. Using this method he expected that both wheels and rail would have a longer life than conventionally laid track. How effective it was can be judged from the fact that the rails never had to be replaced during the line's life. Moreover, right from its opening the Manifold was noted for the smooth running of its stock.

Because of financial problems construction work was delayed until March 1902; and when work started progress was very slow indeed for so short a line. The high standard of permanent way engineering demanded by Calthrop, the many bridges, the one tunnel, poor road access and a serious outbreak of smallpox at Butterton all contributed to this. May 23rd 1904 was to have been the opening day but since the engines and only two of the line's four carriages had just arrived, leaving no time for proper trials to be carried out, the directors reluctantly put back the opening until 27th June 1904. Another, lesser reason for postponing the opening was that the N.S.R. had not yet completed its standard gauge line from Leek to Waterhouses.

The Manifold was opened before it was fully finished and the first few years were spent tidying up loose ends like providing lavatories at stations. From the outset the line was plagued with financial problems which, apart from on Bank Holidays, light passenger receipts did little to alleviate. Milk traffic kept the line alive, especially the introduction of a nightly through milk train to London in 1907. Standard gauge milk tanks were carried along the narrow gauge line on special transporters, flat bed wagons which had rails fitted to the top side at standard gauge.

The transporters enabled any standard gauge rolling stock to be carried along the Manifold line without transhipment of goods at Waterhouses; and in this connection a section of standard gauge track was laid at every station.

For more than two decades the line struggled against mounting financial difficulties. Then, in the early 1920s, a lineside creamery was built at Ecton and a siding laid to it. Thus the line's flagging fortunes were given a welcome boost.

Two locomotives based at Hulme End worked the line on the 'one engine in steam' principle, except on rare occasions when they double-headed heavy trains. They were of a type used extensively in India and had large headlights on top of their smoke boxes. One was named 'No.1 J.B.Earle' after the line's mechanical engineer and the other 'No.2 E.R.Calthrop' after the Chief Engineer. Their original livery was a light chocolate brown with white double lining. This was later altered to standard N.S.R. madder lake with a cream single line. The L.M.S. altered the livery to crimson lake, edged with black and yellow with the railway's insignia on the bunker. In the late 1920s this was altered to unrelieved black. Ugh!

The line's four carriages, which were also based at Hulme End, had primrose yellow livery lined out in black with the class numbers and the legend 'L. & M.V.Lt.Rly.' in a rich emblazoned script shown twice on the sides. This colour scheme was changed by the N.S.R. to match the new locomotive livery of madder lake and, finally, to crimson lake. So both on locomotives and carriages the progression was from good to bad to worse.

With roofs that sloped from a central ridge and a roofed platform enclosed to waist height with highly ornamental wrought iron-work at each end of the third class and the first class end of the composites, the carriages were very popular with the passengers. After the closure of the line these delightful and comfortable (though unheated apart from a stove in the guard's compartment) carriages were kept at Water-houses until 1936 when, sadly, they were burned and the metal work taken for scrap.

Goods and passenger traffic were inseparable, goods wagons being picked up and dropped off en route as the need arose. Frequently passengers had to wait while wagons were unloaded; but this was accepted as being in keeping with the leisurely pace of the valley and nobody minded very much.

The Manifold's original timetable, apart from the addition of Sunday services from 1905, remained the same throughout its life. During the summer months four journeys each way were made except on Thursdays and Saturdays when there were only three. There were three services each way on weekdays during the winter months.

No major townships were served by the Manifold line, the stations were sited too far away from the local villages and, apart from summer time tourist trafffic, there was no steady source of passenger revenue. Milk traffic was good but other freight traffic was limited and this had a detrimental effect on the line. By the 1930s bus and car competition had become an ever increasing threat. Then, in 1933, the Ecton creamery closed and with it went the railway's main life support.

Although the official closure date was Monday 12th March 1934, the last scheduled train ran from Waterhouses to Hulme End and back on Saturday 10th March. With three inches of snow laying on the ground and mist veiling the valley sides, the unheated train set off three quarters of an hour late, carrying only seven passengers. It stopped only once, at Grindon, to allow one passenger to alight; then it continued on its leisurely way to end its life in the way it had lived it - without fuss.

When the line was dismantled the L.M.S. donated the track bed to the County Council which, responding to popular demand, turned it into a footpath. The conversion, which involved little more than levelling and paving the track bed, cost only £6,000; and when the path was complete it was opened by Sir Josiah Stamp, President of the L.M.S. on 23rd July 1937. In 1953 the old Manifold line suffered a further indignity when the footpath between Redhurst and Butterton was re-laid as a road.

Although today most of the line's buildings have gone the walk remains a grand one, winding as it does through beautiful scenery. It is as much 'a must' for anyone not interested in the old narrow gauge line as it is for anyone who is. For it is a generous walk and its delights are - manifold!

A signpost at Waterhouses village indicates the way to the car park on the site of the old goods yard. From there the track goes past the goods shed and continues high above the A523 to the site of the former station. En route it passes a monument erected in 1977 to commemorate the Queen's Silver Jubilee. Some 300 yards past the site of the station the track crosses the main road on a level crossing and continues downhill through a luxuriance of trees, bushes and lush undergrowth. The walking is easy and very pleasant along a six feet wide tarmac surface, fenced on both sides.

Now comes the first of some two dozen river bridges that carried the old railway over the Hamps and Manifold between its termini, the first fourteen of which are over the Hamps. Soon after crossing this river for the third time the site of Sparrowlee station is reached, the gradient levels out and the valley begins to narrow. We are now one and a half miles out from Waterhouses.

The underlying rock in the Manifold Valley south of Hulme End and in the valley of the Hamps is Carboniferous limestone. Being a porous rock, water sinks through it from the beds of both rivers down fissures and sink holes leaving them dry for long periods during the summer months.

For two stimulating miles between Sparrowlee and Beeston Tor there are constant re-crossings of the Hamps, sometimes on bridges still as they were when the line closed, sometimes on bridges where concrete sleepers have replaced the original wooden ones.

Beeston Tor station is on a long curve at the meeting of the usually dry beds of the Hamps and Manifold rivers. The station had no sidings and the waiting room was an old carriage. Yet in a nearby meadow a large wooden refreshment building, now in a sad state of delapidation, was operated by one of the line's shareholders for the benefit of day trippers to Beeston Tor, the height which gave the station its name and where, in 1924, a hoard of Saxon coins and jewellery was found.

Now comes the most picturesque section of the whole walk with the track closely following the River Manifold through an arboreal countryside. After a pleasant half mile Grindon, now an open space beside and to the north of where the road from Grindon village crosses the track, marks the half-way point of the walk and is the place where the long climb to Hulme End begins.

A further three quarters of a mile beyond Grindon is Thor's Cave, the station that served Wetton, one mile distant. It used to have a shelter and until 1917 a refreshment room. But there were few passengers which, considering the distance the Wetton villagers had to travel to catch a train, is not surprising.

Across the river a most spectacular limestone cliff, 300ft. high, towers above the valley. High on this scarp is the gaping mouth of

Thor's Cave which can be reached by using the footpath provided for that purpose. The cave, which is a shallow one, was excavated by the Midland Scientific Association in the 1860s. Some bits and pieces from the Romano-British period were found and there was evidence that it was the site of a late Neolithic burial chamber.

Thor's fissure cave, behind Thor's Cave, has produced implements of the late upper Palaeolithic culture, reindeer and red deer bones, dolphin bones, beads, beaker fragments and buttons as well as a stone axe from the Beaker period and artefacts from Iron Age and Roman times.

Midway between Thor's Cave and Wettonmill is Redhurst Halt where the path widens to allow vehicles along it as far as Butterton. Some half a mile or so along this wider section is Wettonmill station, now a car park; and there is a tea room just across the river.

Swainsley tunnel, overhung with greenery, is not a long one, but its width and height, 12ft.9ins. and 15ft.3ins. from rail to roof, are out of all proportion to the narrow gauge line it was built to accommodate. The reason is that it had to be large enough to allow standard gauge wagons to be carried through it on transporters.

Where, at the northern end of the tunnel, the road turns to the right, the path continues straight ahead to Ecton, once so busy, now little more than a memory. The creamery has gone and nature is reclaiming the old quarry working, hiding them behind ever spreading undergrowth.

About half a mile beyond Ecton the route continues along a very tight curve where the original camber of the rails has been faithfully reproduced on tarmac to good effect.

Hulme End is reached along an embankment with a gradient of 1 in 73 although the terminus itself is on the flat. It should have been an intermediate station for the original intention was to extend the line. It was with this in mind that Hulme End for Hartington, as it was called in the timetable, was chosen to be the line's headquarters. That is why the engine and carriage sheds were built there: that is why it had the only crane on the line. But nothing came of the extension so Hulme End became the line's terminus.

One indirect reminder of the Manifold line still stands in the little village. If you have timed the walk correctly it is well worth a visit for there you can rest in comfort over a pint. The name of this establishment is the 'Light Railway Hotel'.

Rowland Emett's brilliantly drawn Cockle Shell railway and wayside stations at Far Twittering and Fiddling Halt was once scorned by a critic.

'What a waste of draughtsmanship', he pronounced. 'Why do you make such drawings? What good are they?'

Rowland Emett thought for a while, then answered. 'I'll tell you what good they are. They make people smile; and if they do nothing else they will have proved their worth.'

I feel the same about the Manifold Line with its funny, primrose carriages and fussy little engines. I believe that had it not died in 1934 the line would have become a real attraction today. Sadly it has gone and the Manifold Valley is the poorer for it. But at least now we have this lovely walk and for that we should be thankful.

Goods Yard at High Peak Junction. Route 1.

II Northern Cheshire

On 14th April of 979 Aethelred was crowned King of the English. The coronation took place at Bath and it was from there that he sailed with his fleet to Chester, where six Kings of the Cumbrians and the Scots pledged themselves his allies by land and sea.

The following summer unfriendly ships sailed to Chester from the Irish Sea as the Anglo-Saxon Chronicle records: *AND THY ILCAN GEARE WAES LEGECEASTER SCIR GEHERGOD FRAM NORDSHIPHERIGE* (And that same year was Legeceastershire harried by a North-ship-host). Thus we have the first written proof of Cheshire's existence as Legeceaster scir.

Cheshire reached its greatest extent during the early Middle Ages. In 1086, when the Domesday Book was compiled, the county of Chester, as it had then been named, included northwards all Lancashire south of the River Ribble and parts of the Upper Yorkshire Dales. To the south-west it spread across the Dee over Welsh and English Maelor; land which later became eastern Denbighshire and that part of Flintshire squashed between Shropshire and Cheshire.

In 1071 the Norman Hugh d'Avranches, nicknamed Hugh the Fat, was made Earl of Chester. In 1237 the earldom passed to the Crown and the county of Chester has remained a royal earldom ever since.

At about the same time this, the largest of the Marcher Earldoms, became palatinate. This made it an almost independent territory where the King's writ did not run. It could make its own laws, administer its own courts and impose taxes. It retained these powers in full until 1536 and retains the name to this day although now the title is largely nominal.

In 1536, by the Act of Union which brought all Wales and England under the English Crown, Cheshire at last became part of the English realm and sent its first members to parliament at Westminster. By then its territory had shrunk to roughly its present teapot shape. Since then changes have been confined to fairly minor adjustments of its boundary with other counties.

A thousand years ago Wirral, the peninsular between the Dee and Mersey estuaries was twice as long as it is today and the sea lapped Chester's walls, but by 1400 the Dee estuary had become choked to such an extent that access to Chester was hampered by silting sands. This caused concern because Chester was vital for English supplies to

Ireland. Yet with every passing year the silting became worse. So much so that Richard II refrained from extracting rents because of the resultant loss of trade.

Soon after the turn of the 17th century a new quay was built ten miles downstream from Chester at Parkgate. This was used by Irish Packets until the early 19th century; but today Parkgate promenade looks out on a mile of mud banks.

Efforts were made to keep Chester alive as a port by dredging, but the Irish trade shifted to Liverpool on the north bank of the Mersey.

The Wirral peninsular is mostly flat. What high land there is seldom rises more than 200 feet above sea level. Heswall Hill, commanding fine views over the Dee, is only 340 feet high. No Wirral land is higher than that. Apart from its few high points, Wirral is a plateau very similar to the countryside of central Cheshire and like central Cheshire it was once almost entirely covered with oak woodland so dense that the locals said of it:-

> *From Blacon point to Hilbree*
> *A squirrel may leap from tree to tree.*

Today, among Wirral's green, park-like commons, mellow villages are to be found. These charming places increase the interest of this flat peninsular and are typical of those to be found throughout Cheshire. For despite the industrialised Mersey Valley and about half a dozen towns of varying sizes, this lush, leafy county has retained its rural character. Cheshire is rather up-market; but not to the extent that people take their fish and chips home in brief cases. Actually it is a rather nice county where rather nice people live; and its county town, Chester, is more than two thousand years old.

In Roman times it was called Deva or Castra Devana, the camp on the Dee. Later, when the Roman legions had become established, it was given the name Caelleon, city of the legions, by the British Cornovii who lived thereabouts at that time. Within a century the city was generally referred to as Cestre.

The Romans chose with care when they sited Deva at the head of the Dee estuary. It was the lowest bridging point of the Dee and ideally suited to the planned advance along the vital North Welsh coast route and into the Welsh hills.

Throughout its long life Chester has kept the major features of a Roman legionary fortress plan as the basis of its layout, making it unique in Britain. Not even York can make this claim, for present day York has no relationship whatsoever to the fortress buried below its narrow, winding streets.

The best way to see Chester, this gleaming city of spires and towers, is by walking the full circuit of its walls, within which are those magnificent survivors of the Middle Ages, the half timbered rows. Nothing in Europe can compare with these long galleries of shops linked by a covered way between the ground and second floors.

Between Chester and the Pennines lies the shallow dish of rich countryside known as the Cheshire plain. This is divided by the Central Cheshire Ridge, which is narrow, not very high and has a steep eastern edge. It extends northwards from Bickerton to Helsby where, much lower now and broken, it swings east were the Mersey Valley lies across what is structurally the same depression. It is upon the rich soil of this plain that are pastured the hardy cattle which have made Cheshire famous for its cheese. However, cheese is not particularly important to the agriculture of the shire today. Now dairy farming predominates with arable farming, mainly grain and potatoes, a close second.

Under the Cheshire plain between the Central Cheshire Ridge and the Pennines is a huge bed of Keuper Marl overlaid by a thick layer of glacial clay, sand and gravel. This Keuper Marl was laid down in hot desert conditions and contains, at two succesive depths, dried salt lakes from which salt is extracted either as brine or rock salt.

Salt, the most valuable of Cheshire's mineral products, has been extracted as brine from spring or boreholes since Roman times in a salt producing area formed by three towns, Middlewich, Nantwich and Northwich. This area has been known for many centuries as Wichfield or the Wiches.

Rock salt was first discovered at Marlbury near Northwich, about 1670 and the first pit is thought to have been sunk by 1720. Prior to this, brine, which was boiled in lead pans to extract the salt, was the sole source of supply.

Today, rock salt is extracted from only one mine, the remainder being pumped out as brine. Much of the salt is used as a raw material by the chemical factories of the Wiches. Domestic salt from brine supplies most of the home market and is exported. Rock salt is used mainly for clearing snow from roads in winter. A mind boggling three million tons of salt are extracted from beneath the Cheshire plain annually.

Northwich is the modern centre of the salt industry; but this was not always the case. Nantwich was the medieval centre of salt boiling to where packhorses brought salt from Midland villages along ancient 'salt ways'.

Extensive subsidence, an unhappy legacy of uncontrolled salt and brine extraction, had diversified the Cheshire landscape by the collapse of river valleys above salt workings, forming small lakes called flashes. These flashes are particularly rich in flora and fauna. They attract wild fowl which, in turn, attract wild fowlers, bird watchers and fishermen.

Rostherne Mere, comprising some 100 acres and 100 feet deep, is the largest and deepest flash in Cheshire. Now a bird sanctuary, it too harbours a large variety of waterfowl. A local legend tells of how, when the bells were being hung in St. Mary's, a flashside church, the largest rolled into the mere; and that every Easter morning a mermaid rises and tolls it.

Great Budsworth, once the largest parish in Cheshire, lies two miles north of Northwich. It stretched 20 miles south from Warrington to Holmes Chapel and embraced 36 townships. Today all these townships are independent but Budsworth still retains its prefix, Great. The village clusters around its sandstone, hilltop church.

The unobtrusive Cheshire plain is a joyful mix of meadows, meres, swamps or mosses, red sandstone, churches and fine, half-timbered magpie houses in black and white. Wriggling lanes and by-roads abound in what until the early 18th century was, like most of England, a largely rural county where wildlife flourished and game, wild geese, wild ducks and mallard, took to the air in huge flocks large enough to darken the sun.

The red sandstones of the Triassic, bedrock of the Cheshire plain, end abruptly in the north-east of the county on the Red Rock Fault, east of which are the softer sandstones of the Coal Measures with, higher up the western side of the Pennines, the Millstone Grits of the gaunt uplands.

The north-east Cheshire coalfield extended northwards from Macclesfield to Stalybridge and coal began to be worked there in the 18th century. However, its economic importance was minor compared with the Lancashire and Staffordshire coalfields.

From 1926, when the Electricity Supply Act was passed, the many small concerns and supply lines, which until then had supplied relatively restricted parts of the country with electricity, gradually became linked to the National Grid. Now, with electric power available anywhere, the 'coalfield geography' of the 19th century began to crumble and places like Cheshire, which had little coal, could expand industry as never before.

In east Cheshire the new industrial growth was based first on textiles. Woollen cloth has been made in this area since the Bronze Age. In the Middle Ages wool was England's most lucrative industry but

Cheshire's part in it was not very great.

In 1732 Stockport was the first town in the country to set up a silk mill. Macclesfield followed suit in 1743 as did Congleton in 1752. By 1770 there were twelve silk mills in Stockport but by 1800 most of them had been converted to cotton. In Macclesfield and Congleton silk became the dominant industry. Cotton was introduced into both towns in the 1780's but it declined in the slump following the Napoleonic Wars and was never revived in Macclesfield. In Congleton silk and cotton continued side by side until in the 1930's man-made fibres ousted silk.

The 20th century has seen the pace of discovery and invention speed up and new vistas open. Nowhere has this been more evident than in industry, transport and communications; and Cheshire has been vitally affected by these changes. Yet some things remain as constant as the stars in their orbits. For example, it was recorded in 1656 that the women of Cheshire:-

'Are very friendly and loving, painful in labour, and in all other kind of housewifery expert, fruitful in bearing of children, after they are married and sometimes before.'

Yes, some things never change.

Cheshire has a great heritage of natural beauty, its shrinking acres are still vast and many of its towns and villages ae unspoiled. Furthermore, lying at the foot of Lancashire it effectively protects that County Palatine from the Midlands and for that reason alone it is rather special.

6. THE WHITEGATE WAY

Length	:	5½ miles
Opened	:	The Winsford Branch of which the Whitegate Way is part
		for goods traffic - 1st June, 1870
		for passenger traffic - 1st July, 1870
Closed	:	for passenger traffic - 1874
Re-opened	:	for passenger traffic - 1st May, 1886
Closed	:	for passenger traffic - 1st December, 1888
Re-opened	:	for passenger traffic - 1st February, 1892
Closed	:	for passenger traffic - 1st January, 1931
		for goods traffic - 1966
O/S	:	Sheet No.118; Series 1:50,000

63

> *Here at the wayside station, as many a morning,*
> *I watch the smoke torn from the fumy engine*
> *Crawling across the field in serpent sorrow*
> *Edwin Muir*

The Winsford Branch was opened on 1st June, 1870, as part of the West Cheshire Railway Company's plan to serve the salt industry of Winsford. During the 19th century many salt works had developed along the banks of the Weaver Valley on the north side of the town. The L.N.W.R. already served those salt works on the east side of the valley but until the Winsford Branch was built no railway served the west side.

The building of the branch was authorised by the West Cheshire Railway Act of 1862. An earlier Act, that of 1861, had already covered many of the line's features like maximum charges for goods and passenger traffic, and this Act also authorised the building of the line only as far as Falks Junction. The two lines from the junction to Meadow Bank and to Winsford, which came to be known as 'the Winsford extension', were built on land bought privately rather than compulsorily and the plans are dated 1866.

Throughout its life, until the railways were nationalised in 1946, the Winsford Branch was run by the Cheshire Lines Committee Railway Company, the C.L.C. This company was jointly owned by three other companies, the Manchester, Sheffield and Lincolnshire Railway Company (M.S.L.R.), the Great Northern Railway Company (G.N.R.) and the Midland Railway Company (M.R.). The C.L.C., although probably the most important of Britain's joint lines, remained comparatively unknown outside the area in which it operated.

Within four years of passenger trains starting to run on the Winsford Branch to provide a service between Winsford, Whitegate and Cuddington the service was withdrawn. Competition from the main L.N.W.R. was just too strong. Moreover, there was no connection, in those early days, to Chester. So, in 1874, the passenger service folded and was not re-started until 1st May 1886.

This followed a request to the C.L.C. from Winsford Local Board, which was agreed to, provided the trains ran on an experimental basis only. Another factor in the decision to re-open the passenger service, and probably the really deciding one, was fiercer competition from the L.N.W.R. Winsford's L.N.W.R. station was sited a mile or so east of the town; but in 1882, a branch line was opened which brought the L.N.W.R. right into its heart; and the line, besides carrying

NORTHERN CHESHIRE: ROUTE 6

passengers, served half a dozen sidings to salt and other works.

With the salt industry growing, Winsford becoming more prosperous than ever before and connections now to Chester, Wrexham and North Wales, the new passenger service had everything going for it. Yet, unbelievably, the C.L.C. fluffed their chances, operating the passenger side as though they had given it a death wish. The line was run primarily for goods traffic, passengers being of little account. There were only three passenger services a day, each six miles journey from Winsford to Cuddington taking over half an hour. There were no passenger trains as such. Passengers travelled in decrepit coaches attached to goods trains. Anyone using these 'mixed trains' did so in extreme discomfort for the goods wagons to which the coaches were attached had no springs on their buffers; and as if the jolting was not bad enough these unfortunate travellers were subjected to a great deal of waiting as wagons were shunted on and off en route.

On 25th August 1888, a minor accident on the line heralded the line's second closure for passenger traffic. The driver of a mixed train ascending the incline out of Winsford failed to notice that a pair of facing points on one of the sidings had been left open. The train ran into the siding and collided with some wagons of coal, causing a great deal of damage to the rolling stock. One passenger was slightly hurt.

A Board of Trade inspector judged that the many sidings leading onto the line were dangerous and the Board ruled that the passenger service should not be allowed to run without modifications being made to the line. C.L.C. were unwilling to pay the several thousand pounds these would cost and the passenger service ceased on 1st December 1888.

The closure was met with a great deal of disapproval from local people and Winsford Local Board took the C.L.C. before the Court of the Railway and Canal Committee. The hearing took place on 13th and 14th January 1891. The legal aspects of the case went back to the 1854 Traffic Act, before which companies had only the obligation of common carriers. The 1854 Traffic Act compelled a railway company, when it had opened a line, to 'give reasonable facilities' according to their power for receiving, despatching and dealing with traffic. The main argument at the 1891 hearing centred on what 'reasonable facilities' were.

C.L.C. accounts showed that the passenger service had been run at a loss - £85 in 1886, £84 in 1887 and £47 in 1888. Winsford Local Board argued that the losses were fairly small and diminishing. Furthermore, they contended, the line was a feeder with, for example, receipts in 1887 of £796 from passengers travelling beyond

Cuddington. How much, the Local Board asked, could be considered as receipts for the branch alone? C.L.C. worked it out on a mileage basis and credited the Winsford Branch with £249. The Local Board argued that the value of the branch, was much more since few, if any, of the passengers would go from Cuddington onwards, if it were not for the Winsford Branch. They would either go by the L.N.W.R.'s line or stay at home. The Local Board's main argument, however, was that the Winsford Branch as a whole made a profit and that the C.L.C. could not single out and discontinue the passenger service because it was unprofitable itself because this was going against the 1854 Act's provision of 'reasonable facilities'.

C.L.C. countered with three main arguments:-
1) The service was running at a loss and therefore could not be regarded as a 'reasonable facility'.
2) The Company could not afford the capital expenditure involved in modifying the line to meet Board of Trade requirements.
3) This was an attempt to find a legal loophole. The Act of 1861 authorised the building of the line only as far as Falks Junction. The land for the final section had been bought privately, therefore was, in effect, a private line, not under the jurisdiction of Parliament. They could not be told what or what not to do with it.

The Commissioners agreed with the Local Branch's basic argument and the hearing went against the C.L.C. who did not appeal against it. They modified the line to meet the Board of Trade requirements for passenger trains and the service was re-started on 1st February 1892.

At the bottom of the re-opening notices were printed the words 'All Trains are First and Third Class'. Second class was not mentioned, and this is how it came about. In 1872 the Midland Railway Company became the first to admit third class passengers to all its trains and in 1875 it abolished second class altogether. Today's second class is the old third class, promoted in 1956. From the 1870s to 1956 most railways ran first and third class but not second class.

On re-opening, the passenger service provided six trains a day in each direction. By 1910 this had increased to nine trains a day. In addition there were 'specials' to, for example, football matches and shows in Manchester.

During the first World War, when all the railways came under Government control and their resources were pooled, the Winsford Branch did its bit by conveying munition workers to Wincham.

Following the armistice in 1918 the railways, particularly small branch lines like the Winsford Branch, suffered greatly from competition for passenger traffic from buses. Many ex-servicemen, setting up on their own in the bus business, were taken over by shrewd business-men who really set about the thorough development of this promising new transport. It marked the beginning of the decline of the railway system. The rail strike of 1919 and the more serious General Strike of 1926, which severely cut railway services, taught many passengers that road transport was convenient and generally safe. It also saved a walk to the station.

The railways set about dealing with the competition by becoming part of it. In 1928 they received powers from Parliament to buy bus companies into which they could put their own modest bus fleets. These powers enabled a railway company to 'provide, own, work and use road vehicles in any district to which access is afforded by the (railway) system' of the company concerned. In the Winsford area the two parent companies of the Cheshire Lines - by now the L.N.E.R. and the L.M.S. - came to an agreement in 1929 with the North Western Road Car Company of Stockport. It entailed a working agreement between the railway companies and the Road Car Company, with the former subscribing capital and purchasing shares.

Competition from road transport was the major factor in the decline of the railways: yet there were others. The 1921 coal strike didn't help; and the post war economic slump, coming at a time when under the 1921 Railway Act some 120 separate companies were being compulsorily merged into four larger ones, exacerbated an already difficult situation.

As part of this sorry picture of decline the Winsford Branch, being a minor line in competition with Winsford's other railway, was badly hit. Over a six year period which culminated in the demise of the line's passenger service it deteriorated alarmingly, although goods traffic remained profitable. In 1924 the line carried 99,000 passengers: by 1930 the figure was 68,000. Receipts fared even worse, falling from £1,706 in 1924 to £809 in 1930. Running costs, however, increased, giving the line a substantial loss each year.

A Sentinel-Cammell steam railcar was used on the branch between July 1929 and the end of 1930. C.L.C. had four of them, the only motive power owned by the company itself, the remaining locomotives being provided by the L.N.E.R. Although relatively cheap to run, the railcar was unable to stop the continuing losses made by the branch's passenger service.

Matters came to a head when, in 1930, the C.L.C. as a whole lost £6,500 on the whole of their traffic. Economies had to be made and one of the first casualties was the Winsford Branch's passenger service. The announcement was made in November 1930 and the service was closed, for good this time, on Thursday, 1st January 1931.

Salt, consisting almost entirely of types of white salt, was the main goods carried on the Winsford Branch until about 1950, when rock salt also became an important source of revenue.

Before the salt pans were phased out to be replaced by the vacuum process of evaporating brine, coal was a very important part of the branch's business. Large amounts of it were used in the manufacture of salt using salt pans, the ratio being two tons of coal to three tons of fine salt and one ton of coal to two tons of coarse salt. The type of coal used was industrial slack, which is of a higher quality than domestic slack and contains more lumps.

Over the country as a whole the railways largely replaced the canals as a means of transporting goods. The Winsford Branch, however, was an exception in that a lot of coal and salt continued to be sent by boat along the River Weaver until both river and railways were supplanted by road transport.

Generally, most of the salt for export went by river and canal to Liverpool docks, whilst that for domestic use was sent by rail, either by the Cheshire Lines or L.N.W.R.

The Winsford Branch also carried livestock, mail, newspapers, bricks and timber, building materials, food and drink and all the other general supplies needed to support civilized human life within its area. Winsford station had a large warehouse in which all these types of goods were stored before distribution.

Whitegate, a very busy little station with a coal yard, was used for the distribution of agricultural products to the surrounding farms. Just how busy it was in the immediate pre-World War One years can be calculated by a rule of thumb method used at that time when one acre of farmland produced one ton of traffic per annum. There were many acres of farmland around Whitegate in 1914.

Even before the 1914 war the demand for salt was beginning to fall off because many overseas countries had started to produce salt from their own deposits and the production of cheap solar salt in coastal areas around the world was spreading rapidly. These trends helped the decline in goods traffic along the Winsford Branch.

But it was competition from road transport, which started after World War One, that really hit the railways. On the Winsford Branch the decline of goods traffic which had always been much more profitable than passenger traffic, took place over a longer period, surviving the inter war years. Not until petrol rationing was abolished after the Second World War did the decline in goods traffic gather strength. The final blow came in the 1950's when coal production, which had always provided a high proportion of railway freight, was reduced as oil grew in importance as a primary fuel.

The Winsford Branch was hit harder and earlier than many other lines because of competition from Winsford's main line. Winsford-And-Over Station was particularly vulnerable because as the salt pans closed it became isolated from the salt works. For the final decade of its life coal was its main trade.

Just when all seemed lost, the line was granted a reprieve. During the 1950s, rock salt production from Meadows Bank mine increased to keep pace with the increasing demand for the means to treat icy, winter roads. I.C.I. wanted to transport some of the rock salt by rail. The firm successfully negotiated with British Rail to keep open the line from Meadow Bank onwards, the rest of the line into Winsford being closed. I.C.I. agreed to subsidise the line.

The line finally closed in 1966 by which time hardly any bulk rock salt was being despatched by rail because road transport was cheaper. Both I.C.I. and British Rail agreed to its closure, which was understandable and rather nice. Happy endings are so much better than acrimony.

Some 550 yards north-east of the traffic lights at the junction of the A49 and the A556, Ash Road turns right off Cuddington Road into a quiet area with plenty of parking space but, unfortunately, no toilets. Having parked, walk back along Ash Road, cross Cuddington Road and go down the signposted public footpath straight ahead. Continue past a dirt road leading to a quarry on your right and enter a wood along a track muddied through continual use by cattle. After 100 yards the way opens out just before a railway bridge and there, on the left, is the entrance to the northern end of the Whitegate Way, the start of a rare adventure.

Besides its interest as a disused line, the Whitegate Way's most important value is as a 'wildlife corridor' because it provides a site rich in wildlife that is healthy, stable in character and, most importantly, safe for children to visit. In addition it passes through a rich countryside chock full of variety and interest. Easy access is provided by the many leafy lanes and public footpaths leading from it throughout its length.

Because the land through which the Way runs is mainly farmland, the habitat is essentially artificial. And this is where the trackbed scores, because it provides an area which can be colonised by so many species that are missing from nearby fields. The most common plants along the Way are usually those associated with waste ground like brambles, nettles, rosebay willowherb and grasses. When the line was working the trackbed would have been almost free of plants. With the removal of the track and top ballast, the remaining cinder surface has gradually been colonised by plants, usually headed by mosses, colonising from the edges inwards. With the mosses having gained a foothold, grasses like common bent and false oats grass appear with horsetails not far behind.

Many birds have played their part in the seeding of the trackbed. Jays, for example, which are commonly seen feeding on the cinder surface in autumn and winter, store acorns by burying them along the disused line; and in this way assist in the faster spread of oak. Shy birds with white rumps and a raucous alarm call, jays add interest and beauty to the scene. So do the chaffinches, greenfinches, thrushes, blackbirds, wrens, magpies, robins and titmice, all of which make their homes along the Way.

Between the Cuddington end of Whitegate Way and three miles distant Whitegate station much of the trackbed is enclosed in a number of cuttings. On setting off along the Way you climb steadily out of Ravensclough and once the summit is reached the rest of the walk is downhill. At first you go southwards as far as the first over-bridge beyond which the trackbed curves towards the east. Once Whitegate station is passed the Way spends much of its time on embankments, some of which are very high and steep sided. Conditions in the cuttings are very different from those on the embankments and split the Way into two very interesting but contrasting areas.

Badgers build their setts in the soft, sandy soil to the west of Whitegate station and do much of their foraging in the fields surrounding the old line. Sometimes they share their setts with foxes who often take over old ones. Much of the badgers food, which consists of small animals, beetles and refuse, is found on the trackbed in the surrounding area.

Rabbits, finding the sandy soil easy to tunnel, have made a great many burrows in the cutting where they have become pests because of the damage they do. Field-mice, field-voles, shrews and moles share the sandy track-sides west of Whitegate station with the rabbits, the badgers and the foxes. Damselflies, butterflies and moths are all to be found there, fluttering above the Way in abundant variety.

The third overbridge carries Kennel Lane over the Way. It is old and wide and sunk between sandy banks. For part of its length it is bordered with oak trees. A detour along the lane, northwards for half a mile, will bring you to the Cheshire Hunt Kennels. The Huntsmen's horses, a pack of fox hounds and some of the Hunt's employees live there. Over ninety hounds are kept there in roughly equal numbers, male and female. The hounds' enclosure is best seen by going along the lane a bit, past the huntsman's house and going up to a fence. A high wall shields the hounds' pens but you can see an obelisk with an iron-railed surround which was erected in memory of the famous 'Blue Cap', which was rated the fastest fox hound in the country. Legend has it that a weight had to be hung around his neck to prevent him out-racing the rest of the pack. 'Blue Cap' died in 1772.

Returning to the Way, continue along it as it cuts between Abbotsmoss Plantation on its southern edge and on its northern edge, Forest Camp, an area of ground owned by Cheshire Scout Council. The pool which lies close to the Way, at the eastern edge of Forest Camp, is called The Gullery.

Whitegate station has a toilet, a car park and an unruffled history. It was erected in 1870 when the line was opened and since the railway was built to take the most direct line to the salt works at Winsford, the station was sited a mile away from the village whose name it carried in the neighbouring parish of Marton.

Like all C.L.C stations in rural Cheshire the building was a severely practical house-type combining the station master's living accommodation and offices. The ornate wooden barge-boards on the gable ends were typical of C.L.C. buildings. The booking office was at one end of it, next to the station office. A public toilet was at the other end.

A ladies waiting room stood between the station and the bridge carrying the road over the line to Whitegate village. It was demolished in the 1940's.

At first the station had only a single siding and no loop. But by 1899 a loop line on the far or northern side of the line had been added together with another siding. Because the line was single track a loop line was compulsory in order to provide a passing point. This loop proved useful while both goods and passenger trains used the line but later on, when only goods trains were running, it was used as a temporary park for wagons.

The gradient out of the Weaver valley up 'Ocean Bank' was steep enough to strictly limit the number of wagons an engine could pull up it. So a train would pull its maximum load as far as Whitegate station where the wagons were left in the loop, which could accommodate fifty of them at a time. Engine and guards van would then return to Meadow Bank to pick up more to be added to those in the loop and the lengthened train would continue from there.

East of Whitegate station the aspect is more open and the Way runs entirely through farmland. Here, especially on the south side of the track rosebay willowherb predominates, pinking huge patches of embankment in summer. In winter, when the rosebay dies back, underlying bramble stems provide almost the only ground cover.

The north side of the banks attracts plants that prefer damper conditions. Here rosebay, nettles, ferns and bindweed intermingle. Plantain and hogweed prefer the trackbed.

Three quarters of a mile east of Whitegate station, where the Way crosses the road to Whitegate village, a fine example of a late 17th century farmhouse, Falcon Cottage, can be seen on your left. Similar in structure to most of the half-timbered buildings in the area, its timbers are supported on a sandstone sill. The thatch is of Norfolk reeds and has a raised ridge with exposed stitching. It was converted into cottages in the 19th century.

As the Way comes to within a mile of Catsclough Crossing, the end of the walk, it goes along a high embankment which provides excellent views of the surrounding countryside. From this high vantage point, as it passes between two large pools called Poacher's Pools, Brookhouse Farm is seen in a field on the left and another large pool, the Ocean, is on the right. Like so many pools in the area, Poacher's Pools and Ocean are the result of subsidence due to salt mining.

The railway arch over Grange Lane, half a mile from home, became unsafe owing to subsidence and was demolished several years ago. The local children call it 'the broken bridge'. Wildlife abounds here, there are good views and Catsclough Crossing is straight ahead.

The cottage has plaster cladding on its walls and a large chimney at one side of it. It is a railway cottage and the crossing near it marks the end of the Whitegate Way, which does not include the rest of the trackbed down to the road. This is let to the owner of the cottage and is private.

Other indications of the line are a length of track, the sign 'Catsclough Crossing Cottage', the remains of the crossing gates, railway sleepers used for fencing and a drainage manhole cover.

A walk, right, along Catsclough Lane southwards to Catsclough Wood, right along its edge, across Grange Lane and across a field will bring you to Knight's Grange, a sports complex and recreation centre. Once it was a farm and the farmhouse has been converted into a restaurant. Just the place in which to reminisce about the splendid Whitegate Way while someone nips back to Ravensclough for the car.

7. BIDDULPH VALLEY WAY - MOW COP TRAIL MIX

Length :   12 miles including 4½ miles on disused railway
Opened :   for goods traffic - 1859

Closed   :   for passenger traffic - 1864
              for passenger traffic - 1927
              for goods traffic - 1st December, 1963
O/S   :   Sheet No.118; Series 1:50,000

> *The steely train in the stupid green*
> *Of sleepy, sleepy summer tore*
> *An even rent in the placid clean*
> *Cloth of the air with an onward roar.*
> *Genevieve Taggard.*

But that was long ago: nowadays the air remains unblemished by sparks and smoke belching from locomotives pulling train loads of miners from Congleton to the colleries at Ford Green and Biddulph. Sand is no longer carried from Congleton to the Potteries. Coal trains from the Potteries to Congleton are history now. Today the Biddulph Valley Railway is being transformed into the Biddulph Valley Way, a footpath and bridleway that will eventually run to the Potteries. But before this praiseworthy project can reach completion the open cast coal field now sprawling across the disused line will have to be worked out, the area landscaped and a new trackway placed along the route of the original line.

The North Staffordshire Railway Company built it; and did so because the coal and iron barons told it to. So powerful were these industrialists that, had the N.S.R. refused to do so, they would have built the line themselves. Being a small company, the N.S.R. was no match for the combined might of the local coal and steel bosses. It agreed to build the line; and when the agreement was made the coal and iron overlords made it pay their expenses! Authority was granted for the Biddulph Valley Railway in 1854, its main purpose being to serve the extensive rich coal mines and the widespread iron works in the Biddulph Valley. Thus the N.S.R., that 'small octopus of a line', as one of its directors described it, grew another tentacle. And should anyone doubt the line's parentage, everything about it displayed the N.S.R. logo, the Staffordshire Knot, probably the best known trade mark throughout the entire railway system. It was seen on station buildings, coaches, wagons, tarpaulins and the staff uniforms. Yet, despite the famous Staffordshire Knot it displayed so prominently, the N.S.R. was the least known of all the railway companies at the hub of the country's railway system in London. This was because it was a purely local line, although its milk vans were seen on other company's lines and its coaches travelled frequently to and from Euston.

The N.S.R. was at its peak during the Edwardian years. It was one of a few companies, all of whom were larger than itself, which depended on suburban traffic for much of their revenues yet managed to distribute improved dividends because of good management. Bradshaw congratulated the N.S.R. on its achievement in this respect. In the four years prior to its regrouping N.S.R. dividends rose to 4⅜ per cent and gave the company a cherished title, a 5 per cent line. The Biddulph Valley Railway was in good hands.

In 1927 the Biddulph Valley passenger service from Stoke to Congleton was withdrawn. This caused little surprise for the rail journey was used mainly by people shopping at Hanley.

Private mineral trains run by the iron and coal owners abounded on the line, much to the delight of the N.S.R. The L.M.S., however, did not share this enthusiasm and after re-grouping these private trains were no longer welcome as a source of income. In June 1931, they ceased to run.

In 1972 a short stretch of trackbed at Malkins Bank, Congleton, was used by Cheshire County Council in a scheme for converting a chemical tip into a municipal golf course.

Timbersbrook, a pleasant village sheltering behind and to the south of The Cloud, an eminence offering tremendous views over the Cheshire Plain and the Peak District, makes an attractive start to this excellent walk. Gritstone houses, slumbering in their rural setting, make it difficult to believe that Timbersbrook owes its existence to industry - a silk mill, a dye works and a quarry. A restful place these days, Timbersbrook once teemed with activity. At one time, every day was filled with the hiss and clatter of steam wagons and horse teams bringing in the coal. So dense was this traffic that many of the villagers complained about the damage being done to the village road.

In 1961 the silk mill was closed. It was demolished in 1976.

Timbersbrook is within an Irish mile of being the half-way point of the Mow Cop Trail which has its northern terminus at Rushton, three miles away. There, to the east of the A523, three splendid walks, the Mow Cop Trail, the Gritstone Trail and the Staffordshire Way, meet. It has parking facilities, a picnic area with tables and toilets.

On leaving Timbersbrook car park turn right and 100 yards down the road on your left a Mow Cop Trail marker on a fingerpost points the way (Mow rhymes with cow, incidentally). Follow the Trail across meadows to join the disused Biddulph Valley Railway and turn left along it. The trackbed will take you along a valley carved by melting glacier broth at the end of the last Ice Age. For the first mile and a bit of railway walking the Mow Cop Trail and the proposed Biddulph

Valley Way are one.

Like so many other disused lines this one is quickly becoming a haven for wildlife. Flowers grow along it in great variety, adding charm and colour to the scene; and their presence attracts many beautifully marked butterflies. Birch and goat willow are prominent among the colonising trees: trees that provide food and shelter for many of the birds to whom the trackbed has become home. More than 60 species of birds have been identified along it. Once across the second bridge, which carries the trackbed over the A527, you enter Staffordshire and spend most of the next half mile or so in cuttings which become shallower as you move through them. Where they thin to open trackbed a farm, Whitemoor Farm, can be seen on your right and slightly to your rear. As you enter another cutting a little way ahead the Mow Cop Trail turns right along a path which very soon turns right again, then left to go straight ahead, passing in front of Whitemoor Farm. Continuing in the same direction, north-west, the path makes a sharp left turn just past where another path branches to the right. The way is now south-westerly, past bracken beds where foxes often rest, to Nick i' th' Hill.

The Mow Cop Trail leaves Nick i' th' Hill most pleasantly through fields and Willocks Wood. It runs close to the county border along the famous gritstone ridge called Congleton Edge, 700ft. high, from where the views across the Cheshire Plain are spectacular.

Millions of years ago a break in the earth's crust caused the sandstone beneath the Cheshire Plain to sink relative to the dark, rather forbidding millstone grit rocks of the hills. This split, known as the Red Rock Fault, is responsible for this splendid ridge which stretches along the very frontier of Staffordshire where the county's wild moorland descends to the green pastures of Cheshire.

Congleton Edge has more than its fair share of quarries. The Mow Cop Trail threads between them as it goes along the county boundary towards its destination, Mow Cop village. Those on the top of the ridge and some at its base supplied gritstone for building purposes. One, at least, on the Cheshire Plain, was a sandstone quarry. Close to the end of the Mow Cop Trail the most impressive of these quarries has for a centrepiece a giant gritstone block, known today as the Old Man of Mow. It was left by the quarrymen as they prised out the surrounding rock. It is frequently ascended by rock climbers.

Mow Cop village, which sprawls around a great, rocky hill nearly 1,100 feet high, is now the property of the National Trust. In the middle of it Mow Cop Castle marks the southern end of the Mow Cop Trail. Randle Wilbraham of Rode Hall, down on the plain, had it built

Mow Cop

in 1754 as an eyecatcher. So, although it looks like a ruined castle it is a folly. The rock on which it stands and from which the village gets its name, Mow Cop, stems from 'Moel Cop', meaning bald rock.

In 1807 Hugh Bourne, a Stoke carpenter, held a great camp meeting at Mow Cop from which stemmed the Primitive Methodists with a membership of 100,000 and 5,000 chapels. At one time 38 of these chapels were on the slopes of Mow Cop. In 1932 they became re-united with the Methodists.

At one time there were five mills making fustian, a velveteen-like cloth, in Mow Cop. They have gone now, but others remain to make surgical dressings and nylon.

Many of the village's inhabitants are miners who work in Biddulph and Stoke-on-Trent.

Leaving Mow Cop Castle, turn right and retrace your steps for a short distance, first along Castle Road, passing the Mow Cop Inn on your left (if the hours are against you), then along Congleton Road to where Towerhill Road joins it from the right. Turn right and continue along Towerhill Road for about a mile as far as a crossroad where turn left along Akesmoor Lane, passing a farm, Towerhill, on your right as you begin to walk along it. Continue along the lane to where, half-way

76

along the third field on your right, a path will take you to the disused
line as it cuts through the western limits of Biddulph, goes diagonally
across a corner of a long field and continues close to a hedge on its left
to enter a lane which goes past Woodside Farm, on its right, shortly
before reaching the disused railway.

From here the way is left, northwards along the line, first with fields
on both sides but with houses not far away on your right.

Once the first overbridge is passed, houses press close to the trackbed for about half a mile when more open country is reached.

Just past an embankment with a wood at the end of it on the right, a
road on the left crosses the trackbed on a bridge. Immediately beyond
this bridge there are some railway cottages on the left. Here you have a
choice of routes. You can either leave the trackbed and take a path
behind the railway cottages which, after less than half a mile veers
slightly left to join the Mow Cop Trail, close to the little cutting where
it leaves the old line for Nick i' th' Hill. Or you can continue up the
trackbed to the same place. The choice is yours: and if you continue
up the trackbed, to where the Mow Cop Trail leaves it, another choice
quickly follows. Either keep to the track or follow the Trail. All three
variants lead to the same place.

The way ahead is the same as on the outward journey, passing
Whitemoor Farm, to where, just before the path makes a sharp left
turn, another path branches to the right. Follow it northwards over
the county border, back into Cheshire, passing close to the delightfully named Hollybush Farm on your left. A quarter of a mile beyond
this farm the path changes direction, bending to the right, and after a
similar distance reaches the A527 close to the Castle Inn public house.

Cross the A527 diagonally towards the right and continue northwards along the full length of Mill Lane to a T junction with Reade's
Lane, which cross and follow the footpath along the side of Dane In
Shaw brook on your left. Your course is parallel and close to the trackbed on your right. After half a mile the path begins to close in on the
trackbed and joins it exactly where the Mow Cop Trail does, coming
from the other direction.

From here what appears to be the correct route to complete the walk
is back along the path you used on setting out; and to be sure, this is a
valid one. But there is another way, a slightly longer and more interesting one.

Continue walking northwards along the trackbed until you reach the
Macclesfield canal. Pass under it and turn left onto the towpath and
walk along it in a north-westerly direction, with The Cloud sitting on
your right shoulder for a quarter of a mile to where a metal footbridge

spans it. Use this bridge to recross the canal and follow the path across fields to Timbersbrook and the completion of a fine walk.

Macclesfield canal, which shares with the Peak Forest the distinction of being the highest navigation in the country at about 500 feet above sea level, is 28 miles long and almost entirely rural. One of the last waterways to be built, well after the peak of canal building, it was opened to traffic from Hardings Wood to Marple, where it linked with the Peak Forest in 1831. It was the last link in a chain from Manchester through the Potteries and the Midlands to the south of England.

The Biddulph Valley Way and the Mow Cop Trail intermix very well. The airy views from dramatic Congleton Edge contrast well with the more intimate habitat for wildlife much of the old line has become. The ratio between trackbed, road, footpath and towpath walking together with the several choices of route available all combine to make this a walk to be tackled again and again. It has so much to offer; and that is the essence of a good walk.

8. THE WIRRAL WAY

Length :	12 miles
Opened :	Hooton to Parkgate - 1866
	Parkgate to West Kirby - 1886
Closed :	for passenger traffic - September 1956
	for goods traffic - May 1962
O/S :	Sheets No.108 and 117; Series 1:50,000

While in the swift and crowded train our journey we pursue,
How bright a world of waters is depicted to our views!
Blent with the whistle's jarring sound, how strange it seems to hear
The gentle ripple of the wave steal softly on the ear!
Maria Abdy.

The Wirral Way is like a commercial waiting for a sponsor. For the first eight miles of its journey from West Kirby down the peninsula the sea, washing the Dee Estuary, is never far away from its mani-cured lawns and its carefully tended parkland surroundings. It is a pampered line, well cared for by a dedicated staff of full and part-time Country Park Rangers, P.R. people, information assistants and clean-ers who, between them, manage to keep it in apple pie order. This is as it should be for the walk was purpose built as an escape from dull urbanity for 1½ million Merseysiders.

The track follows the course of the only true country branch line in the Wirral, the first part of which was opened in 1866. It was 4½ miles long and ran from Hooton on the G.W.R./L.N.W.R. joint Birkenhead Railway to Parkgate. In the same year the Hoylake Railway opened a single line from Birkenhead to Hoylake and also got powers to extend down the peninsula to Parkgate; but the only part that was built was from Hoylake to West Kirby. This was opened in 1886.

Throughout its length the line's over and under bridges were built for double track but only a single line was laid. It carried eleven trains each way on weekdays and four on Sundays, serving the local stations. In October 1923, the only through service from the Wirral Railway was inaugurated, a through coach from New Brighton to London, Euston. The railway provided a pleasant rural ride with interesting views across the Dee Estuary. Apart from a rock cutting at Neston there were no engineering features of note.

The trains were operated by both the L.N.W.R. and the G.W.R. throughout the line's life, the only exception being the withdrawal of Sunday trains after World War II.

The immediate post war years saw the decline of passenger traffic. Thurstaston, Caldy and Kirby Park stations were closed in 1954 and the line closed for passenger traffic in September 1956. Goods traffic continued to serve all the stations except Caldy, which never had goods facilities, until May 1962.

Today, with the line's cuttings no longer echoing to the rumble of steam trains, the sounds are different, for the abandoned railway is now the backbone of a country park developed by Cheshire County Council and the Countryside Commission. This park, properly named the Wirral Country Park was one of the first two country parks to be opened in Britain and is not, as one would expect, an area of flower-beds, play areas, football pitches and carefully tended lawns, although parts of it, particularly around Thurstaston, are definitely top drawer. No - this country park is built on a much grander scale. It is a vast stretch of open countryside set among towns and farmlands. The route of the disused line has footpaths and bridle ways leading from it giving easy access to various places of interest along the line and enabling people to plan circular walks, all of which adds interest. The park was opened by Lord Leverhulme in 1973 and is today the envy of many local councils throughout the land.

Since the Wirral Country Park is a place of contrasts its wildlife is rich and varied. Here are to be found all sorts of wild creatures from badgers and foxes to newts and frogs; and because of its proximity to the mud flats and cliffs of the Dee Estuary its bird life embraces waders like gulls, oystercatchers and lapwings. The Wirral Way, running along its full length, cloaks itself in the park's diversity with the nearby trees and bushes in the cuttings holding the eye and the distant views across the Dee Estuary to the Welsh hills playing a similar roll from the airy embankments.

The Wirral Way is open every day throughout the year and one Ranger is always on night patrol. The Rangers are there to help the public and to protect the park. These very approachable people are easily identified by the distinctive green clothes they wear.

From July to September there are guided walks to areas of natural and historic interest and lectures are given at Thurstaston Visitor Centre. A slide programme and exhibits, also at the Visitor Centre, introduce people to the park's story. There you can discover all about the forces that shaped the land, learn of the rise and fall of Deeside ports and find out about the transformation of the railway into the Wirral Way and of the animals and plants that live there. Schools and other educational groups are catered for and teachers' information packs are available from the Visitor Centre. All this is only a part of what the Wirral Country Park has to offer so it is little wonder that it has become a source of pride to the fortunate people who live on the Dee side of the Wirral peninsula.

The Metropolitan Borough of Wirral and Cheshire County Council, who jointly run the line and pay its costs have, between them, magically transformed a dreary derelict into a Cinderella ready for the ball. Since the line was purchased from British Rail in 1969 for £98,000 about £250,000 has been spent on developing it and building the excellent Visitor Centre. Annual running costs are around £100,000, which is a small price to pay when you consider that it is available for the whole of Merseyside.

As good a way as any to explore this or any other disused railway line is to begin at one end and walk to the other. My son-in-law Stephen and I chose to start from West Kirby, and at the end of town had our first look at the Wirral Country Park which thereabouts stretched from the track to the estuary shore.

Before long we reached Caldy station, now a car park and picnic area. During the years between the two world wars private horse drawn carriages would convey their very important owners between the wayside stations, including Caldy, and the huge houses with their large gardens where they lived in some style. Many of Liverpool's powerful shipping magnates and other important businessmen lived along the Deeside of the Wirral peninsula and they expected their means of travel to be on a par with their living standards. In compliance with the wishes of these important people the L. & N.W.R., who ran the line jointly with the G.W.R., and whose trains contained first, second and third class carriages, added 'club' carriages which, with their armchair seats and bridge tables, were infinitely superior to even first class compartments.

As we discussed these luxurious 'club' carriages we viewed in the estuary a different kind of club, a sailing club, and edging the Wirral Way on both sides, a golf club. The links was attracting its fair share of golfers; but many walkers share my view that golf is a good walk spoiled.

For most of its length the track is split into two paths, one for horses and one for walkers. But we saw no people on horse back and few on foot until we were past the golf links. From then on the numbers increased as, some two miles out from West Kirby we approached Thurstaston station, now the hub of the line and the whole Wirral Country Park.

The famous Visitor Centre on the site of Thurstaston station attracts some half a million people annually; and not all are walkers. To this spic and span complex of pleasing buildings peeping from behind trees and shrubs also come bird watchers, fishermen, horse riders and picnickers. Campers make full use of its discreetly hidden campsite which has space for sixty pitches and is open throughout the year. All these and the rest of the facilities came into being with the Wirral Way so all are comparatively new. All the old railway buildings went years ago. All that remains of the original station are the platforms and the clearly defined route of the line.

From Thurstaston the Way continues southerly to Heswall which was once a village and is now a small town. This came about firstly because a number of small landowners sold their estates for building purposes and secondly because it became a favourite resort for the residents of Liverpool and Birkenhead. Heswall has a fine, sandy beach with grassy mud banks beyond. Paul McCartney has a house there and his brother, Michael, still lives in this desirable spot.

Heswall station had a passing loop from which the driver could only return to the single track when he had been given a token by the signalman controlling the section. Today the station is no more, although some railway cottages remain.

On leaving the site of Heswall station the outlook varies greatly between the landward and seaward sides of the track. The view to landward is of the older, lower and rather superior part of the town. Called the Lower Village, it spreads southwards for almost a mile.

Look the other way and you will see flatlands where deep, shifting channels carry streams to the estuary through dangerous mud banks and salt flats.

This is an ornithologists' paradise for these marshes are particularly rich in the organic life on which so many waders feed. It is not unusual to see flocks of up to 100,000 of them settle in these shallow waters, knowing that the pickings are good. Kestrels, lapwings, curlews, greenshanks and sparrow hawks share this plentiful food supply with oystercatchers, short eared owls and many other species; and what a privilege it is to be able to observe them from such close quarters.

The Dee Estuary began to shrink *circa* the fourteenth century when Chester, which for almost four hundred years had been the most important port on the north-west coast, began to silt up. By the sixteenth century Chester had lost its importance as a port and was eventually left high and dry. The estuary, which was once twenty miles long, is today, only half that length and Shotwith, Burton, Neston, Parkgate and Heswall have all followed Chester's suit.

Within living memory boats moored at Parkgate and its open air baths were washed clean with sea water at each high tide. Now only exceptionally high spring tides manage to touch the harbour wall and the baths were closed in 1942 because of silting.

Sir Wilfred Grenfell, the explorer, was born in Parkgate and Emma Lyon, later to become Lady Hamilton, spent a holiday there with her mother in 1784. Nineteen years later someone else with a certain reputation visited the resort, staying at the Talbot Inn: Mrs.Fitzherbert, lady friend of George IV. Handel is thought to have written his *Water Music* in Parkgate while waiting for a packet to take him to Dublin for the first performance there of his *Messiah.*

Near Neston the way goes through a sandstone cutting about a quarter of a mile long. So damp is it that a sewage pipe placed in it by the local council when the line closed, has now, like the rocks themselves, become so overgrown with mosses and moisture-loving plants that it is hardly visible. Nature is doing a good job in that cutting.

Not only is Hadlow Road the only surviving station on the line, it is very likely the best preserved old railway station in the country. Everything about it is in apple pie order from the huge Bovril sign high on the station wall and the seat and the milk trolleys on the platform to, inside, the tickets, the timetables, the scales, the posters and the rest of the railway station memorabilia. The signal box is not original. It is a recent addition, having been brought in from Cheshire; and my goodness! it certainly enhances the character of the station, as

Hadlow Road Station on the Wirral Way

do the crossing gates at the end of the platform. The station is opened every morning and left un-attended for the rest of the day. Anyone can wander around it at will yet nothing is ever disturbed. It is as though the ghosts of station staff long dead are standing guard, keeping it safe.

The Wirral Way is a walk I shall not forget in a hurry, that's for sure. Nor, I suspect, will you once you have walked it and savoured what it has to offer; for it really is a spanker. The large sums of money lavished upon it have raised it high above the ordinary run of disused lines. Today, rich rewards await all who tread this gentle walkway or horse-ride the adjoining bridleway: rewards that cannot be evaluated in financial terms. For who can price a glorious sunset with the sea's edge running gold or cost singing larks rising from a cutting? These rewards are of the senses and the spirit and, as such, are the best rewards of all.

9. THE MIDDLEWOOD WAY

Length :   11 miles
Opened :   for passenger traffic - 2nd August, 1869
             for goods traffic - 1st March, 1870

Closed   :   for goods and passenger traffic - January 1970
O/S   :   Sheets Nos.109 and 118; Series 1:50,000

> *'No poetry in railways!' foolish thought*
> *of a dull brain, to no fine music wrought.*
> Charles Mackay.

'Tewiffic!' enthused Dr.David Bellamy, jumping for joy at the new walkway. The occasion was the official opening of the Middlewood Way on May 30th 1985 at Higher Poynton station, now a beautifully landscaped picnic area. David, as the botanic man insisted on being called, unveiled a plaque there, further marked his presence with a tree planting ceremony and delighted onlookers and councillors alike by removing his shoes and socks and wading through a mucky pond.

Bubbling over with approbation, bearded Bellamy was clearly impressed with the Middlewood Way and lavished praise on the Stockport and Macclesfield councils who, with D.O.E. grants of £1.3 million have done such a fine job in reclaiming the derelict railway track and turning it into a nature treasure trail.

The next day, together with Stephen Barker, who has accompanied me on countless walks, I saw for myself just what made the Middlewood Way so special and learned something of the problems facing the North Staffordshire Railway and the Manchester, Sheffield and Lincolnshire when they combined to build the Macclesfield, Bollington and Marple line in the early 1860's.

As far back as 1849 the North Staffordshire Railway, (N.S.) having reached Macclesfield, found the way to Manchester blocked by the ever-jealous London and North Western Railway, (L.N.W.) The N.S. therefore suggested a branch to Whaley Bridge to link with the proposed Manchester, Sheffield and Lincolnshire Railway, (M.S.L.) from Hyde Junction; but nothing came of it. Throughout, the L.N.W. was obstructive and refused to allow any traffic to Manchester to pass via Macclesfield, insisting that it went via Crewe, thus ensuring a greater L.N.W. mileage.

In 1863 a Macclesfield businessman, Thomas Oliver, in an effort to give a fresh lease of life to Bollington, then an important cotton town suffering from depresssion due to the American Civil War, promoted a scheme for a local line to be built from Macclesfield to Marple via Bollington. The line would also carry Kerridge stone from local quarries and coal from the collieries of the Poynton area.

Both the N.S. and the M.S.L. were enthusiastic about the scheme, the N.S. because it could become a new route to Manchester independent of the L.N.W., which was becoming increasingly obstructive; and the M.S.L. who saw it as another outlet to the south. The *Macclesfield Courier and Herald* proclaimed M.S.L.'s enthusiastic General Manager, Edward Watkin, to be the inspired leader of the scheme, second only to Thomas Oliver.

With such support the scheme prospered and the line was authorised on 14th July 1864. The N.S. and the M.S.L. were both empowered to subscribe £80,000 for its construction and work it when open.

Yet almost immediately the original purpose of the line to provide the N.S. with an independent route to Manchester was lost because the L.N.W., alarmed at the success of the M.B.M. came to an amicable traffic agreement with the N.S.

Now that the urgency had gone out of the scheme the construction of the line slowed considerably despite there being no major engineering problems apart from a low, 23 arch viaduct at Bollington and two deep cuttings on the approach to Marple Wharf Junction. When, at long last, it was opened for passenger traffic on 2nd August 1869, the M.B.M. was single line only, on the 'up' side of a double bed. Four single platform stations, Marple Rose Hill, High Lane, Poynton and Bollington served it. Initially there were four trains each way on weekdays and two each way on Sundays. Goods depots were opened at Rose Hill and Bollington and a goods service began on 1st March 1870.

In 1871 the line was doubled throughout at a cost of £16,000 and second platforms were provided at all four stations. By 1872 a link had been made just north of Poynton station with Lord Vernon's colliery railway system, the line curving to westwards in a wide arc to enter the colliery. A great deal of traffic was carried along this branch to and from the M.B.M. until the last colliery closed in 1935.

The original Macclesfield terminus was a temporary one sited close to the L.N.W. Hibel Road station. For two years the M.S.L. General Manager tried to persuade the L.N.W. to partner the N.S. and M.S.L. in building a station to serve all three lines but the ever suspicious L.N.W. refused even to consider it. Faced with the L.N.W.'s interminable intransigence the N.S. and M.S.L. opted to go ahead without their problem rival. Together they built a link from the M.B.M. to join the N.S. main line a little south of Hibel Road station. It was opened in 1873 and the original terminus near the L.N.W. Hibel Road station became a goods depot. Still the L.N.W. remained obdurate and refused to allow any through N.S.-L.N.W. trains to use the new joint station, the Central. This decision meant that both the Central station and the M.B.M. line were deprived of much of the connectional usefulness; and the M.B.M. settled down to a purely local existence.

A bridge carried the M.B.M. line over L.N.W's Stockport-Buxton line at the northern end of the L.N.W. Middlewood station. In 1879 the M.B.M. authorities opened a station almost directly above the L.N.W. Middlewood station for the interchange of passengers. Earlier, in 1876, a curve connecting these two lines to provide better facilities between Macclesfield and Buxton had been proposed; but it did not materialise until 1885.

It was an elaborate affair of a type normally only found at the most important and busiest of junctions. It contained a flyover which carried the 'down' line from Macclesfield over the Buxton line to link with the 'up' line to Buxton, so avoiding problems with down Buxton trains. It was the only 'flying' junction on the south side of Manchester. High hopes were expected of it but the curve was not a great success and soon services along it were confined to the summer months.

However, through goods trains used the curve regularly and exchange sidings were added. A daily early morning goods from Macclesfield to Buxton used the curve. It was known as the 'knotty' after the nickname of the N.S. which used the Staffordshire knot as its company badge. It ran until after World War II and when it ceased the curve was used mainly for storing old coaches.

From Marple Rose Hill the M.B.M. flanked the Pennines all the way to Macclesfield. Its stations were all small and unpretentious. Initially Rose Hill, situated on the 'up' side of the line, comprised a small, one storey brick building with a low pitched slate roof which extended to form a canopy. Inside were four rooms, all entered from the platform - the Porter's Room, the Station Office, a General Waiting Room-cum-Booking Office and a Ladies Waiting Room and lavatory. A brick built Gents. adjoined. As business expanded greater facilities were called for and a similar office block was built on the 'down' side.

When Rose Hill station was built the only house in sight was the Railway Inn. But soon afterwards houses began to be built more on the Rose Hill side of Marple. Not until after World War I was the area around the station developed.

High Lane was built on the Stockport-Buxton turnpike road half a mile away from the little settlement from which it took its name. It was surrounded by fields then: it remains surrounded by fields today. It really was out in the sticks. Gas lighting never reached High Lane and it remained oil lit until the 1970's.

There were no houses at Middlewood, which really was situated in the middle of a wood, with no road access. There was little local traffic but a fair amount of toing and froing between the M.C.M. High Level and the L.N.W. Low Level stations.

The Middlewood Way is certainly one of the finest examples of skilful conversion of a derelict line that I have come across and much of the credit must go to the Macclesfield Groundwork Trust - motto: *Linking Town ... With Country* - which provided so much expertise. In three brief years the line as far as Bollington has been transformed from an eyesore to a most pleasing trail which provides excellent walking, riding and cycling facilities well away from road traffic. Stout fences separate the bridlepath from the path used by cyclists and walkers. Within the sheltered cuttings there is a choice of routes for all except horse riders. You can either keep to the cutting bottom or, should you prefer it, take either of the paths built along the tops of the embankments from where right along the route, there are always fine views of the Cheshire Plain, the urban skyline and the Pennine foot- hills. Bridges have been repaired, more than 28,000 shrubs and 8,000 trees have been planted and miles of ditches dug.

The five evenly spaced picnic areas attract a lot of people, many of whom are content to sit at the stout tables provided, eat their sand- wiches, drink their beverages and watch the passing parade. Nothing much happens at these places but many people come and go. The walk attracts walkers and cyclists in roughly equal numbers. People on horse back are thinner on the ground. Yet because the Middlewood Way slices through 'horsey' country the bridleway is seldom devoid of equestrians; and this is as it should be.

There are car parks at Rose Hill, High Lane, Higher Poynton and below the viaduct at Bollington.

At Bollington, having crossed the viaduct, the Middlewood Way continues for a short distance to where the old M.B.M. bridged a street. There it comes to a full stop three miles short of its destination. Plans are well advanced to complete the development, originally held up because a lorry depot straddles the track, now that the depot owners have agreed to move to another site, thus removing this solitary obstacle. Meanwhile the way ahead is via a very exciting detour.

Cross the aforementioned bridge and continue along the course of the old line for about 150 yards towards the lorry depot. There, to your left, you will find a signposted path across Tinker's Clough wood. Take it, using the sloping path down to a stream, which cross,

Part of the Marple Lock system at that end of the Middlewood Way

and climb up the other side of the valley, still on the path which will bring you to a bridge over the Macclesfield canal. Go down to the towpath and turn right along it for a quarter of a mile to where another bridge crosses the canal. Now leave the towpath and turn right along the road for 150 yards to where it bridges the old M.B.M. line. Cross the bridge and at the right-hand far side of it take the signposted steps down to the track. This continuation of the Middlewood Way, still a cinder track, will take you along a descending 2½ miles long slope into Macclesfield where, on a bridge over a road, a line of concrete posts linked with metal marks the end of the walk.

The Macclesfield canal, meandering gracefully through the Pennine foothills roughly parallel to the Middlewood Way, makes an interesting divertisement. To the left or Bollington side of the bridge leading from Tinker's Clough wood stands the huge Adelphi Mill, a proud reminder of the town's strong association with cotton. Adjacent to the bridge, on the far side of the canal, two luxurious dwellings enhance the site of a converted mill, the Bee Hive. What a delight these superior houses are and how well they blend with their restful surroundings!

Perched on a hilltop overlooking Bollington is a white landmark, a folly, called White Nancy. The origin of the name is obscure but the three likeliest explanations all have merit. (1) There used to be an ordnance column on the site and Nancy is a corruption of the 'nance' part of ordnance. (2) Both Mrs.Gaskell, wife of the folly's builder, and her daughter were called Nancy. (3) The lead horse of a team of eight used to drag a heavy marble table uphill to be placed inside the folly was called Nancy. You can take your choice!

The table is still there. Once access to it was through an oak studded door but, because of a very real fear that vandals would damage it, the folly's entrance was sealed with the table still inside.

Although the Middlewood Way, certainly from Marple to Bollington, looks complete, the Macclesfield Borough Council and Stockport Metropolitan Borough Council say that other facilities will be added as opportunities arise; and that, as with the work already done, in future work the ranger and warden services will be the key to progress.

Strong as is the Way's great appeal, it holds yet another valuable asset in the number of alternative routes and circular walks it provides. The Ladybrook Valley Walk bisects the Way at Middlewood station while close to Higher Poynton are to be found the old tramways of the Poynton colliery inclines. Still at Higher Poynton an interesting uphill walk to southwards along a quiet country road leads, after a couple of miles, to magnificent Lyme Hall in the middle of Lyme Park Country Park. Roaming this undulating parkland is a large herd of red deer. Close to Lyme Hall the Gritstone Trail begins its tortuous journey, skirting the Pennines roughly parallel to but much higher up than the Middlewood Way. Much closer to the Way, and, again roughly parallel to it is the Macclesfield canal.

III Lancashire

Lancashire, originally Lancastershire, has been the subject of more misconceptions than perhaps any other English county, mostly based on the 'observations' of people who have never set foot in this ancient County Palatine. Quite unfairly it has been described as a dreary industrial agglomeration of mines, mills, workshops and ugly towns set in a countryside where the grass grows black, whereas it is well endowed with beauty, charm and even grandeur. Lancashire has within its boundaries scenery any other county would be proud to possess.

Some of the towns *are* drab and parts of the countryside *are* despoiled; but the Coronation Streets of yesteryear have all but gone and great tracts of Lancashire are entirely free from the murk of industrialism. Much of the county is given over to farming with its broad acres of golden cornfields, smiling meadows and sweet pastures. At its northern extremity it shared, until, for no good reason, bureaucracy decreed that the boundaries be altered, some of the finest lake and mountain scenery in Britain.

At the south-western extremity of Old Lancashire, on the north bank of the River Mersey, to which it owes its eminence as one of the foremost ports of the world, lies Liverpool. Today it has gone metropolitan, this great hearted city with its flair for humour, its own language and its five miles of docks. Technically it may be part of the new 'county' of Merseyside but to historians and sentimentalists this city of cathedrals is still part of Lancashire.

Liverpool came into prominence in the 17th century through the Irish trade and now trades with every country in the world. It is a great sprawl of a place that would take half a lifetime to explore. But to savour it simply walk along the floating landing stage from the pier head. It is a fine vantage point from which to watch the ships coming in from all over the globe. And how's this for a piece of Lancashire grandeur seen from the same place? Liverpool's 'big three', the Cunard Building, the Port of Liverpool Building and the Liver Building on which two Liver birds perch and whose four clock faces are bigger than Big Ben's.

Manchester, Roman Mancunium, now part of Greater Manchester, proudly offers more Lancashire grandeur. Its town hall is a palatial piece of Victorian Gothic, its once black cathedral now stands clean and golden, the great circular bulk of its Central Library is a gem and its Free Trade Hall, traditional home of the Hallé Orchestra, is magnificent.

The John Rylands Library is an exquisite argosy filled with priceless treasures. Inside, illuminated medieval manuscripts, many with jewelled bindings, are housed along with a priceless collection of Biblical and calligraphic art. Outside, John Rylands, the self-made former Wigan weaver, whose memorial it is, and his inspired widow whose vision it was, stands guard in marble effigy.

Manchester is Piccadilly, Market Street and the Manchester Ship Canal. It is a great commercial centre, the home of national newspapers, northern edition, Italian ice-cream makers and great beers like Boddingtons, Chester's Bitter, better known as 'Lunatic Broth', Threlfall's Ales and Swale's.

West Lancashire is flat and the coast, north of Liverpool, makes a convex curve via Formby and Southport to the Ribble Estuary. The sands and spreading dunes along this shoreline have a quiet charm all their own while inland many pleasant villages dot the rich agricultural land that spreads eastwards to the edge of the industrial area.

Southport has Lord Street with its genteel arcades and ornate shops, its wrought ironwork and its trees. It has its sands which spread right across the estuary to Lytham St. Anne's; but it has no sea. The briny simply isn't there. Land is being reclaimed from it watched by the pier which defiantly juts out into a sea of sand.

Southport is a very pleasant town, in an attractive setting. It has a first class theatre, the Floral Hall, and the Royal Birkdale golf course is on the doorstep.

Long before the M6 was built, the main north to south route was through Preston, the 'priest's town', the administrative centre for the Duchy of Lancaster and the setting for many battles throughout history. It was at Preston that, in 1791, John Horrocks, having decided that being a quarry owner and maker of millstones was not his way to a fortune, set up first as a weaver, then a trader, before opening the Yellow Mill and becoming one of the earliest manufacturers and founding the firm whose cotton products were to become world famous.

At Walton-le-Dale the Ribble is joined by the Darwen which, from the moors of its birth, flows through wooded dales. It skirts the foot of an eminence on which sits historic Hoghton Tower where James I was lavishly entertained in 1617. It was there that he knighted the loin of beef and when he and his hangers-on left, his host, 'Honest Dick' de Hoghton, faced a stretch in Fleet Prison for debt.

At the old Unicorn Inn at Walton, Jacobites hatched their plots. Joseph Livesey, founder of the teetotal movement was born at Walton and it was there, in St. Leonard's churchyard than an Elizabethan necromancer called Edward Kelly, practiced his black arts one midnight.

East of Clitheroe, one of Lancashire's most famous landmarks, Pendle Hill, gives extensive views of the wild Bowland fells and the full length of Ribblesdale from Yorkshire's Three Peaks to the coast.

The Lancashire Witches were real people who lived in the Pendle villages in the reign of James I, who himself believed implicitly in the power of witchcraft. Their story is well known through Harrison Ainsworth's famous novel *Lancashire Witches*. The most notorious of them was Elizabeth Demdike. She brought up her children to be witches and instructed her grandchildren in witchcraft. Such handing down in families of the secret art was common practice. To ensure a good feast at the sabbaths the Lancashire Witches simply went to the house of a well-to-do farmer and helped themselves to what they liked from his pantry. This was also the custom in many other localities and the covens were so dreaded that the farmers made no protest.

The River Hodder, which joins the twisting Ribble a little below the Lower Hodder bridges is a clear, unsullied stream which drains the Forest of Bowland. It is a beautiful lure to the haunting solitude of Little Bowland. I defy anyone to view the Hodder Valley from the limestone heights around Whitewell, which offer fine views of the upper Hodderdale, the distant fells which gave the river birth, and the dales of Whitendale and Brennand and fail to be impressed.

At the western edge of a majestic sweep of moorland that is Longridge Fell, close to the dreamy hamlet of Chipping, is Parlick Pike from the top of which are excellent views of the Bleasdale Fells and the great, flat expanse of the Fylde, which goes all the way to Lancashire's holiday coast.

The Fylde, derived from the Old English 'gefilde', refers to the coastal plain of the Ancient Hundred of Amounderness. It stretches northwards from Lytham St. Anne's to Lancaster and is an agricultural and horticultural area. It is a gently undulating land of attractive villages and windmills.

Old time Fylde folk were either 'moss-ogs' or 'sand grown uns' and they were, and still are, great talkers. They used to hold forth in a rich dialect but, sadly today the Fylde dialect has almost died out.

In outlook nearby Blackpool is a million light years away from the Fylde. It is a brash, noisy and vulgar place, and yet, because it accepts this, it is honest with itself. Its Pleasure Beach is the largest pleasure centre in Europe and its Illuminations are the greatest free show on earth.

In 1415 Blackpool was called 'Le Pull', which became 'The Poole', then the 'Poole of Layton' and, finally it got its present name, which means a small pool with a black, peaty bottom.

The road from Blackpool going north through residential Bispham and Cleveleys will bring you to the expanding resort of Fleetwood. It has a fishing industry, passenger shipping and high hopes of becoming a container base serving the oil industry.

Lancaster, on the Lune, is deceptive. Built of grey stone it can look dull in cloudy weather. But little exploration is needed to uncover a dignified county and castle town. The medieval and neo-Gothic castle is neighboured by Georgian streets and houses and down by the Lune there are some 18th century warehouses.

Two hundred years ago merchant ships from the West Indies called there to unload their cargoes of sugar, rum, tobacco and raw cotton. They would then sail away carrying cloth, lime, stone and millstones. When Glasson Dock was built at the Lune's mouth in 1787, Lancaster's importance began to wane. Now Glasson Dock has declined too.

History is ever close at Lancaster. The Romans forded the Lune there; Danish raiders sailed past it, up the Lune, in their long ships; Normans, seeking conquest, swept northwards through Lancaster, harrying; and similarly minded Scots came through it plundering. It has seen the passing of armies heading north to wage war with Scotland and experienced the clash of battle between Cavalier and Roundhead. Scottish armies of the 1715 and 1745 rebellions came quickly south through Lancaster and returned through it to their homeland even quicker. But of the Wars of the Roses Lancaster saw nothing. These were not wars between the counties of Lancashire and Yorkshire but between the Houses of Lancaster and York, which was an altogether different kettle of fish. No 'roses' battles took place on Lancashire soil.

Morecambe has style. As a holiday resort it has taken a middle course which can best be illustrated like this: where Blackpool burgers take fish and chips home in popular tabloids and those in haughty Lytham use briefcases, Morecambe folk use *The Guardian* and *The Times*.

There is a bracing twang of ozone about Morecambe that attracts convalescents. Its superb sunsets, when the western horizon runs golden as the sea swallows the sun, cause lovers to drool and the quicksands of Morecambe Bay give people with mother-in-law problems food for thought. For ornithologists the shoreline to the north of Morecambe is paradise.

North of Carnforth, the 'crane ford' where herons once settled on the river Keer, lies Warton, a village of grey stones with a very strong American link. President George Washington's ancestors lived there for about 300 years before moving to Sulgrave; and it was their coat-of-arms with mullets, five pointed stars, and bars, stripes, that inspired the American flag. Every fourth of July Old Glory flies proudly over Warton.

The caves below Warton Crag are among the oldest human dwellings in Lancashire.

Until the local government re-organisation of 1974, Lancashire had a lakeland 'north of the sands' of which it was justifiably proud. The Three Shire Stone at the top of Wrynose Pass which marks the meeting of Cumberland, Westmorland and Lancashire bears only one name, Lancashire.

Yet despite this loss, vast acres of matchless delights give lie to the county's grim industrial image. Without a doubt Lancashire's claim that it is well endowed with scenery of a praiseworthy quality is a valid one.

10. THE DOWNHOLLAND BRANCH

Length :	A five mile circular walk embracing Haskayne Cutting Nature Reserve and a section of the Leeds and Liverpool canal.
Opened :	for goods traffic Meols Cop, Southport to Barton - 2nd September, 1887 for goods traffic Barton to Hillhouse Junction - 1st October, 1887 for passenger traffic - 1st November, 1887
Closed :	for passenger traffic - 26th September, 1938 for goods traffic - 19th January, 1952
O/S :	Sheet No.108; Series 1:50,000

Every night when the moon is bright
The miller's ghost is seen
The mill wheel turns though the night is still...
He haunts the station, he haunts the mill
And the land that lies between
The old Irish legend in 'Oh, Mr. Porter', recited by
the toothless Harbottle (Moore Marriott)

The more I saw of this lovable little branch line the more I was reminded of that very funny thirties film, *Oh, Mr. Porter*, which was all about an incompetent station master, Will Hay, who, aided and abetted by Graham Moffatt as the fat boy and Moore Marriott as old Harbottle, cleared an Irish branch line of gun runners posing as ghosts. True, no windmill waves its arms to the vast, west Lancashire sky, no miller's ghost - with its ear 'ole painted green - walks on moonlight nights and no station master as grossly inefficient as Will Hay ever worked on the line. But there is a delicious atmosphere about it that sets it apart from other lines, stimulates interest and makes it a joy to walk.

The line's birth was far from carefree with a rival company vociferously condemning the 'unholy alliance' that produced it. This is how it came about.

In 1882 the Lancashire and Yorkshire Railway had a monopoly of Southport trains. But that year the tiny West Lancashire Railway Company broke this monopoly by completing their line from the town's Derby Road station to Preston's Fishergate.

Also that same year the Southport and Cheshire Lines Extension from Aintree to Southport's Lord Street was under construction. Again in 1882 the W.L.R. tried unsuccessfully to obtain powers for a connection in a tunnel to the Southport and Cheshire Lines Extension to give it access to Liverpool. Although it was staving off impending bankruptcy, the West Lanky, as railwaymen referred to it, sponsored a seven miles long, double track link line, the Liverpool, Southport and Preston Junction Railway, as an alternative means of achieving this. And because of this sponsorship of the L.S.P.J. by the West Lanky, the rival L.Y.R. directors saw it as an unholy alliance.

The line crossed rich, flat farmland to join the Cheshire Lines Extension near Altcar and Hillhouse and should have been easy to build. But this was not the case because at many places along it boggy ground made construction difficult.

When the L.S.P.J. opened in 1887 the Cheshire Lines Extension was just three years old. Trains ran between Southport and Altcar and Hillhouse to connect with trains on the Cheshire Lines Extension but none ran directly from Preston, avoiding Southport. So the L.S.P.J. did not become a through route from Preston to Liverpool except for freight traffic. Moreover the area through which it passed was very sparsely populated and passengers were few. The line never prospered and to make matters worse other West Lanky ambitions failed. Expensive renovations were needed to the engines, rolling stock and even the rails. It all became too much for the despairing directors and in 1897 'this miserable pretence of a railway', as one disillusioned shareholder called it, was absorbed by the L.Y.R.

Throughout its decade of independence, the Downholland branch, as the line had come to be known, was used by only a handful of trains daily. Following its takeover by the L.Y.R. it fared no better. At the turn of the century only four passenger trains a day were using it. Operating costs were too high and to make matters worse Southport's electrified tramways were nibbling at suburban rail traffic. In 1906 the L.Y.R. retaliated by introducing a steam railmotor service between Southport and Altcar and Hillhouse; and four new halts were opened along the line. There was a single coach attached. This 'right queer looking 'osity' made its debut in July 1906, and became known as the Altcar Bob.

Altcar Bob lifted the branch from the ordinary to the extra special simply by being it was, 'an 'osity'. A nimble little vehicle, it was train that behaved like a bus; and it never needed turning. Travelling engine first, fireman and driver shared the footplate: travelling coach first, the fireman stayed on the footplate while the driver went to a special compartment at the far end of the coach which was equipped with remote control gear. It travelled quickly between frequent halts to pick up passengers and was able to stop and start with little effort and small cost, something not possible with the more usual branch trains.

The locals loved Altcar Bob and welcomed the frequent service it gave to Altcar and Hillhouse to connect with the Cheshire Lines Services to Liverpool.

The four halts established when Altcar Bob came into service where at Butts Lane in Southport and beside the over-bridges at Heathey Lane, Newcut Lane and Plex Moss Lane. At each halt a flight of steps led down the embankment to the side of the track. There were no platforms. When Altcar Bob stopped to pick up or set down, neat little folding steps were extended from the coach and the passengers used these.

During the hours of darkness, travellers waiting at the halts for Altcar Bob would stand beneath oil lamps thoughtfully provided by the L.Y.R.; and had the rail motor's drivers been able to see them, all would have been well. Unfortunately they were too dim to be seen and more often than not Altcar Bob would steam past leaving would-be passengers to stare in disbelief at the firebox glow and the lights of the coach as distance and darkness swallowed them. Clearly steps had to be taken to ensure that people waiting at these halts were not over-looked. A solution had to be found. It was; and it was a classic one that would have done credit to Will Hay's Irish branch line. The answer was matches. As Altcar Bob rushed towards each halt, throwing fire and sparks and smoke into the night, one of those waiting for it would strike a match and hold it high. The driver would see it, Altcar Bob would sigh to a stop, collect its passengers and with a hiss of steam gather speed and be on its way.

Tickets for people who boarded and alighted at the halts were issued by the guards who doubled as conductors. The last two regular guards, Jimmy Drake and Harry Lindley, like so many of their predecessors, loved the line, working alternate shifts and taking on the extra unpaid duties of conductor with a will seldom to be found beyond their own special branch. For it was a happy place worked by men who wore their pride in it on their sleeves; and it showed. Part of a team they might be but their different personalities were never allowed to merge into uniformity. Regulations were never broken, only severely dented, and the travelling public was never inconvenienced. It was just that along the line, away from the stuffy confines of Southport, the men felt free to express themselves in their own special ways.

One guard was in the habit, whenever his railmotor was waiting at Barton to start its return trip, of borrowing a bike, pedalling to the nearby Blue Bell pub and knocking back a couple of jars of the brown stuff; and where was the harm in that?

Pheasants were reared in fields adjacent to the line and sometimes one would be hit by Altcar Bob. Whenever this happened the driver would stop the railmotor and run back along the line to collect his booty; and where was the harm in that?

Many of the pheasants were in the habit of sitting close to the track, watching the railmotor go past. They congregated there in large numbers, often standing in rows. It was too good an opportunity to miss and many a fine bird got a free ride on Altcar Bob, felled by a well aimed lump of coal. It was good sport and the knowledge that a gamekeeper could be watching made the adrenalin flow that much faster. For if a driver was seen throwing a missile at a pheasant, let alone hitting it, the matter would be reported to the shed master at Southport. Gamekeepers are like that: no sense of humour.

Pheasants were not the only wild creatures to be had along the line. There were also hares and rabbits. So game rotas were drawn up to ensure fair distribution of the spoils. One driver recalled that while he was still a fireman his driver and the guard would take turns to have any pheasants that were 'won'. If either a hare or a rabbit was hit he, as fireman, was given the chance of having it. But since he did not like rabbit pie and jugged hare his driver and the guard shared those too.

The regular crews frequently received other benefits in the shape of farm products like eggs, poultry and root crops donated by local farmers with whom they were on Christian name terms. People living close to where the old line used to be still recall the story of the cabbage given by farmer Tom Sumner of Halsall to driver Billy Maudsley for his church's Harvest Festival. It weighed thirty two pounds.

The Downholland branch created legends like rabbits create offspring; and it all stemmed from the fact that it was a happy line where everyone knew everybody else. Even the trailer that was sometimes attached to the railmotor coach helped to enhance the friendliness with its one-class saloon and reversible, basketwork seats.

Harry Marshall, J.P., who was a driver on Altcar Bob for more than twenty years, has become part of the legend of the line. A man of many parts - keen Rechabite, lay preacher, Sunday School teacher, Co-op board director, infirmary director, union stalwart, unpaid instructor to anyone preparing for his promotion exam - Harry had a stone coffee pot which he always had with him while driving. It stood on the firebox flap so that the contents could be kept warm.

Another man, Tommy Shaw, began his working life as a lad porter at Barton. Progressing through the grades, he ended up commanding the line from Kew Gardens to Altcar and Hillhouse. Despite his success he never lost the common touch and as station master of Shirdley Hill thought nothing of being first to leap into a wagon to help with the unloading. His devotion to the line was such that he declined promotion in order to remain there. So proud of it was he that he was tempted to think of it as his own. His wife, too, was proud of the Downholland branch and was very supportive to Tommy. On one occasion, at Christmas, a railmotor driver recalled, she met his train with hot mince pies, a huge jug of coffee and an invitation to 'Come on, lads, fill your cans up'.

The first rival to the railcar was the bicycle, particularly in warm, dry weather. Then, with improved roads and frequent buses, which gave people almost doorstep services, passenger receipts began to shrink. The private motor car accelerated this trend and on Saturday, 26th September 1938, passenger working along the Downholland branch terminated.

When the sad day arrived it was not Altcar Bob, the railmotor, that made the final trip. The honour went to a more conventional train which was also called Altcar Bob. For some time it had been used regularly on the Saturday night runs and its roll had been to deposit passengers from Southport at their respective stations before returning empty and without stopping to Southport shed. That was how the run was scheduled, but a passenger train's final trip is rather special. So once the last passenger had been safely delivered, the now almost empty train became the focal point of the passenger service's farewell festivities. Almost empty because apart from driver Gordon Binks, his fireman and the guard, all Tommy Shaw's family and a few others closely connected with the line remained on board for the return trip.

At Shirdley Hill the engine was festooned with flowers and streamers. Messages were written in chalk all over it: 'Goodbye Old Friend': 'Farewell Old Faithful' and many others. There were chalk marks everywhere. So many, revellers turned up to join in the tribute that had Altcar Bob, the railmotor, been used it would have been too small to accommodate them all. They had a singsong, with sentimental numbers like 'Auld Lang Syne', and driver Binks kept blowing the engine's whistle as hard as he could. Last tickets were purchased from the guard and coal from the bunker was snatched as a keepsake. People shouted and cheered and sang. Fog signals placed on the track exploded under the train's wheels and, as the train hissed over the level crossing to vanish under Heathey Lane bridge, tears welled in many a watcher's eye. The last passenger train had gone to become another legend of an unusual and very happy line.

Freight trains continued to run but road competition was becoming even stronger and by the late forties only one train a day worked the line. The last train to use it did so on Saturday 19th January 1952. That was the day Jim Rimmer retired. He had been born the year before the line was opened and was the last full-time employee to work at Shirdley Hill station.

A few year later the lines which had continued to be used as storage sidings were lifted and the stations were demolished.

In 1935 a bore hole was sunk near Barton station. It produced up to 150,000 gallons of water a day for the steam railmotors. Because of this bore hole the North West Water Authority took an interest in that section of the Downholland branch from Halsall through Barton station to Chisnall Brook.

In 1978 the Water Authority leased it to the Lancashire Trust for Nature Conservation who today manage it under licence.

In 1896 when the British Association held its annual meeting at Liverpool the chapter of its guidebook dealing with botany suggested an excursion to Barton station. Particular mention was made of the water-loving plants that thrived thereabouts. Ninety years on, despite intensive draining of the surrounding agricultural land, there are still

Haskayne Cutting Nature Reserve

some very wet areas on and close to Barton station where sedges, rushes, forget-me-nots, yellow flag and other water lovers grow.

Trains arriving at Barton station from either direction did so along Haskayne Cutting. The station was midway down it and at its widest part. Today the remains of the station mark the entrance to Haskayne Cutting Nature Reserve. Under the terms of the licence granted by the Water Board to the administering Trust visitors to the reserve are required to carry a permit which is, in fact, a most attractive and informative guide.

The Lancashire Trust for Nature Conservation is a voluntary, charitable body dedicated to preserving wildlife - which means seeing to its welfare, not pickling squirrels! All its members are dedicated nature lovers: none more so that the Haskayne Reserve's indomitable manager, Barbara Yorke.

What good company she proved to be! Time and again, as we progressed through the reserve she drew my attention to an item of interest that otherwise I would have missed. She spoke of past achievements and plans for the future of the sanctuary. As we talked it occurred to me that if enough people of Barbara Yorke's determination and outlook involved themselves in nature conservation the future would become much brighter for our rich heritage of flora and fauna; and of course, for our descendants yet unborn for whom we carry the torch.

A good starting place for this fine, five miles long circular is at the entrance to the Haskayne Cutting Nature Reserve on the site of Barton station, grid reference SD358089. To reach it turn into Station Road from the Maghull to Southport road (A567) at the Blue Bell Inn, Haskayne. The entrance to the reserve is on the left-hand side of the road immediately before it bridges the old Downholland line.

It is clear from the outset that the Trust takes its responsibility very seriously. Many shrubs have been planted on the approach to the old platforms and marker posts, five of them, have been placed at irregular intervals between the station site and the end of the reserve's south-western section four fifths of a mile away.

Some cylindrical rock cores, two feet in diameter, are scattered around close to the bridge at the end of the station platforms. They are from the bore holes sunk there in 1935. Common lizards, I was told, bask on them in summer, if it is hot enough; but it was too cold for basking the day I was there.

Of Barton station only the platforms remain. Between them willow shrubs are colonising the damp ground that once carried the track. Immediately behind one of the platforms where the cutting side inclines steeply, strawberry plants grow in wild profusion. From the platforms the goods sidings, grass covered now, are easily discernible. Near the platforms, where mortar from the station buildings has begun to crumble and penetrate the soil, the lime-loving lady's fingers with their yellow, red and purple flowers prosper in the limy soil.

Leaving behind the station's remains and the overgrown goods sidings, the trail follows the narrowing cutting south-westerly; and almost at once the different types of flora stress the different types of soil to be found there. Along the bottom of the cutting patches of yellow loose strife can be seen. These plants which proudly carry yellow flowers on tall stems are ideally suited to damp conditions. They were so named by the Greeks who believed they were capable of ending strife between oxen and horses harnessed together on the same plough. On the higher ground of the cutting sides patches of heather thrived; and heather needs dry, acidic conditions.

Rampant willow scrub was taking over the cutting until, in 1979, young people working for that admirable body, the British Trust for Conservation Volunteers, began a programme of scrub control. Many of these shallow rooted shrubs were removed, but enough have been allowed to flourish to provide excellent cover for the many kinds of birds frequenting the cutting. More than sixty kinds have been seen there including the willow warbler.

Grass, when left to mature and die back, gradually builds up a thick mat of dead grass that restricts the growth of small plants. The Trust tackles this problem by setting fire to it every third year and as a consequence the higher, drier ground becomes dotted with mauve scabious in late summer.

At other times of the year, other flowers predominate: coltsfoot and marsh marigolds in the spring: lady's smock in early summer: midsummer sees the great variety of grasses at their best and the marsh orchids are out: heather turns part of the embankment into a purple carpet in the autumn.

Small tortoiseshell butterflies, fresh from hibernation are attracted to the willow catkins in April and midsummer sees common blue, large skepper, meadow brown and gatekeeper butterflies charming the place with their presence.

Near post three, where sandstone outcrops begin to appear on the cutting sides and the soil is thinner, beautiful ferns peep from their shady, humid homes. One, the mountain fern, is usually found in hilly areas and is not common on the Lancashire coastal plain.

Walking through Haskayne Cutting on a glorious summer day is like being in a pretty room with a blue ceiling.

The low embankments towards the end of the cutting produce a mass of flowers, particularly in midsummer. They come in various colours and sizes from the tiny milkwort to the tall rosebay willow-herb.

Suddenly there are no confining embankments and you find yourself in the middle of a rich agricultural land under an immensity of sky. In winter pink-footed geese in their thousands converge on these flat lands to feed on waste grain and potatoes left from the harvest.

Continue to where a road bridge, seen ahead, crosses the trackbed and go left along the road to the first turning on the left which will bring you to Haskayne village. Keep on through the village to the Leeds and Liverpool canal, which cross, and take the footpath on your left, which runs parallel to the canal in a north-westerly direction to join another road which meets it at right angles. Turn left along the road, back over the canal and walk along the towpath on your right to the second bridge, where leave the canal and go left into Halsall village.

Many disused railway lines and canals share therapeutic qualities and this section of the Leeds and Liverpool canal and the Down-

The Downholland Line in Haskayne Cutting Nature Reserve

holland branch have this affinity.

The Leeds and Liverpool is the last remaining trans-Pennine water-way. From a junction with the Aire and Calder Navigation at Leeds to the Mersey at Liverpool it runs for 127 miles. Between Leeds and the summit there are 44 locks and 46 on the Liverpool side. There is a mile long summit tunnel on it at Foulridge and a smaller one near Burnley. At its highest level it is almost 500 feet up. The canal is wide but because the locks east of Wigan cater for boats no longer than 62 feet, the traditional narrow boat cannot use it.

The stretch between Haskayne and Halsall is one of considerable rural beauty.

At Halsall turn left along the A567 for a few hundred yards before turning right at the first junction. Soon after the road bends to the right the road bridges the Downholland branch. It is here that you rejoin the trackbed on the left-hand side of the bridge and continue along it towards the site of Barton station.

Immediately beyond the first bridge you come to, some steps lead down the embankment to the trackbed. This is the site of one of those famous, badly lit halts where to stop Altcar Bob on a dark night the traveller had to strike a match and hope that the driver would see it.

Immediately beyond the second bridge you come to are the remains of Barton's platforms and the end of a most interesting and informative walk.

Cause for celebration: and where better to celebrate than at the nearby Blue Bell Inn, Haskayne, a watering hole much favoured by many a Downholland branch line employee. It also has Leeds and Liverpool associations for several pieces of canal memorabilia hang from its walls. 'Station master' Will Hay, old Harbottle and 'porter' Graham Moffatt would have felt at home there and I'm sure you will too.

11. RAINFORD JUNCTION - RAINFORD VILLAGE CIRCULAR

Length :	3 miles
Opened :	1st February, 1858 - Rainford Junction-St.Helens
Closed :	for passenger traffic 18th June, 1951 - Rainford Junction-St. Helens
	for goods traffic 6th July, 1964 Rainford Junction-St. Helens
O/S	Sheet No.108; Series 1:50,000

Few buildings are vast enough
To hold the sound of time,
And now it seems to him
that the one that held it better than all the others
Should be a railway station,
                    Thomas Wolfe.

This walk begins at Rainford Junction, a still open station on the Liverpool and Bury line which passes just to the north of Rainford and was opened by the Lancashire and Yorkshire Railway in 1848.

Two years earlier, responding to the opening up of a coal field around the isolated mining village of Skelmersdale, the Liverpool, Ormskirk and Preston Co. obtained authority in its Act of 1846 to build a branch line from Ormskirk to Skelmersdale. However, nothing was done to implement the Act.

In 1853 the East Lancashire Railway, successor to the L.O. and P., obtained an Act to extend the branch beyond Skelmersdale southwards to Rainford.

In 1853 the St. Helens Railway and Canal Co. obtained powers to build a line northwards to Rainford.

A bridge across the L.Y.R. joined the two lines which were opened in 1858. Both sections were double track and there were spurs from both directions to join the L.Y.R. at Rainford Junction.

In 1864 the St. Helens Railway and Canal Co. was absorbed by the L.N.W.R. and running powers between Rainford Junction and St. Helens were granted to the L.Y.R.

In 1906 the L.Y.R. introduced railmotors between Ormskirk and Rainford. Steam passenger trains worked the L.N.W.R. portion of the line. There were eight passenger trains on weekdays, none on Saturdays and three on Sundays running between Rainford and St. Helens.

In later years the railmotors, which for so long had run between Ormskirk and Rainford only, worked right through to St. Helens, calling at Rainford Junction en route. A halt which served Rainford village was opened on the L.N.W.R. section and this was the only centre of population south of Rainford Junction the line served.

Surprisingly the line remained open for passenger traffic until 1951. Freight traffic used the line until the early sixties.

Both sections of the line were dismantled soon after closure.

I left Rainford Junction railway station, crossed slantwise to my right to the Junction Hotel side of the road and bridged the L.Y.R., revelling in the crisp clarity of the vast Lancashire sky above me. I was about to walk an interesting circular the most exciting part of which would take me along an embankment that once carried the double line from Ormskirk to St. Helens. The path I took led me across a small piece of typical west Lancashire countryside with little effort on my part for flatness predominates in that part of the county. It was a good walk, an easy walk that I enjoyed. Here are the detailed route directions.

Having crossed the bridge turn left and go along the edge of a field following the side of the L.Y.R. Cross a stile at the end of it and, still edging the railway line, cross a second field to where a bridge carries a farm track over it. Leave the field over a stile, cross the track and with the line still on your left, make for a second bridge over it. Turn right here along a farm track and at a crossing of tracks turn left towards Red House Farm.

Continue along the farm track which is wide now, ignoring a footpath sign pointing to the left just past the farm. After about a quarter of a mile a road is reached. Turn right along it for about 80 yards to where the road bends sharply to the right. At this point leave it by turning slightly to the left and continue in the same direction as you were taking before the road curved. Go along a footpath with some trees on your left. Keep on it for half a mile, edging the open aspect of Holiday Moss on your left. The footpath bends to the right past some rhododendrons and enters Rainford village.

Where the footpath meets the road turn left along it, then sharp right at a bend with an Ormskirk sign, down Cross Pit Lane to where the route of the disused L.N.W.R. line cuts across it.

The embankment on which this old line used to sit runs straight as a die, northwards, towards the still operating L.Y.R. swinging to the right only at the last minute to continue alongside it to the road which is where the walk started.

It was built by navvies who, during the construction of the railways, not only worked together but lived together in shanty towns miles from anywhere, far removed from the sobering influence of family and home. A few of the luckier ones found billets in local villages but even these places were down at heel and overcrowded. Moreover the men were overcharged, a problem they usually overcame by simply leaving the lodgings without paying anything.

Usually one end of a shanty was the sleeping area. There the men slept, two to a bunk, lightly stacked from floor to ceiling. For pillows they used their kits but more often than not they were too drunk to care.

An assortment of dogs, usually bullhounds and lurchers, shared these rough quarters. The navvies used them for poaching or fighting.

The kitchen was at the opposite end of the shanty to the bunks. In it was a rough dresser and a rickety table with its motley collection of mugs and basins. An assortment of pots was fixed to the wall with hooks.

Guns were hung over the fireplace and hanging over a roaring fire was a large copper in which meals were cooked.

Several strings, attached to notched pieces of stick which were placed across the rim of the copper, disappeared into the steamy water. A navvy's meal was attached to the other end of each string. One would be potatoes, another bacon and cabbage, yet another something different. The notches on the sticks identified the owner, the quality of the meal being cooked at the other end depended on the owner's ability to provide. Sluttish women camp followers saw to the cooking and the notched stick method was the only sure way they had of seeing that the navvies got their own food.

On many contracts men would not be employed unless they took part of their pay in beer. On all the contracts drink was a major problem. Beer was the commonest drink, with whisky and gin coming close runners-up when funds could stretch to them. Where whisky was forbidden, as it sometimes was by the magistrates, it was brought to the site in kegs marked paraffin. Publicans living close to a shanty town did a roaring trade, frequently doctoring the beer to make it look stronger. Navvies often sold shovels for ale and even when all their money had gone they still bought more by selling the shoes from their feet.

So the railways were built by rough living, hard drinking, hard fighting men who frequently stopped work to knock the living daylights out of each other and generally terrorise the neighbourhood. In such conditions the wonder is that the embankment between Rainford Junction and the village was built at all, let alone in a straight line.

There is nothing to be gained in scenic value by getting onto the embankment while it slices through the village. So continue along the road, the B5203, to a junction where continue to the right to the fifth street on your right, almost at the end of the village and you will reach the embankment as it escapes Rainford's confines.

St. Helens Metropolitan Borough Council owns the embankment and has plans to develop it as a linear park.

A footpath runs along the embankment's western side; but walking along the old trackbed is much better because there is more to see. When the day is tranquil, when the wind is holding its breath and when only a few high-flying wisps of cirrus lie on an otherwise clear blue sky, the trackbed comes into its own.

12. RAMSBOTTOM - IRWELL VALE
(with, for good measure, a look at the Ogden, Alden and Lower Rossendale valleys)

Length : 2½ miles with a 5½ miles loop at the Irwell Vale end.
Opened : 28th September, 1846 - Clifton Junction-Rawtenstall
Closed : for goods traffic - 4th December, 1980
        for passenger traffic - 5th June, 1972 -
        Bury-Rawtenstall
O/S : Sheets Nos.109 and 103; Series 1:50,000

Then hurrah for King Steam, whose wild whistle and scream
Gives notice to friends and to foes,
As he makes the dust fly, and goes thrundering by,
So stand clear, and make room for King Steam
Ned Farmer.

107

The Normans knew Rossendale's River Irwell as a clear stream in a swampy, thinly inhabited wasteland. For five hundred years, until Tudor times, all Rossendale was a royal forest and as such had restricted access and little development took place. It was not until the 16th century that tenants with leases set about turning those bleak heights into fertile farmland. Many of the small farmers supplemented their incomes by spinning and weaving in their own homes. From many of these homes hamlets and villages developed. Landowning families became established, some great houses were built and green parks landscaped along the Irwell valley. During the latter half of the 18th century Rossendale's rural image changed dramatically and rapidly as the new Lancashire mill owners moved in.

Many of the great houses became the homes of these new industrialists, green parks shrank before spreading bleach grounds, the Irwell ran dirty and uninviting, spindles whined, looms clattered and mill chimneys were planted instead of trees. King cotton had arrived and within a hundred years much of east Lancashire's prosperity was dependent upon it. The cotton spinning towns became established close to Manchester's northern limits while the weaving towns were situated further north in the Blackburn and Colne area. Rossendale was hedged between these spinning and weaving zones where they were more or less equally balanced. Conditions there were just right for bleaching and dyeing, the water was soft and the numerous small streams were easily harnessed for power.

Rossendale had one big drawback - its communications were still at the pack-horse stage and this did not please the local industrialists and businessmen one bit. In September 1843, they called a meeting at Bury to consider the best means of bringing the railway from Manchester through Bury to Rawtenstall, a manufacturing village in the Irwell Valley about 2½ miles from Haslingden. The line was authorised on 4th July 1844, as the Manchester, Bury and Rossendale Railway. At the same time a nominal company was floated under the title of the Blackburn, Burnley, Accrington and Colne, Extension Railway to extend the main line of the M.B. and R. from Stubbins Junction, just north of Ramsbottom to Accrington, with branches from there to Blackburn and Burnley. The Act was obtained in 1845 together with the amalgamations of the M.B. and R. and the new undertaking became the East Lancashire Railway in 1846.

The E.L.R. line was routed along the Irwell Valley through hilly country. Pauling and Hanfry, who had been awarded the contract to build it, encountered many problems both with the difficult terrain and bad weather. The Irwell was crossed numerous times, the first being on a viaduct of thirteen arches at Clifton. It took the threat of the Rossendale Company to complete the job themselves to ensure that Pauling and Hanfry made a satisfactory job of the project. Yet even with this threat parts of the permanent way were left in such a shoddy state that large sections had to be completely re-layed.

From Bury right along the Irwell Valley through Ramsbottom to Rawtenstall the line was double track. Beyond Rawtenstall, through the narrow gorge above Waterfoot it became single.

Extensive sidings and a substantial coal depot sprawled along the west side of the Irwell on the northern outskirts of Ramsbottom. Once free of them, the line ran along a mile long embankment to Stubbins bridge, pressed close to the river by the valley sides.

It was at Stubbins Junction, now no longer there, that the Rawtenstall line diverged from what was to become the main line to Accrington. On leaving Stubbins station the Rawtenstall line caused an optical illusion by seeming to drop below the level of the Accrington main line. In fact it continued along a level section and then climbed at 1 in 132 for just over a mile towards Ewood Bridge. It was the Accrington line, climbing at a gradient of 1 in 78, that caused the illusion. Stubbins station, of which only the platforms remain, never served the Accrington main line which was routed not through but around the back of it.

Just before entering Alderbottom cutting there is a good view to the left, of the Alderbottom viaduct on the Accrington main line, now on a higher level. Once through the cutting, the Accrington main line can be seen again, curving to the left; and the bridge at Lumb can also be seen. The line's gradient is now about 1 in 254 all the way to Ewood Bridge station.

From Irwell Vale the moors beckon on all sides; and the call is too strong to resist. The line continues to Bacup; the discerning walker alights at Irwell Vale and heads for the hills.

On Saturday, 14th February 1981 the 'Rossendale Farewell' railtour, the final passenger train from Manchester to Rawtenstall via Heywood and Bury, departed Victoria station at 11.05 and arrived at its destination at 13.45. It left Rawtenstall ten minutes later and arrived back in Manchester Victoria at 15.30. On board this trip into nostalgia were many members of the East Lancashire Railway Preservation Society, who now own that section of the line from Bury to Rawtenstall. The line is still operational and this could have put a damper on its potential as a railway walk but for the Irwell Valley Way.

The Irwell Valley Way is a path leading from Castlefields in the

Ramsbottom Station

centre of Manchester to the village of Weir in Rossendale. It is a journey not only along the river valley but also back in time, exposing the development of south-east Lancashire. Its route is northwards, through industrial towns and attractive countryisde, to where, in Rossendale's upland villages, the development began.

Between Ramsbottom and Irwell Vale it lies cheek by jowl with that stretch of the East Lancashire Railway Preservation Society's line that forms the basis of this walk. Because railway and riverside path lie side by side, or near enough, following the Irwell Valley Way's distinctive dragonfly logo provides a rare opportunity to observe and enjoy the railway from a slightly different angle. Moreover, at almost any point it is possible to shift from riverside walk to railway and vice versa without fuss; and all this adds interest.

Ramsbottom makes a good start to the walk because of its association with the new manufacturers who settled along the Irwell and transformed it out of all recognition. In 1805 the three Grant brothers came to Ramsbottom and built the village of Nuttall. It was made up of a print works, spinning and weaving sheds, dyeing and finishing shops, cottages for the workers and a mansion for themselves. They also built a Presbyterian church and a pub, the Grant's Arms. The

110

Grants frowned on drinking yet, knowing that to many of their employees beer was food and drink, they gave their workers weekly 3d vouchers which could be spent at the Grant's Arms. Charles Dickens modelled Charles and Edwin Cheeryble, the two prosperous and kindly merchants who befriended Nicholas Nickleby, on the Grant brothers having met them in 1838. Today nothing much remains to remind the people of Ramsbottom of those three ambitious Scots immigrants who did so much to put Ramsbottom on the map. Not even Grant's Tower remains, which is a crying shame.

The Irwell Valley Way leaves Ramsbottom along the river's eastern bank where it remains as far as Stubbins where it crosses to the west bank and immediately goes right, first through public gardens, then allotments, before continuing along the riverbank.

This is a most exciting section because that part of the railway north of Stubbins through Chatterton and Strongstry and on, almost to Lumb, is the site of the proposed Stubbins Nature Area. Future generations will derive great benefit and pleasure from this admirable scheme; and the organisation to thank and support is Rossendale Groundwork Trust.

There was a riot at Chatterton in 1826. A lot of people were put out of work by power looms which had been installed in the mill. They reacted angrily and remove plugs from the looms. This allowed steam to escape and the machines were rendered useless. The army was called on to quell the protest and nine people were killed and many more wounded.

Beyond Strongstry the river is recrossed and the way ahead is left, through a gate. The path is under the railway and along the river. At Lumb the river is recrossed and the way is upstream along the riverbank.

At Irwell Vale, a pleasant village set among meadows, leave the Irwell Valley Way and go to the bridge at the entrance to the village where the six and a half miles long loop begins.

Irwell Vale, a typical Lancashire mill village, was designated a conservation area by Rossendale Borough Council in the 1970's.

The way ahead is northerly, along Irwell Vale road, past a red brick mill and along an attractive meadow. The mill has a datestone, 'T.A. and S. Ltd. 1952'.

Soon a double gate with a stile beyond is reached. Go over the stile and take the grassy track across the meadow. Cross another stile and continue along the path which becomes increasingly wooded, alongside the River Ogden. Soon the path goes under the tall arches of the viaduct that used to carry the line from Stubbins to Accrington. The river upstream of the viaduct is very lovely and was at one time called 'Little Blackpool' because of the numbers of bathers who swam there.

The path continues over another stile and along the riverside, passing, on the opposite bank, a flat, grassy area which is the site of Ravenshore Mill, which as early as the 17th century was fulling cloth. Soon after going through two gates a pretty hamlet is reached. The O/S map calls it Holme Vale but its other and more descriptive name is Snig Hole. Once eels thrived here, in the Ogden's rocky dubs, and the local name for eel is snig.

The way forward is along an unsurfaced road, which becomes surfaced alongside some memorial gardens. When the Bridge End Hotel is reached turn left into Helmshore Road and after passing under the bridge carrying the Holcombe Road fork right along the tree-lined Sunnybank Road. The site of Sunny Bank Mill is a little way along this pleasant wooded valley.

Joseph Porritt began his woollen business here in 1866 and his mill grew until it stretched from one side of the valley to the other. At one time Sunny Bank Mill was the world's largest producer of paper-makers' felts. In the early 1900s the longest loom in the world was housed there.

Turn right along a surfaced road, passing some cottages, and continue uphill, past Ivy Lodge and another dwelling nearby, converted from some cottages. Both these properties are thought to pre-date the Industrial Revolution in the Aiden Valley.

Soon, on the right in well wooded grounds, Tor Side House can be glimpsed. Joseph Porritt built it for his own occupation. In the early part of this century it was extended and remodelled. It was given the name Tor Side House and between 1949 and 1982 housed the offices of the Ministry of Agriculture's Great House Experimental Farm.

Before long, on the left-hand side of the road Great House Farm, with its sinister sounding 'experimental' connotation, comes into view. Ahead are two pairs of semi-detached cottages with, behind them, Tor Hill itself, which rises to 1,114 feet. Cross the farmyard and go through the double metal gates adjacent to the top farm building, when immediately turn left onto a well defined path. The way is now past a farm building called Halliwell's, through a gate and on, past two more buildings, Trickling Water and Fall Bank Farm. These buildings are on the spring line. Leaving Fall Bank Farm through a gate, the path crosses a meadow, passing below an isolated tree just beyond a farm building. Then it is through a gateway in a wall and a fence ahead. The path then goes past another isolated tree which stands at the side of Spring Bank Farm.

For many years Robert 'Rough Robin' Pilkington lived at Spring Bank Farm in the 'township of Pilkington' as the upper part of Aiden is still known. He got his nickname because he invariably referred to the weather as 'a bit rough'. He enclosed common land on the adjoining moor but refused to pay his rates. Consequently during the depression of 1826, he was refused relief. He appealed to the Government for redress saying he lived in the township of Pilkington. The name stuck and he was dubbed the Marquis of Pilkington.

At Spring Bank Farm site the path veers to the left, following the course of a retaining wall. Soon a row of hawthorn trees marks the path which, after going through a gate, follows a well defined green track across open moor to the Aiden Brook where it flows over some pleasant little waterfalls. The way is on the south side of the brook and is clearly defined. It climbs steeply up the moor, with the ruins of Goose Pits Farm on the left, to the right-hand corner of a wall near the skyline.

The views here are terrific, especially towards the north. On a clear day Pendle Hill and Ingleborough can be seen to the left of Tor Hill.

Turn left on the path at the edge of the moor alongside a stone wall and after half a mile look out for a stone cairn with a small upright stone near it. The cairn marks the spot where Ellen Strange was murdered.

Legend has it that Ellen Strange lived with her parents at Ash Farm, Hawkshaw. She had a lover, a pedlar called Billy from Stone Fold. One day they were seen to leave Haslingden fair together. They were going to Ellen's home, calling at the White Horse Hotel on the way. She never reached home. She was murdered on the edge of the moor. Billy, the pedlar, was tried at Lancaster where he pleaded guilty to the crime. He was executed at Lancaster and his body hanged in a gibbet on Bull Hill.

Continue along the path by the stone wall at the moor's edge to a gate where a number of tracks converge. Go through it and follow a walled and rather boggy track called Stake Lane where you will see, a few yards along it, Robin Hood's well.

The origin of the name Stake Lane is obscure. Either it was because it was once staked out with poles or markers or because bulls were tied to stakes there while terriers attacked them. It was supposed to tenderise the meat.

Even less is known of Robin Hood's well, a bit further along the lane. Its association with Robin of Sherwood is slender. However, a Robin Hood festival used to be celebrated annually in Bury until 1810, so maybe there is a genuine connection with the famous outlaw.

Stake Lane becomes surfaced where it gives access to Dowry Head. Keep on it and at Aiden Road turn right and right again along the track behind the White Horse Inn. Cross Helmshore Road and go through the gate to the left of the cottages. Now on a well defined track go through two gates and past a farm and cottages at Ravenshore.

Once across the old railway bridge there are some grand views through the woods of the Irwell Valley below. Ahead is Irwell Vale village, the end of eight splendid miles of varied and interesting walking.

13. RAWTENSTALL - BACUP

Length : 5 miles
Opened : Rawtenstall to Waterfoot (Newchurch) -
4th March, 1848
Waterfoot (Newchurch) for passenger traffic -
1st October, 1852
Waterfoot (Newchurch) for goods traffic -
1st February, 1853
Closed : 5th December, 1966
O/S : Sheet No.103; Series 1:50,000

> *Late at night in the station*
> *It is cold; the gas lamps shine,*
> *Down pointing pyramids of yellow light,*
> *In a long, solemn line*
> *Vivian de Sola Pinto.*

The Bacup branch, that part of it which runs east to west and for about five miles shares a narrow gorge with the twisting, infant Irwell, is quite pleasant despite a certain amount of industrial despoilation over the past two hundred years. An abundant and regular supply of water was an important factor leading to the spread of industrial development in the area: another was the coming of the railways. Rossendale's damp climate was well suited to the woollen, cotton and felt trades that became established there. There was an abundance of stone in the area which was used for roofing and paving and rail was the most economical means of transporting it.

Two companies, the Manchester, Bury and Rossendale Railway and the Blackburn, Burnley, Accrington and Colne Extension Railway amalgamated in 1844 to exploit and open out the area. The Manchester, Bury and Rossendale Railway was continued along what was to become the Bacup branch railway, being opened first from Stubbins, just north of Ramsbottom to Rawtenstall and extended by stages to Bacup.

On Friday 25th September 1846, the East Lancashire Railway, formed by the amalgamation of the above two companies, was formally opened from Salford to Rawtenstall. A special train of directors and friends travelled the line from Salford, via Clifton Junction, the southern end of the East Lancashire Railway and on to Rawtenstall, where in a large, new weaving shed not yet containing machinery, the party had a celebratory meal.

In May 1845, surveys were made for the extension of the line to Bacup and in July 1846 an Act was obtained for this purpose. In January 1847, the contract for the work was let but in May work beyond Newchurch was suspended, possibly because of the expense of Thrutch tunnel. However, the rest of the work continued and on Saturday 4th March 1848, the line from Rawtenstall to Newchurch was opened.

On 17th August 1848, the railway between Stubbins and Accrington was opened and this relegated the line from Rawtenstall to Newchurch to branch line status.

Although the construction of the line had come to a temporary halt at Newchurch, Bacup remained the ultimate goal. Already £3,400 had been paid out for the land and the cost of completing the line was estimated at £47,700. Everything, including the construction of the tunnels and stations was contained within one contract; and the contractors took possession of the land on 27th October 1851. In April 1852, the miners and the stonemasons went on strike and during the summer months the weather was terrible. Yet despite these setbacks the link with Bacup was made and the branch opened for passenger traffic on 1st October 1852, and for goods traffic, using Bacup's new goods station on 1st February 1853.

In May 1856, tenders were advertised for the building of waiting rooms at the intermediate station at Stacksteads and in 1857 a new station was rebuilt a little higher up the valley than the original wooden structure. It was renamed Waterfoot in August 1881. More importantly, because of increasing traffic on the branch it was decided to double the line between Stubbins and Rawtenstall from where it remained single, passing through the narrow gorge above Newchurch in two tunnels. When this section was doubled in 1878-81 there was no room for an additional track in the gorge so it was carried though

Rawtenstall West Signal Box

the Thrutch tunnel further into the hill. At that time the old single line tunnel at Bacup was enlarged.

While all this was going on negotiations were taking place for the merger of the East Lancashire Railway with the Lancashire and Yorkshire Railway. The amalgamation took place in 1859.

For much of its life the Bacup branch had to contend with road competition, especially from the Rossendale Valley Tramways which operated a service between Rawtenstall and Bacup from 1888 to 1909: the last regular system of steam trains in the streets of England. But it was competition the branch was quite capable of taking in its stride. In fact the tramway system was regarded disdainfully by many of those working on the Bacup branch.

Bacup became a 'closed' station on 8th June 1904, when ticket barriers and gates were erected to restrict free access to the platform. In April 1917, as a wartime economy measure, Clough Fold station was closed but re-opened when hostilities ended.

On 5th December 1966, the section of the Bacup line between Rawtenstall and Bacup was closed.

From Rawtenstall to Clough Fold the trackbed has been made into a road; and further up the valley it is partly built over. The only part that is walkable is from Waterfoot through all three tunnels to just east of Stacksteads; and this section is being made into a linear park.

14. BAXENDEN BANK

Length   :   2 miles
Opened   :   17th August, 1848 - Stubbins-Accrington
Closed   :   5th December, 1966 - Stubbins-Accrington
O/S   :   Sheet No.103; Series 1:50,000

> *Jump jolt,*
> *Engines that bolt*
> *H. Cholmondeley-Pennell.*

This is a peep into the future for the two miles long notorious Baxenden Bank is destined to become a linear parkway. However, there is no need to wait for that to happen before doing the walk. The locals have been perambulating up and down it for years.

Baxenden Bank came into being as the northern end of the Stubbins to Accrington line which transferred the Rossendale railway into a through route from Manchester and Bury to Accrington, Blackburn

117

and Preston. From Stubbins, 442 feet above sea level, the line climbed over a spur of the Pennines to reach its summit at Baxenden. For five miles it climbed through hilly country with fine scenery to reach, in a big wet cutting, its highest point. The line's route brought immense engineering problems, all of which were overcome and it opened on 17th August 1848. From Baxenden summit the line dropped steeply for two miles to Accrington station almost 300 feet lower down.

From the line's opening, Baxenden Bank, with its severe 1 in 40 gradient, was an operating problem. Sand drags, the first ever to be used on the E.L.R., were installed on it in 1903 to retard any runaways. Accrington station, at the foot of the bank, was the scene of a most remarkable piece of operational skill when in 1914 the E.L.R. introduced a slip coach to stop there from the 4.25 p.m. Salford to Colne express on Mondays, Wednesdays and Thursdays. As it descended Baxenden Bank this ten coach train slowed to a 5 m.p.h. speed restriction through the station and slipped a coach. It was a tricky operation because, despite the use of train brakes in descending the bank the driver had to restore vacuum so that the slip-guard would be left with enough brake power to stop his coach in the platform after it had been separated from the train. Because of the curve through the station the driver passing along it could not see if the stop had been successful so a man had to be stationed at a suitable place on the platform to signal to him that all was in order. On Tuesdays and Fridays, the busiest days on the Manchester Cotton Exchange, when there were a good many mill owners returning from the city, the Accrington section of the Salford to Colne express was run as a separate train. Fortunately there were no untoward incidents with the slip coaches but in a train of 50 wagons some ran out of control down the bank, derailed on a sand drag and hit a locomotive.

In 1908, at a time when 242 trains were passing through Accrington station every day, it was described as 'inconvenient as any to be found in the north of England' with 'internal accommodation of a primitive condition'.

Freight traffic included the famous Accrington bricks, some of which support Blackpool tower, cotton wares, soap, wringers and billiard tables from the factory of E.J.Ridley.

In 1857-8 a mechanics' institute, news room and assembly room, called the Peel Institute, was built to commemorate Sir Robert Peel, the founder of the police force, whose family was the biggest employer in the town. Today this interesting building, with its Corinthian portico above a carriage porch, is the Town Hall.

The market hall was built in 1867 by the Local Board of Health. Its wide-spanned roof is supported on iron columns behind an entrance that looks like a Roman arch.

Of all the stone viaducts built by the E.L.R. the most impressive one, built on a sweeping course of 19 arches, dominates most views of the town centre. It carries the line from Blackburn to Burnley some 54 feet above the River Hyndburn.

Following the closure of the Subbins to Accrington line, most of Baxenden Bank remained in the ownership of the British Railways Board. Some was purchased by Lancashire County Council and part was bought privately.

Eventually the two miles long length of trackbed (3.3km) along Baxenden Bank was all purchased by the Lancashire County Council under a reclamation scheme so that the disused railway and its associated derelict land could be developed as a public open space, trees planted, grazing land developed, hedges planted, stone walls rebuilt and fences repaired. The scheme incorporated a footpath from the vicinity of Accrington town centre to near the borough boundary.

Lancashire County Council leased the land to Accrington Borough Council for a term of 99 years, subject to a peppercorn ground-rent if demanded, and Accrington Borough Council is responsible for the repair and maintenance of the boundary walls, fences, structures and all the landscape works. The reclamation scheme is designed to keep maintenance to a minimum.

The scheme, which has a total estimated cost of £353,500, is designed to accommodate a pedestrian route only, with no horse riders, motor cyclists and push bikes being allowed on the footpath. However, because of the considerable demand for these facilities the overall design of the scheme will make it possible to provide for all these non-pedestrian users at a future date if desired.

A few years ago two bridges on Baxenden Bank were demolished, one at Shoe Mill, in the middle of the walk, the other where Nuttall Street and its continuation as Mount Street meet. Because of financial constraints and technical difficulties little further progress was possible. A start was made in 1987 on the first part of the scheme.

The Baxenden Bank walk begins at Nuttall Street.

South from Nuttall Street the old trackbed will become the footpath for the full length of the walk, so whether it is trackbed now, before the transformation is complete or later, when the chrysalis stage has passed and a thing of pristine loveliness awaits you, the route remains the same.

From Nuttall Street go along the trackbed, where, on each side of it, the existing vegetation is being retained and as reclamation work progresses, more will be planted. Soon you pass Rothwell Avenue where a second access road will be provided with trees. The Council hopes to acquire the large piece of rough grassland adjoining Woodnook Water and regrade and restore it to open space.

The cutting between King George V playing fields and Priestley Clough is going to be filled with spoil from the Nuttall Street embankment to bring the path to the level of Rothwell Bridge, the underside of which will also be filled. This bridge will become the third access point for walkers.

On now, towards Shoe Mill through some of Accrington's most attractive scenery. It is here that the Accrington Heritage Trail crosses the trackbed in search of more of Lancashire's industrial archaeology. There is a footpath from here up to Bedlam and here, also, a footbridge crosses Woodnook Water at the south end of which the route continues through a cutting to Hurstead Farm where a further pedestrian access point will be provided.

A final access point will be at Bridge Houses where steps will lead down into the cutting. Here, where an overbridge serves Alma Court and Bridge Houses, is where you should make your exit.

The remainder of the trackbed as far as the borough boundary will have pedestrian access and will be planted with trees.

Here, then, is a trackbed which although good to walk along in its present state, will become a jewel in Accrington's crown once this reclamation work has been completed. For showing considerable foresight and initiative Accrington Borough Council is to be congratulated.

15. WHITWORTH CIRCULAR VIA HEALEY DELL VIADUCT

Length :   4½ miles
Opened :   for goods traffic - 5th October, 1870 - Rochdale-Facit
           for passenger traffic - 1st November, 1870 - Rochdale-Facit
Closed :   for passenger traffic - 16th June, 1947 - Rochdale-Bacup
         for goods traffic - 12th August, 1967 - Rochdale-Whitworth
O/S   :   Sheet No.109; Series 1:50,000

Along the windswept platform, pinched and white,
The travellers stand in pools of wintry light,
Offering themselves to morn's long slanting arrows,
The train's due, porters trundle laden barrows.
Seigfried Sassoon

The Rochdale to Bacup branch was not built to be a money spinner. Back in 1860, when the L.Y.R. directors were promoting it they were all fully aware that it would never pay its way. They also knew that if they did not build the line a rural company would be delighted to do so; and the attitude of the L.Y.R. directors was 'let 'em'. However, they were in a minority, so the line was built.

It was not an easy task. Rough terain caused severe constructional problems and costs soared. Even the building of the large viaduct at Rochdale was fraught with difficulties. Landslides impeded progress to such an extent that not until the 1870s was the line opened, and then only as far as Facit.

From Rochdale to Wardleworth the track was double: from Wardleworth to Facit it was single. Not until 1881 was the extension from Facit to Bacup completed. It was double track, many of the gradients were severe and its summit, at 965 feet, was the highest throughout the entire L.Y.R. system.

Traffic receipts were poor, but this was no surprise. As time passed they went from bad to worse. Competition was strong, at first from the electric trams and later from buses. The effect was predictable: dwindling receipts. Yet somehow the passenger service managed to survive until 1947.

Goods traffic fared rather better but gradually the freight trains decreased until only one train a day was running to Joseph Taylor's coal yard at Whitworth station in 1968, when the line between Whitworth and Facit was closed. On 12th August 1967, the rest of the Rochdale to Bacup branch was closed.

This splendid walk starts in Whitworth at the car park where Market Stret and Hall Street meet. The way is westerly along Hall Street. When Wall Bank Drive is reached, turn left and, just beyond a lodge, which once served a mill, turn left again onto a footpath. This soon bears right and runs between some houses on the right and the site of a former dyeing mill. Cross a stone bridge and immediately turn right down a short incline, which brings you to the trackbed of the former railway line which is the *pièce de résistance* of the walk. The way is southwards now, along a path with the River Spodden on your left.

The part of the valley through which you are now walking looks far better than it used to, thanks to a bit of government help. For this is land that has been reclaimed with the aid of a Government Derelict Land Grant. The hope is that eventually this facelift will become an extension to Healey Dell Nature Reserve.

The small valley on the right is the site of Broadley sidings and a little way along it is Spring Mill, one of the oldest factories in the area.

121

There used to be a little tramway worked by drum and cable leading from Spring Mill to the sidings. Cloth from the mill was brought down along it in small wagons, which ran onto a high banking above the sidings and tipped directly into L.Y.R. wagons. On the return trip vats of acid for bleaching were frequently carried.

A rubbing mill was also located at the siding and another tramway brought stone from a quarry on the edge of Rooley Moor. The quarry tramway closed in 1900 but the Spring Mill tramway worked until 1947.

Just beyond where a wooden bridge crosses the route there are two L.Y.R. boundary stones, one on a path going down to the river and the other 200 yards along the disused line on the site of the Broadley signal.

Broadley Wood Mill, tucked away in the wood rising on the right, used to manufacture corduroy. The business went bankrupt in 1930. Now all that remains of it are ruins and the remains of two lodges which used to feed the mill with water. The ruins are haunted, supposedly by the mill's owner.

Just north of Broadley station a level crossing once carried a footpath over the line to Broadley Wood Mill. The station platform is still there, on the right, and a track branching off, up a ramp to the left, was the former station approach.

The gap in the station platform is where the signal-box stood. Because the line was single track it was operated by a 'tablet'. Using this safety method no train could pass from one section of the line to the next one until driver and signalman had exchanged tablets, which were housed in black shoulder pouches.

From the ramp across the trackbed from the station platform a detour can be made through the prettiest part of the Healey Dell Nature Reserve. Take the track which branches from the ramp to Station Road, turn left along it then along the footpath on the right at the east end of the bridge over the river.

Here, where the river churns and roars through a narrow gorge it is known as the 'the thrutch'. Steps lead down to the river at a place where some rocks have been hallowed out in the shape of a church window. This is the thrutch's 'Fairies' Chapel'.

There is a fine view upstream of waterfalls while downstream is all that remains of a single stone arch across the river on the site of an old corn mill which dates from 1676 and was powered by a water-wheel.

The Healey Dell viaduct which strides so splendidly across the Spodden was constructed in 1866, in part by local labour using picks and shovels. Steam cranes were also used. Built of stone, it stands 105 feet high and has eight spans of thirty feet. When in 1967 the line was closed the viaduct was in danger of falling in disrepair. However, a main sewer was relaid down the trackbed and it is carried across the river by the viaduct.

The path climbs up, going under the viaduct and joins a tarmac surfaced lane. The way is sharp left along the lane which soon reaches Healey Corner at the junction of Market Street and Shawclough Road.

By sticking to the course of the old railway you go under a bridge carrying Station Road and soon you are on the viaduct being rewarded with magnificent views of the wooded valley below on either side. At the end of the viaduct take the footpath on the left-hand side which will bring you to a tarmac road which climbs up, through trees to Healey Corner.

You can, of course, having taken the detour under the viaduct to Healey Corner, walk down the tarmac road and up the footpath onto the viaduct, thus seeing it from every angle. Is there no limit to this walk's versatility?

The Rochdale-Whitworth boundary stone is at the southern end of the viaduct on the right-hand side. On the left, up the hill, Healey Hall stands in a landscaped setting. Built on the site of a 13th century house, this 18th century hall is now a listed building. Sir Samuel Turner, a former owner, sold the land to the L.Y.R. but reserved the right to have the trains halted at the bottom of his garden to pick him up each morning and set him down again each evening. The path Sir Samuel used and which remains private is still there, going up the hill from the end of the viaduct to the hall.

It was a later owner of Healey Hall, Richard Heape, who developed Healey Dell and laid out the paths in the 1920s.

Leaving the old railway the route now crosses Market Street, ascends narrow Ending Rake Lane, goes under an arch into open country and continues straight ahead. Soon after going through a metal gate a small white house, Hopwood Hall comes into view. At the turn of the century a rifle range at the side of the hall was used by the Rochdale Volunteers.

The little valley along which you are walking once supplied paving setts for the street of Rochdale.

Soon the valley opens out and you are given a fine view of Hamer Pasture and Brown House Wham reservoirs with, beyond, the towns of Littleborough and Rochdale.

The way ahead is uphill along a stony lane, by the wall above Hamer Pasture Reservoir which was completed in 1846 by Rochdale Corporation Waterworks Company. Apparently it leaked and is now disused.

At the end of Brown House Wham Reservoir the way is left, up the moorland track. Quieter now, this track has had a very busy past. Every Shrove Tuesday the Syke Hunt would go along it to course hares on Brown Wardle. Coal from Brown Wardle and lime from Clitheroe were carried along it on the stout backs of Galloways. On Sundays the faithful passed this way to Hallfold Chapel.

Climbing steadily the track reaches the Man Stone Edge, passing on the left, a huge boulder, the Man Stone, which gave the edge its name. The Man Stone carries the imprint of a giants hand and is said to have been thrown there from Blackstone Edge.

The views from the Edge are grand, especially to the wild moors to the north. Where the way bifurcates take the left-hand fork and continue, with flat roofed, red brick Lobden golf course club house on your left, ignoring the track coming in from the right. Descend towards the tower of St. Bartholomew's church. At a cattle grid the moor is left behind and the walk continues along Whitworth Rake to Whitworth Square, on the right just past a park.

At the far side of Whitworth Square you will find the old Red Lion Inn with its datestone, IMT 1674.

Here, over a pint and a bar snack, is where to reflect on how, at the beginning of the 19th century, 'the Whitworth Doctors' put the place on the map.

The doctors, the most famous of whom were Dr. John and Dr. George Taylor, lived in Whitworth House on the north side of Whitworth Square, close to the Red Lion. Originally farmers and blacksmiths by trade, the Taylor family became famous for their bone setting skills. They also made and applied ointments, salves, bandages and splints. All the family joined in, the men folk, their wives, sons and daughters all working together as a team. People came from far and wide to be treated by them and the charge was the same for rich and pool alike: eighteen pence a week. Often rich patients gave them handsome presents, but if a poor person could not pay, nobody ever asked for the money.

Returning to Whitworth Rake turn right along it, bear right into Church Street and this will bring you to the car park where it all began but where it need not end.

Whitworth Square, including Church Street, was designated a Conservation Area by Lancashire County Council in the 1970s. For anyone with a spark of interest in the Industrial Revolution a closer inspection of the old buildings and interesting sites to be seen there is most rewarding. Vying for attention are 17th and 18th century farmhouses and cottages, 17th century shippons, an old parsonage, a church and a chapel, an obelisk to the Taylors, stocks and another pub, the Dog and Partridge, which also provides bar meals.

Anyone wishing to walk the trackbed to four miles distant Wardleworth will be well rewarded for it passes through some very interesting country. From the car park in Whitworth follow the direction for the circular walk as far as the south end of Healey Dell viaduct and simply continue along the trackbed.

Just south of the viaduct there is a curious double bridge. The original one, along with its approach embankments, slid down the hill during construction. A new one was built almost on the same spot, only slightly closer to the hillside.

Either way, doing the circular or keeping to the trackbed to Wardleworth, this walk is a winner because the wealth of industrial archaeology it contains is delightfully held in a beautiful setting. This walk makes happy memories.

16. BRINSCALL - WHITE COPPICE CIRCULAR

Length :   4 miles
            The joint L.Y.R.-L.N.W.R. line around which this
            walk curves was:-
Opened :   for goods traffic - 1st November, 1869 -
            Blackburn Cherry Tree-Chorley
            for passenger traffic - 1st December, 1869 -
            Blackburn Cherry Tree-Chorley
Closed :   for passenger traffic - 4th January, 1960 -
            Chorley-Feniscowles
            for goods traffic - 3rd January, 1966 -
            Chorley-Feniscowles
O/S   :   Sheet Nos.103 and 109; Series 1:50,000

May a star lead you,
The wind be at your back,
The road rise to meet you,
And God hold you.
In the hollow of his hand.
Old Gaelic blessing for travellers.

If you are one of those people used to taking country walks along tracks and lanes but who have hitherto neglected disused railway lines, this is just the introduction you need. Twice the route cuts across the Lancashire and Yorkshire Railway and the London and North Western Railway joint line midway between Cherry Tree and Chorley allowing you to savour its flavour but at the same time giving you the choice of either embracing it or keeping it at arms length as fancy decrees. Choice is the keynote of this pleasant ramble which makes a fine introduction to walking disused railway tracks.

Being circular it gives you a choice of starts; and Brinscall is as good as any. This Victorian-looking village, which once supplied labour for the mill in nearby Wheelton on the other side of a hill, sprawls along a rift below Anglezarke Moor. Although some of the older houses look a bit down in the mouth, Brinscall is not and never has been depressed: a lively local council sees to that. And the cheerfulness of the local inhabitants is a real, Lancashire tonic.

The walk begins in a car park behind Brinscall baths from where you turn left into Lodge Bank and continue parallel to the track of the L.Y.R.-L.N.W.R. on your right. To your left the smooth waters of the Lodge are backed by deciduous trees with conifers rising above them. Beautiful enough in its summer greenery, I suspect that the view across the Lodge on a clear day in autumn will be breathtaking.

Anyone living close enough to Brinscall to be able to visit Lodge Bank regularly can, by taking the same walk day by day, become immersed in the scene. As part of this happening, the animals and birds making their homes there will become used to your presence and no longer become alarmed as you pass by. You will become accepted by these wild creatures and in this way will enjoy a new found freedom because simply by being there on a daily basis you will have become, perhaps without realising it, a natural part of this beautiful countryside. More importantly, having been accepted by the local wildlife, you will have gained a rare freedom, a real freedom and one to cherish.

Soon the road becomes a stony track which reaches a crossroad of paths, the right-hand one going under the disused railway. However, the way is straight ahead through a gap at the side of an iron gateway. Cobbled now, the track becomes arched by trees. Before reaching the end of the cobbles, turn right to cross under the disused railway line going through kissing gates on either side of it. The shell of a ruined house is directly in front of you at a junction of two paths, where the way ahead is now left, over a cattle grid and across a long meadow on a straight, clear path.

Just beyond a second cattle grid you pass a pond and a large house before continuing through landscaped parkland belonging to the house. The pond used to be a mill lodge and the mill to which it belonged, known as Blue Dye House, is now this large house, pleasantly converted. After crossing a third cattle grid the track passes some cottages and a fourth cattle grid, beyond which it passes, on the right, the end of the drive up to Logwood Mill Farm.

As its name implies, Logwood Mill Farm has associations with the dyeing industry. As Logwood Mill it was probably where tannin was extracted from various barks in the mid-nineteenth century.

Continue straight ahead, past the drive entrance, to a tarmac road where turn left across a bridge and climb uphill. At a T junction turn left again, away from the tarmac road and over the bridge across the disused line.

Immediately after crossing the bridge take the right-hand one of two facing gates and follow the path across a long field, keeping close to the hedge on your left. At the far end of the field cross a stile in the corner to enter a small copse with a ditch on the right. Leave the copse over a stile on the right leading into another long field and cross it keeping close to its left-hand boundary. Leave it via another stile, close to another one a few feet away which appears to be superfluous.

Keeping a barbed wire fence to your left and a depresion with a marshy area to your right, continue straight ahead, through a gap in the fence and aim for the wooden bridge. Cross it and continue straight ahead with the hedge to your right and at the end of it climb another stile onto a track. Go straight ahead for a little way then turn right down a tree-lined track at the end of which cross the bridge near some cottages and turn left along a tarmac road towards White Coppice cricket field. To reach it go through the gate on your right onto a cinder path, ignoring the tarmac road to White Coppice Farm, and this will bring you to the cricket field, which enter.

One of the greatest honours a Lancashire village can bestow upon its sons is membership of the local eleven. Such is the hold of the game on these friendly folk that few, if any, villages are without an area set aside for playing this most English of games. Most villages can count on enough enthusiasts to field one eleven and many, calling on the surrounding district for support, can muster two. But for choice of setting, few can match White Coppice cricket field for its harmony of colour, restful greens predominating, against ascending moorland.

Originally a weaving village, White Coppice is a lovely little place, awash during the cricket season, with colourful roses and summer bedding plants. It is a contented village because only people having this happy outlook could become such dedicated gardeners.

Leave the cricket field going eastwarts past the pavilion and cross a bridge over a man-made water course known as the Goyt, which channels Liverpool's reservoirs at Tockholes to those lower down at

127

Anglezarke and Rivington. Continue uphill along a broad track to a Rambler's Association sign where turn left; but ignore its direction. Instead, follow the path overlooking, on your left, the lodge and a cone shaped hill known locally as The Lowe. Any Scrooge not wishing to make a donation to the village cricket match, should one be in progress when he is there, can have a good view of it from this undulating track, which narrows as you progress along it. I make this observation in the sure knowledge that such meanness is unacceptable to the walking fraternity, so the collection is quite safe.

Where there is a bifurcation of paths just beyond the water lodge take the higher, right-hand one. Cross an old ruinous wall and go over an old track in a gully coming up from a bridge. Keep straight ahead and soon a wall and some trees will appear to your left. With the Goyt channel always below it on the left, the path continues through slopes of bilberry and bracken which in summer becomes head high to most people. Soon Wheelton plantation appears ahead. After passing several trees the path bears left across flatter ground towards a bridge over the Goyt. Cross a stile just before reaching the bridge and turn right into Wheelton plantation.

Take the broad path through the trees, climbing steadily and where the trees on the right of it thin to a grassy area take the downhill path to your left, close to a stone wall. After about 100 yards the track begins to go uphill and is now walled on both sides. Where the path turns sharp right then left a ruined house can be seen through the trees on the right. This is Heather Lea. Continue along the path, now topped with stone chippings and lined with silver birch trees and pines. After about half a mile there is a well-maintained wall on your left. Where the track makes a sharp bend look over the wall and you will be staring into what used to be a quarry and is now the 60 feet deep Hatch Brook ravine. This is not the place to take a short cut.

Go through the gate ahead and continue downhill. Soon the track gets a tarmac surface and houses appear on the right. You have returned to Brinscall. Now all that remains is for you to find where you left the car. Turn left into School Lane, then first left and past some terraced house. Then, *voila?* Before you know it there's the car park and, with any luck at all, they'll be open.

17. PRESTON, BAMBER BRIDGE AND WALTON SUMMIT PLATEWAY TRIANGULAR

Length :   4¾ miles

Opened :   for passenger traffic - 2nd September, 1850 -
Bamber Bridge and Lostock Hall Junction-Preston
for goods traffic - November, 1850 - Bamber Bridge
and Lostock Hall Junction-Preston

Closed :   for passenger traffic - 5th December, 1966 -
Bamber Bridge and Lostock Hall Junction-Preston
for goods traffic - 7th October, 1968 - Bamber Bridge
and Lostock Hall Junction-Preston

O/S   :   Sheet No.102; Series 1:50,000

> *Through the cold morning sped the train,*
> *The nearer fields loomed bleak*
> *Out of the mist; but it was in vain,*
> *Beyond their bounds, to seek*
> *Familiar landmarks.*
>
> Gilbert Thomas

For centuries Preston has commanded the only highway to Scotland
west of the Pennines. Standing at the lowest point on the Ribble to be
crossed by a bridge, it was, in Daniel Defoe's day, the place to which
the local gentry resorted in the winter time. And it was at Preston
during these cold months that prestigious great balls, assemblies,
musical evenings and the like were held.

With the rise of industrialism Preston suffered the disadvantage of
being some distance away from the coal fields. However, with the aid
of spring tides vessels of 150 tons could navigate the Ribble. Further,
John Rennie, the engineer of the Lancaster canal from Wigan to
Walton, set about building a large aqueduct to carry the canal across
the Ribble Valley. Shortage of money prevented this and a tramway,
or plateway connection was built instead. Its opening on 1st June
1803, improved the town's industrial prospects.

The plateway was double track with a gauge of 5ft.0ins. over the
outsides of the plates. It ran from the canal basin in Preston under
Fishergate in a tunnel, then descended a 1 in 6 incline which was
worked by a Boulton and Watt engine and an endless chain to the
Ribble which it crossed on a wooden bridge. Once across the bridge a
long embankment led to the foot of another incline from which the
plateway crossed fields to reach the canal's southern section at Walton
Summit.

The cost of hauling coal along the plateway was one shilling per ton
plus four pence per ton for the use of the Company's wagons.

The plateway remained in use until 1859.

Where the Ribble bends around the foot of Avenham Park three

Avenham Park, Preston

bridges cross it, the one furthest upstream being a footbridge built in reinforced concrete to the same design as its wooden forerunner, the one that carried the plateway. It is from this bridge, known today as the Tram Bridge, that this interesting walk begins.

Cross it to the southern bank, which is a vast grassy area and continue along a heavily wooded embankment which has three arches next to the river through which excess water flows when the Ribble in spate bursts its banks. As you continue along this arboreal way you will see another embankment closing in on you over to your right. This is the trackbed of the line which used to link Preston North Union station with the Ormskirk to Blackburn line at Bamber Bridge and Lostock Hall junctions.

At the appropriate place, join it and continue along it, back to where the line used to cross the Ribble. The embankment along which you are walking was originally a viaduct but all the arches except the three closest to the Ribble were filled in when it was converted into an embankment in 1884-6. Parts of the viaduct can still be seen between the Ribble and the site of Whitehouse North Junction.

The bridge crossing the Ribble to your left carries the electrified line from Preston to Wigan.

Until recently it was possible to return to Avenham Park by crossing the central bridge on a footpath. Originally it was a cast iron structure but in 1930 it was replaced by steel spans. The footpath across it remains to this day. But although access to this footpath is straight-forward from Avenham Park, this is not possible from the southern bank of the river. Nor is the prospect inviting. The whole structure of the bridge, in my opinion, is unsafe and I would discourage anyone from making use of it, as a means of crossing the river.

As the bank is approached, descend the embankment on your right and walk along the riverbank, upstream, to Tram Bridge, seen clearly ahead. Climb up the embankment onto the plateway, turn left along it, recross the river and prepare to celebrate the completion of a neat little triangular walk which has more than its fair share of interest.

18.   LANCASTER TO GLASSON DOCK

Length :   6 miles
Opened :   for goods traffic - 2nd July, 1883
            for passenger traffic - 9th July, 1883
Closed :   for passenger traffic - 7th July, 1930
            for goods traffic - 7th September, 1964
O/S   :   Sheet Nos.97 and 102; Series 1:50,000

> *The sun shines,*
> *The coltsfoot flowers along the railway's banks*
> *Shine like flat coins which Jove in thanks*
> *Strews each side the lines.*
> *D.H.Lawrence.*

The development of the Lune Estuary probably began when the Romans chose to build a settlement at Lancaster. The hilly site suited them well because it offered a commanding position overlooking the Lune which at that point was fordable at low water and navigable by ships at high water.

Slowly at first, then increasing in volume down the centuries, trade developed to such an extent that by the late 17th century Lancaster was handling cargoes from places as diverse as the West Indies, the Americas and the Baltic.

In 1680, during the most rapid increase in the port's trade, a local merchant, John Hodgson, built a sugar refinery in Lancaster. This refinery was almost certainly the very first factory, as opposed to a cottage industry, to be built in England.

During the 18th century, because of silting in the Lune which made navigation upstream to Lancaster increasingly difficult, especially for the larger vessels which were now being used in preference to smaller ones, trade began to decline. In 1740 moorings were constructed off Fishnet Point, Glasson, for the unloading of the large vessels which could no longer be accommodated at Lancaster.

In 1749, following pressure from the merchants and ship owners of Lancaster, an Act of Parliament was passed authorising the setting up of a Port Commission to improve the channel up to Lancaster and the building there of a stone quay complete with warehouses. A charge toll on ships and cargoes would be charged to pay for this work. The quay, named St. George's Quay, together with its associated buildings, was constructed soon after the Act was passed.

In 1767 New Quay was built downstream of St. George's Quay to accommodate larger ships.

In 1789 a wet dock large enough to hold 25 ships was built at Glasson to enable larger vessels to serve Lancaster without the necessity of sailing up the silting Lune Estuary. Communications between the two places were either by small boats or by road, but because of the distance, Glasson's rapid initial growth did not continue.

Lancaster merchants involved with the slave trade petitioned Parliament in 1789 to oppose its abolition; but to no avail. In 1792 slaves were freed in the West Indies and in 1807 Britain abolished the slave trade throughout the Empire. Following the defeat of Napoleon at Waterloo in 1815 Britain was hit by inflation and a trade depression. That year also saw Lancaster's prosperous association with the West Indies collapse. As a result, Glasson's deep sea trading came to an end. Coastal trade, however, continued, allowing both Glasson and Lancaster to maintain viable ports.

Meanwhile in 1797 the first part of the Lancaster Canal, which would link it with Preston, was opened. In 1826, the year following the opening of the first public railway in Britain, the extension of the Lancaster Canal to Glasson Dock was opened and between then and 1830 a large canal basin with direct access to the main dock had been opened. This allowed small vessels to reach Lancaster, Kendal and Preston. Although this branch of the Lancaster Canal had been planned to revive the trade of the Lune it had the effect of diverting shipping from Lancaster.

Carlisle Bridge, built in 1845 to carry the Lancaster to Carlisle railway over the Lune downstream to St. George's Quay, had so low a clearance under it that it effectively made the quay useless. Consequently the Lancaster and Carlisle Railway Company agreed with the Port Commissioners to pay for a new jetty below the Carlisle Bridge and to contribute £10,000 towards improving navigation in the Lune.

In 1883 in an attempt to give speedier access to Glasson Dock, the L.N.W.R., which had leased the canal since 1864, opened a five miles long branch line from the north end of Lancaster station. The line had one intermediate station, Conder Green, a mile away from Glasson Dock. Passenger traffic was never heavy and, following the opening of Preston Dock in 1892, freight traffic declined. But the line remained open for passenger traffic until the depression of 1930. Freight trains ceased in 1964.

A small, commercial port still functions at Glasson Dock. It is used mainly by pleasure craft passing through it between the estuary and the extensive moorings in the canal basin.

Glasson Dock makes a fascinating start to the walk because it is a busy marina with plenty going on: ships loading and unloading; tourists wandering up and down inspecting the moored craft; owners working on them; seabirds squabbling over discarded scraps and gulls screaming.

Follow the old track eastwards from the station master's house, all that remains of Glasson station, cross the River Conder, then continue northwards to the picnic area at the site of Conder Green station a mile from the start. There old level crossing posts at the car park entrance explain why Conder Green came into being. The crossing keeper's cottage at Conder Green and the station master's house at Glasson are the only remaining buildings along the line.

A good half mile further on are the rotting and overgrown remains of a wooden platform. It was built close to Ashton Hall for the exclusive use of the Hall's then owner, a Mr. John Starkie.

Two miles further on, at Old Cliffe, that part of the walk which is actually along the old railway ends and we say goodbye to the trackbed. Because the line cuts through salt marshes it would be reasonable to expect the vegetation growing on it to be the same as the surrounding countryside. But because the trackbed ballast is limestone it supports a rich variety of lime loving plants.

For many years sheep have grazed on the salt marshes and as a result much of the vegetation is grass, mostly red fescue, thrift and English scurvey grass.

The contrast between the limestone loving plants of the trackbed and the surrounding salt marshes is so marked that, with a little imagination you could be walking along a toned-down version of Dorothy's yellow brick road in Oz.

Do the walk late in late September when the musty autumnal smell is strong and every gust of wind brings a shower of leaves out of the trees, as I did, and great will be your reward. For, in addition to the usual flocks of waders, wildfowl - mallard, shelduck and wigeon - are to be seen there. All these birds are attracted to the Lune Estuary because the mud flats are rich in worms, shellfish and shrimps on which they feed. Nowhere else in Britain supports as large a number of wintering and passage birds as the Lune Estuary; and for this reason it has been designated an area of special scientific interest.

The old line makes an excellent viewing point and from it you will be able to see how the graceful movements of all these beautiful birds etch the day with loveliness. They are a constant joy, these glorious creatures and a never ending source of wonder.

Somewhere among the redshanks and the oystercatchers you are likely to come across a thingumajig or two. Should this happen, and I do hope it does, make a note of the bird's markings and any other characteristics. Follow this up with some research at your local library and before you know it you will be hooked on ornithology; and all because you had decided to spend some time walking along an old railway line.

Between Aldcliffe and Marsh Point the route follows the bridleway and horse riders as well as walkers and cyclists are able to use it. From Marsh Point the way is along roads by Lancaster's riverside to Green Ayre station, which is now a small riverside park.

19. LANCASTER - WENNINGTON: TO BULL BECK

Length :	6 miles
Opened :	17th November, 1849
Closed :	for passenger traffic - 3rd January, 1966
	for goods traffic - 5th June, 1967, except the section from Lancaster Castle to Green Ayre which was closed to goods traffic on 8th January, 1968, but retained as a link to Lancaster power-station until this closed on 1st October, 1976.
O/S :	Sheet No.97; Series 1:50,000

A little child at morning tide
Was journeying by train;
She saw the shining landscape glide

By the clear window pane.
Roden Noel.

Green Ayre has come full circle: grass to grass in four generations: green area to railway station to small riverside park in 130 years. And as a reminder of the 'little' North Western's Railway, of which it was an important part, a crane from the disused warehouse at Hornby has been erected on the station site. It's a nice gesture, a fond remembrance of an interesting branch.

Work began in 1846 on the building of a branch line from Clapham to Lancaster to link West Yorkshire towns with a western port for the supply of raw materials and to serve as an outlet for manufactured goods. As part of this development work began that same year on the building of a station at Lancaster on the site of a former shipyard. It was named Green Area, a name it kept until the end of 1870 when it became Green Ayre.

The newly formed North Western Railway Company was authorised to do this work by an Act of Parliament which received royal assent on 26th June 1846. On 16th July of that year the N.W.R. became part of the London and North Western and from then on people referred to the N.W.R. as 'little' to avoid confusion with the L. and N.W.

A further Act authorised a harbour to be built at Poulton -le-Sands together with a 3½ miles long line, the Morecambe Bay Railway, to meet the N.W.R. at Lancaster. At the beginning of the 19th century Poulton-le-Sands had a population of some 500 people and was gaining a reputation as a small resort. When the railway opened on 12th June 1848, there were 1,300 people living in this fishing village and 50 years later it had become a fashionable sea bathing resort with a population of almost 12,000 and a new name, Morecambe.

Because of its situation on Morecambe Bay, the harbour was known as Morecambe Bay Harbour. When the line to Lancaster was opened work had only just begun on the harbour which never did get finished in the form originally envisaged.

In 1906 the Midland Board decided to electrify the line, Castle station through Green Ayre to Morecambe Promenade. On 1st July the electric service was inaugurated between Green Ayre and Morecambe and, on 14th September of that year, between Green Ayre and Castle station. It was one of the first electric train services in the country. Alternating currents at 25 cycles, 6,600 volts, was used; and because the line was short and the voltage was high there were no sub-stations.

The installation caused a lot of interest because instead of a third rail overhead equipment was used. The trains built for this service remained in use for more than forty years, by which time they were more or less clapped out.

Steam hauled trains replaced the electrified system on 12th February 1951, and while they were in use work began on converting the original Midland installation to a 50 cycle system at 6,600 volts A.C. Experimental runs of the converted electric stock began towards the end of 1952 and the line was re-opened as an electric system on 17th August 1953. Between October 1955 and March 1956, electric services were again suspended for modification of the overhead equipment. So this small experimental system became a laboratory for B.R.'s high voltage electrification on which work would shortly begin.

On 17th November 1849 the line from Green Area to Wennington was opened. It was a very pleasant, 10½ miles long run along the broad Lune Valley through an agricultural landscape patched with woods. Between Caton and Halton the Lune made a severe loop which the line crossed on two girder bridges. About a mile west of this loop, on the south bank of the river, stood Halton station, which served Halton village on the north bank. A wooden bridge across the Lune linked village and station until 8th February 1869, when it was washed away in a flood. In September of that year the present iron bridge replaced it.

Lancaster is rich in historic and architectural treasures, two of which are its castle and the Ashton Memorial. In the second half of the 11th century William the Conqueror offered a gift of some land at Lancaster to one of his supporters for the purpose of building a fortress on it to defend one of the principal routes to Scotland. Work began on the keep right away and additions were made to the castle from time to time. Eventually its military importance declined, so weakening Lancaster's position in the county. In 1798 Lancaster relinquished to Preston its position as head of county government and in 1835 additional assize courts were set up at Liverpool and later, at Manchester.

For 700 years Lancaster Castle dominated the skyline. Then Lord Ashton decided to build a hilltop memorial in Williamson Park to the memory of his wife. Taking three years to build (1906-9) it stood 150 feet high. When it was finished some called it the grandest monument in all England. Others saw it as a useless thing, an extravagant folly to end all follies. These views were opinion. What is fact is that it has usurped the castle as Lancaster's dominant skyline feature. Both buildings are open to visitors and both are well worth a visit.

Half a mile after leaving Green Ayre, the start of the walk, the river flows over Skerton Weir. Built over 300 years ago, it was completely reconstructed in 1976-77 as part of a scheme to minimise the risk of tidal salt water flowing further upstream. A large fish pass with an electronic fish counter has been incorporated into the centre of the weir and this is an important help for salmon and sea trout.

A further half mile upstream the old line passes through one of the arches of the aqueduct carrying the Lancaster-Kendal canal over the Lune. This remarkable structure merits more attention from visitors than it gets for it really is a masterpiece of civil engineering. It stands 60 feet high and is 600 feet long. Its arches are supported by four piers, three of which are in the river. The fourth is on the southern bank. Built by John Rennie, the aqueduct was opened in 1797. During its construction Rennie had a lot of problems to face: sudden rises in the river level, flooding of the coffer dams, bad weather and lazy, drunken workmen.

The canal carried by the aqueduct is no longer a trade route. These days small pleasure craft and anglers have taken over.

That part of the Lune as far upstream as Skerton Weir, being tidal, attracts an infinite variety of bird life. Both migrators and residents feed on the featureless mud in their hundreds, particularly in winter; and because their feeding habits differ, the various species are all able to share the same stretch of mud. Oystercatchers, with their strong bills, are ideally adapted to opening the hard shells of cockles and mussels, ringed plovers and redshanks pick up surface dwelling worms and shellfish and dunlins, dashing hither and thither, probe for small snails and worms and other choice creatures that lie in the mud's surface layers. During the summer months the swans which glide so gracefully along the river's channels wear tiny cygnet tails.

Natural shrub has been augmented with willows and alders planted by men and women who, as Cicero said to his friend Atticus, are prepared to say 'I care more for that long age which I shall not see than for my own small share of time'. This is a favourite habitat of long tailed tits, linnets, reed bunting and bird book toting ornithologists.

On the higher, better drained ground close to the trackbed the profusion of wild flowers encourages butterflies and bees. In this way nature's peace flows into you as sunlight flows into trees. The wind blows its freshness into you and the storms their energy while cares drop off like autumn leaves.

Half a mile west of Denny Beck car park, on the south bank of the Lune from Halton, the award winning modern bridge carrying the M6 over the river, arches cleanly across the placid water from one fringe of trees to another.

A toll-bridge built by the railway company to give access to the former station on the Lune's southern bank is well worth crossing for the village on the north bank has a lot of character. Mainly residential, but with some industries sited there, Halton has been around for a very long time. There are records of a Saxon castle once standing on the hill above St. Wilfrid's church, still known as Castle Hill. The shaft of an 11th century cross in the churchyard shows both the Crucifixion and the Sigurd Saga.

Trackbed and river continue to hug each other for a further half a mile upstream of Denny Beck. Then at a gentle bend the Lune begins a broad loop while the disused line goes straight ahead, like the string to a bow, to rejoin and cross the river close to Crook o' Lune. Between Forge Bank Weir and Crook o' Lune on the river's southern bank the intake for the North West Authority's Lancashire Conjunctive Use Scheme is to be found. Reasonably well camouflaged, this pipe enables 82 million gallons of water a day to be pumped from the river to pass through a massive underground pumping station in nearby Quernmore Park.

Half a mile west of Caton, slightly north of where the river takes a sharp bend at Crook o' Lune, the trackbed crosses it twice, the second time - if you are walking or cycling from the Lancaster direction - in the company of another bridge which carries a by-road from Caton to Halton. The riverside hereabouts is particularly lovely with smooth waters gliding between pebbly beaches and grassy banks. Here, too, the scenery is enriched with tall trees that, in autumn, add new life to the countryside, changing its personality in a most beautiful way as the deep greens of the summer leaves slowly change to yellow and reddish-brown as they die. The fallen leaves replenish the earth, injecting the soil with fresh vitality which the winter months will slowly process ready for a resurgence of life in the spring.

East of the by-road from Caton to Halton the trackbed ceases to be a cycle cum footpath and continues to Caton Green as a footpath only. And what a pleasant footpath it is! Many flowers are becoming established on its newly landscaped banks and in the grassy margins they co-exist with established grasses. Many, like the knapweed, are very attractive to bees and butterflies which delight the eye and add charm to this pleasant walk.

But all is not newly established. Close to Caton two examples of more mature vegetation are a fern-clad bank and the marshy pockets at the bottom of the cutting sides where the great willow herb and the sweet scented meadow sweet thrive. Medicinally, meadow sweet has

138

the same properties as aspirin.

Near Thurtell Cottages both the maiden hair spleenwort, a tiny fern, and feverfew with its pungent, yellowish leaves find root in old mortar. Feverfew used to be a popular herb of the physic garden and has been used against fever. Infusions were taken to ease colic, aid digestion and as a tonic.

Caton dates from the days of the Norse settlers and the records of its parish church, St. Paul's, date from the times of Henry III. At the end of the 18th century Caton had a mixed economy with families making their livelihood from both agriculture and industry. Hand-loom weaving dominated many villages, especially south of the Ribble. But in Caton, as elsewhere in Lancashire at that time, many families relied entirely on agriculture for a living.

In 1774 Parliament repealed the ban on English printed calicoes, although they were still subject to a heavy excise, and this became the signal for the great expansion of English cotton cloth production. Cotton quickly became very popular indeed.

Thomas Hodgson built his cotton mill on the site of a corn mill where Artle Beck tumbled to the water meadows flanking the Lune. There he was assured of a constant supply of fast flowing, soft water and plentiful woodland provided the raw material for bobbins and machine making.

Thomas Hodgson was not the only entrepreneur to harness Artle Beck, which by 1800 was providing a reliable source of power for three other mills. With several mill owners depending on Artle Beck for power water, rights were carefully defined in the leases and these frequently became the cause of heated arguments among the mill owners involved. In all Thomas Hodgson built three cotton mills on Artle Beck and converted a former forge into another. The first one, Low Mill, remained the largest.

Low Mill continued to produce cotton warp until the 1970s, thus becoming one of the longest surviving of Lancashire's late 18th century cotton mills.

These days Caton is a modern residential development with much of its architectural interest centred in Brookhouse, its picturesque suburb, where old cottages group around St. Paul's, Caton's parish church.

East of Caton, trackbed and river come together like reunited lovers to bring this delightful walk to an end among the sand and shingle banks of the Lune.

20. CLAPHAM JUNCTION - SEDBERGH

Length :	including detour at Sedbergh end - 21 miles
Opened :	Skipton, through Clapham to Ingleton - 30th July, 1849: single line
	Ingleton-Low Gill for goods traffic - 24th August, 1861
	for passenger traffic - 16th September, 1861
Closed :	Clapham-Ingleton - 1st June, 1850
	Re-opened as double track - 1st October, 1861
	Clapham-Low Gill for passenger traffic - 1st February, 1954
	for goods traffic - 19th June, 1966
O/S :	Sheet Nos.97 and 98; Series 1:50,000

> *So still, so still; a faint scream in the distance,*
> *Then silence and the train*
> *Crashes in, a golden horse, fiercely triumphant,*
> *Tossing his fiery mane.*
> *Vivian de Sola Pinto.*

The name Clapham Junction almost invariably brings to mind that huge metropolitan conglomerate of points which not so long ago became associated, in the title of a novel, with a rude gesture. But the Clapham Junction which marks the soutern end of the Clapham to Low Gill line can knock its London namesake into a cocked hat in every respect except size. For a start the delightful village it serves sits prettily in the middle of a limestone area famed for its underground passsages and pot-holes of which perhaps Gaping Gill is the best known.

Clapham Junction lies about a mile away from the bottom end of the village it serves and to the south-west of it, sharing its isolation with a pub.

From the station the gleaming line to Bentham curves away to west-wards; but our way is in a more north-westerly direction and, for a little bit, on British Rail property. After the first bridge Ingleborough dominates the view to the right magnificently. The air was sharp that mid-winter morning Ron and I walked the trackbed and Ingleborough was capped with snow. It was a grand sight.

Beyond the bridge the trackbed was rather wet, which was no problem. However, just ahead and spread across our path four frisky, red stirks eyed us with rather more interest than we thought healthy. They moved towards us and their advance seemed to me to hold

Clapham Junction - the northern version. Our route goes straight ahead to Ingleton and beyond

menace. Fortunately there was an embankment handy which we climbed with alacrity and had passed the critters before they realised what had happened.

At the far end of the embankment a wire fence marks the end of the B.R. part of the track. The next section belongs to Mr. E.Townley of Nutta Farm who, like so many farmers who own stretches of disused

141

line, is quite agreeable to allow walkers to use it provided they abide by the country code and do no damage.

The next fence, a wooden one with a metal gate at one end of it, marks the end of Mr. Townley's land. From that point on, to where the B6480 crosses the trackbed on an embankment, you are walking on land owned by Mr. D.Robinson of Low Birks. Mr. Robinson shares Mr. Townley's views on people wishing to walk the old line.

Where the B6480 crosses the track go left along it, away from the trackbed to avoid Green Close Farm land which begins on the far side of the road. After about a third of a mile the road bends to the right and continues in this direction for a further half mile, keeping parallel to the trackbed, before curving to the left. At this point leave the road and cross the field on your right to regain the old line where a bridge crosses it, a third of a mile away.

Thin lids of ice were riveted to all the large puddles lying in profusion along this part of the trackbed. Ron and I avoided them by keeping to the top of a cutting, returning to the trackbed where a bridge crossed it. Just beyond the bridge an awkward wire fence, separating Mr. Smith's piece of track from that of Mr. Hodgson, faced us. But it looked far more formidable than, in fact, it was, and soon we had it to our backs.

Now the old line made a pronounced curve to the right as it approached the point where the A65 swept across it. Over to our right as we closed on the A65 along an embankment, snow capped Ingleborough towered, end on, in haughty splendour. It was a beautiful site.

Once across the road, woods close in on the line and soon a wire fence spreads across it, beyond which the way is through the middle of a spread of pine chalets, Pine Croft.

A council depot built on the trackbed on the outskirts of Ingleton makes further progress along the trackbed impossible. But by continuing along the field to the left of it where a road set at right angles to the line of approach is reached through a stile, the site of the old Midland Railway station, now a community centre, is reached. The way ahead is past the community centre car park to where the River Greta is spanned by a viaduct and down the steps on the right-hand side of the trackbed.

We descended to the valley bottom along a steep, winding street, crossed the Greta and followed the road uphill with the viaduct on our left and continued along the road to the site of Thornton-in-Lonsdale on the outskirts of town. In so doing we were following in the footsteps of the railway passengers of old who, before the M.R. and the L.N.W.R. kissed and made-up, were obliged to cover this part of their journey on foot from one company's station to another. However, whereas those early travellers would probably have been unaware of what lay beyond the embankment on their right - the one that used to carry a mineral railway from Meal Bank Quarry to the main line - Ron and I, having explored the area many times, knew that Ingleton's pride and joy was hiding there.

For four and a half beautiful miles the 'Falls Walk', as this jewel is known, leads up the charming valley of the River Doe, through Swilla Glen to Pecca Falls; and a little further on, the dramatic Thornton Force. Here, in a natural amphitheatre, the Doe slides over a limestone crag to drop sheer for forty six feet into a pool. Above Thornton Force the walk swings right along Twistleton Lane below Twistleton Scar End past Twistleton Hall and Beezley Farm where at Beezley Falls, it joins the River Greta for a very spectacular return to Ingleton.

If ever there was a walk not to be missed this is it. For here nature has excelled, mixing light and shade, high drama and serenity in full measure. Now fearsome milk churns, the two rivers spume into deep, dark dubs; now they splash gently into airy, sun-dappled pools. There are limestone bastions thrusting magnificently from bewitching woodland glades; open moorland offers extensive views and Beezley Farm offers pints of milk. It is almost too much!

Thornton-in-Lonsdale has a church, a 17th century inn and little else. The church tower is Perpendicular but the rest of it is much more modern having been largely rebuilt by the Victorians and again in the 1930s following a fire. From the interior its good, solid construction in various shades of sandstone is seen to advantage. The church clock chimes pleasantly on the hour while from the far end of the churchyard there are some distant views of Ingleborough.

The inn's little porch carries the date 1679 and there is a beautiful coat-of-arms above its black and white door. Called the Marton Arms, it is a very pleasant hostelry. We couldn't resist sampling its falling down water and discovered that, in keeping with such an inn, it was both old and peculiar.

Across the railway from the inn a narrow lane leads to a large house set in its own grounds which, some 200 years ago, was the scene of a dastardly murder. It was the home of Lady Barbara Redmayne, a comely lady who was made pregnant by someone of a lower station than herself. When her father became aware of his daughter's condition an almighty row ensued. This ended with Lady Barbara killing him. She fled to a nearby nunnery where, in the fullness of time her baby was born. Whether or not she was brought to justice is not clear;

143

but on many a moonlit night her shade has been seen crossing the next railway bridge up the line from the one near the Marton Arms, reflecting, no doubt on her crime as she returns to haunt her old home.

About a mile on from Thornton-in-Lonsdale we came across some buildings which turned out to be kennels; and a little further on where, for a short distant the A65(T) has been built over the old line, we made a slight detour to avoid a short section of trackbed signposted 'private'. Where the road makes a smart left turn and the trackbed reappears, we stayed on it for it quickly makes an equally smart right turn and runs parallel to the old line. After a mile of road walking, soon after passing a road entrance on our right, we reached what had been a wayside station. It was easily identified and had a weighbridge at its entrance. Here we rejoined the line and continued along it to Barbon. At one point we entered a field to skirt a short section of the trackbed which had become a garden attached to a wayside cottage. Otherwise there were no snags.

Anyone wishing to explore nearby Kirkby Lonsdale should continue along the A65(T) for about a mile instead of rejoining the trackbed at the wayside station. I thoroughly recommend a visit to this delightful place for so much about it pleases. Built of limestone it shows a comfortable face. Possibly the only ugly thing about it is its market cross: almost everything else looks good; and there is a view of the broad Lune Valley from near its parish church, St. Mary the Virgin which Ruskin called 'one of the loveliest in England - therefore the world'. The parish church has a Saxon foundation but most of the building is 12th century. Although it commands an elevated position above the Lune, buildings hide the church from the town.

Perhaps Kirkby Lonsdale's greatest attraction is the Devil's Bridge, a medieval, graceful structure with three ribbed arches. The bridge was built in the 15th century to replace one reputed to have been built by the Devil. Many regard it as the finest old bridge in England and it is listed an an ancient monument.

We arrived at Barbon under a bridge beyond which the trackbed became a tarmac road which we followed to a T junction. There we turned left and close to the church which was immediately to our front, entered a field through a five-barred gate and regained the track at the far end of some land on which a bungalow had been built.

Barbon's parish church of St. Bartholomew is not all that old. It was built in 1893 to replace a chapel. But when seen against a background of trees and fells it looks superb.

From Barbon northwards to where it crosses the River Rawthey near Brigflatts, the track continues up that part of the lovely Lune

Not Colditz! - but the ridiculous lengths some people go to, to prevent access to walkers. This is a bridge over the River Rawthey just south of Sedbergh.

Valley bounded on the west by undulating uplands and on the east by the high unbroken barrier of Middleton Fell.

I like Middleton Fell and find its solitude compelling. Its pathless heights attract even fewer people than do the Howgills. For anyone with a hint of Garbo in his or her make up, a visit to Middleton Fell is a must. But take care for should you meet with a mishap while on that lonely upland help may be a long time in coming. Because of its remoteness Middleton Fell is definitely not the place for any but the experienced fell walker. The valley bottom, on the other hand is; and to follow the route of the defunct line that zips up it is great fun.

About three miles north of Barbon we came across a medieval manor house, Middleton Hall, which looked in pretty good shape despite its age. Tucked away behind its massive curtain wall and sitting in an enclosed courtyard, the hall itself, a fine 15th century structure, looked little changed since the first of the Middletons occupied it ten generations ago.

A little to the north of Middleton Hall the trackbed and the A683 lie side by side for almost a mile. Then the trackbed begins a gentle curve eastwards which brings it to the River Rawthey close to Sedbergh and the end of the walk.

A fine bridge spans the river at this point but we cannot use it. A stout walkway crosses the bridge but it is out of bounds. For at each end of the structure, a very strong tall wire fence has been erected and the doors built into it to give access to the walkway are locked. British Gas, we later discovered, has erected these barriers because the bridge carries a gas pipe which, once on our side of it follows the route of the trackbed we have just come along, southwards for some seven miles or so. The gas pipe is buried under it.

In order to reach Sedbergh a detour is necessary; and in such congenial surroundings this is a joy. The way is upstream with the Rawthey on your left to where, all too soon, the River Dee pours into it. Then it is up the Dee, briefly, to Abbot Holme Farm from where a road will take you over the river to nearby Catholes. Then the way is left and left again and along another delightful road which has come down Dentdale to reach Sedbergh most pleasantly across the Rawthey.

21. LOW GILL - SEDBERGH

Length : 6 miles
Opened : for goods traffic - 24th August, 1861
           for passenger traffic - 16th September, 1861
Closed : for passenger traffic - 1st February, 1954
           for goods traffic - 19th June, 1966
O/S   : Sheet No.97; Series 1:50,000

I stare into the night
While others take their rest,
Bridges of iron lace,

146

A suddenness of trees,
A lap of mountain mist
All cross my line of sight
            Theodore Roethka.

The year was 1846 and England was in the grip of railway mania. London was already linked by rail to most of the country's principal towns and now the eyes of the railway promotors were on Scotland. In Lancashire, the Lancaster and Carlisle was under construction and in Yorkshire the Leeds and Bradford was extending to Skipton and Colne. If a line from Skipton could be extended to the Lancaster and Carlisle, a route would be established from the manufacturing towns of Yorkshire to Scotland. To achieve this end the North Western Railway Company was empowered to build a line from the Leeds and Bradford north-west of Skipton to join the Lancaster and Carlisle at Low Gill, south of Tebay, with a branch from Clapham to Lancaster. It was all part of a larger scheme that included the building of docks and a harbour at Morecambe and a line from there to Lancaster.

Construction work began but by then, because of rapidly rising costs, it was decided not to proceed with the Low Gill line beyond Ingleton. Instead emphasis was concentrated on the development of the Lancaster and Morecambe branch. It was not until 1857, when the Lancaster and Carlisle obtained an Act to built a line between Low Gill and 18½ miles distant Ingleton to provide a connection with the Midland Railway via the North West Railway, that any more progress was made in that direction.

There had never been any love lost between the L.N.W.R. and the M.R. In 1859 the North Western Railway Company was leased to the M.R. and the Lancaster and Carlisle to the L.N.W.R. When the double track from Low Gill to Ingleton was completed in 1861 the L.N.W.R. and the M.R. found themselves end on to each other at Ingleton, their termini separated by the deep gorge of the Greta, spanned by a connecting viaduct. The M.R. doubled the 4½ miles of track between Clapham and Ingleton, re-opened the line and restored the passenger service on 1st October 1861. A new station at the southern end of Ingleton viaduct came into use a few weeks later and passengers were at first compelled to walk between the two Ingleton stations, which were half a mile apart and separated by the deep-sided Greta Valley. The L.N.W.R. station was built in the village of Thornton and not in Ingleton itself. Moreover, the timetable from Ingleton to Low Gill was prepared so that connections were missed. So instead of becoming a meeting place of two important companies, Ingleton

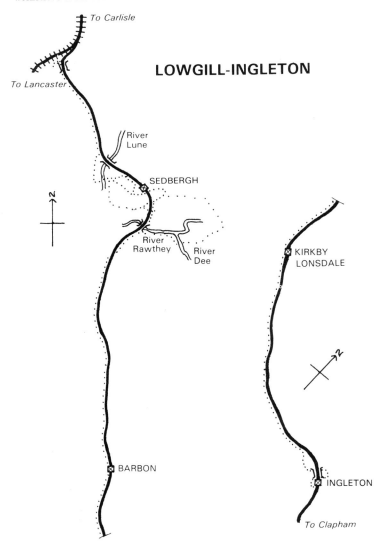

LOWGILL-INGLETON

had become a point of confrontation between two of the country's railways whose friendship had ended.

Later, when through trains between the Midland line and Tebay were introduced, the M.R. complained of intolerable obstructions by the L.N.W.R. Yet by the summer of 1862 a reasonable service was in operation between Kings Cross and Carlisle using the Clapham to Low Gill line. Passengers leaving Kings Cross at 9.10a.m. and changing at Leeds reached Carlisle by 5.45p.m., only 35 minutes slower than the 10.00a.m. from Euston which anyone continuing to Scotland could catch and be in Glasgow by 9.30p.m. The return journey via Low Gill, Clapham and Leeds took only ten minutes longer to reach Kings Cross than the direct run from Glasgow took to reach Euston. However, despite this reasonable service the M.R. remained aggrieved to such a degree that on 16th July 1866, it obtained an Act for the construction of the Settle-Carlisle line.

This development so alarmed the L.N.W.R. that it offered the M.R. new conditions for through traffic which were so attractive that the latter was delighted to accept them. The M.R. then tried to abandon the Settle-Carlisle project which, on reflection, it now saw as an extremely expensive undertaking. The L.N.W.R. saw this too, and realised that the new line to Scotland would be a mistake. So in November 1868, it reached a settlement with the M.R. which allowed the M.R. to use the line from Ingleton all the way to Carlisle over Shap.

A Bill for the abandonment of the new line was deposited but the North British and the Glasgow and South Western Railways petitioned against the abandonment and the M.R. was forced to go ahead with the construction of the Settle-Carlise line.

With the completion of the Settle-Carlisle line in 1876 the Ingleton route lost its main line status. M.R. and L.N.W.R. trains continued to meet at Ingleton but traffic along the line never developed except when the Settle-Carlisle line was blocked with snow. Between 1910 and 1913 the M.R. routed one express daily along it during the summer months. On 1st January 1917, the L.N.W.R. station at Ingleton was closed to passenger traffic and all its trains then stopped at the M.R. station. Somehow the line's passenger traffic survived two world wars. It was not until 1st February 1954 that it was discontinued. The line remained open as a through freight route until 1966 and was dismantled soon afterwards.

We stood the three of us, overlooking a valley bathed in lovely, glaucous light. From across the Lune Gorge the Howgills towered with Fell Head prominently stretching into the winter sky. This was the site of Low Gill Junction, the northern end of our walk and we had reached it travelling southwards along the B6257 which branches from the A685, the Tebay to Kendal road near the summit of Dillicar Common. Just beyond where, in quick succession, this secondary road passes under the M6 and the main line from Euston to Glasgow, a signposted minor road on our left had brought us to the disused line we were seeking.

Low Gill Junction, which lies close to a row of railway cottages, is the start of the walk. But between the junction and the road bridge we had crossed to get there the trackbed belongs to British Rail and since it is close to the electrified main line anyone caught walking along it could be fined £200. So we retraced our steps to the bridge and only then did we clamber down to the old line. This we did on the bridge's southern side and found ourselves outside B.R.'s domain. A wire fence stretched from one side of the bridge to the other across the trackbed marked the boundary.

Following a gentle downwards gradient, the old track runs along a high embankment describing a graceful curve which continues across a fine sandstone viaduct. This proud structure possesses eleven arches, the tops of which are all made of brick. There it stands, in honourable retirement, a credit to its builders who, goodness knows how, managed to manhandle those huge slabs of stone into place and construct a thing of usefulness and beauty.

Walking towards it I wondered if it had been built on sheep's wool as had several other Westmorland viaducts, especially on the Settle-Carlisle line. Sheep's wool is a very absorbent material and during the construction of the railways through this glorious part of England, because it was so plentiful and so cheap, the railway engineers used it as a foundation for the rubble.

On both sides of the viaduct the trackbed is clear of undergrowth. Yet step onto it and at once you have to wind your way across between an abundance of saplings which, if allowed to grow, will eventually make crossing the viaduct chancy. The alternative will be to leave the trackbed along a track crossing a field on your right to join the B6257 which will take you down to the bottom of the narrow vale, up the other side, there to rejoin the trackbed. It seems such a shame that, through lack of simple, inexpensive, remedial action now, this fine example of railway engineering could become ruinous and too expensive to repair in a few years time.

An inviting track leads under the viaduct to the Lune, passing, while still in the shadow of the tall structure, a grand Westmorland farm, Beck Foot, which looks as though it has been there since the

150

year dot. There is an appealing non-conformity about it, the accumulation of a succession of alterations made to satisfy the fancies and changing requirements of generations of owners.

About a quarter of a mile beyond the farmhouse the track crosses the Lune on a most graceful 17th century bridge, brook of Lune Bridge, not quite wide enough to take a large car. Scratch marks on the parapet walls tell of close encounters with such vehicles, so should you linger a while on this elegant structure, your attention held by the smooth, shallow waters below, the green, well wooded lower slopes of the valley and the dominating Howgill tops, and you hear a car coming, run for it or you could become a road accident statistic.

Southwards from the viaduct, the trackbed runs roughly parallel to the B6257, keeping between it and the river, far below, passing through the small and scattered community of Firbank.

Firbank has strong associations with George Fox, who sowed the seeds of Quakerism there in fertile soil. It was from on or near a rocky outcrop, known today as Fox's Pulpit, that on Sunday 13th June 1652, he preached for three hours to a large gathering on the new Christian sect he had founded. Many people became convinced of the truth of his teaching, that Sunday on Firbank Fell, and the meeting went a long way towards establishing the Society of Friends as a viable group.

From the walker's point of view it is rare good fortune that trackbed and road run side by side immediately before the former swings away to cross Waterside viaduct, the central span of which is a cast iron arch flanked by three stone arches at each end. The viaduct is securely fenced off because the floor of the high central span is very exposed, making a crossing highly dangerous. So forget it; and instead, make further progress along the aforementioned road.

The way ahead is downhill, past the farm that snuggles against the viaduct, and along the valley bottom. Soon the A684 is reached and the way is left along it to where the beautiful, old Lincoln's Inn bridge crosses the Lune.

This mellow, twin-arched, humpbacked structure was built in the 17th century to assist horse-drawn vehicles to cross the Lune. It was wide enough in those days to accommodate all the equipages using it, but it is unsuited to the requirements of modern traffic. Yet such is its charm that to have it replaced with a much wider modern bridge would be unthinkable. Its contribution to the riverside scene is immeasurable and far outweighs any inconvenience to drivers using the A684.

On the eastern side of Lincoln's Inn bridge a choice of paths

A rare sight on a disused railway is iron girders remaining on a major viaduct. This is Waterside Viaduct at Sedbergh on the line north to Low Gill. The walker is strongly advised not to cross this bridge but to follow the detour described in the text.

presents itself: an upstream walk to rejoin the trackbed at Waterside viaduct or a downstream walk along, for me, an old friend, the Dalesway.

Once back on the disused line Sedbergh station, now a private residence on the edge of town, is a pleasant mile away. Beyond it the A684 scythes through the trackbed which curves in a southerly direction to where a bowstring deck-girder bridge spans the Rawthey near Brigflatts. The bridge is padlocked and cannot be crossed. Moreover, near a cutting to the south of the A684 serried conifers bar the way. So it is advisable to take the A684 into Sedbergh.

The trackbed approach to Sedbergh is a very pleasant one; but the southwards alternative along the Dalesway is even better. Leave the Lune going right to a gap in the fence ahead and on to a gate, beyond which turn left. After a short distance turn right to Luneside Farm.

Depart Luneside Farm through a gate and continue southwards alongside a hedge to a green lane where turn left and left again to High Oaks Farm.

From High Oaks Farm turn right at a gate leading to a green lane

152

and continue up a field and over a small hill, where turn sharp left. After a few yards go through a gap in the hedge ahead and cross a beck in the top corner of a field. Now go down the field, parallel to a hedge and through the remains of a stile to the Sedbergh to Kirkby Lonsdale road, where turn left along it.

Go down the green lane soon to be seen on your right, through a gate and then left. Continue through a field to the river from where the way is along a pebbly bank, past a clump of trees. Now turn away from the river and turn sharp right at Grid Reference 637913. At Brigflatts go over a wooden stile between a fence and the river and continue upstream to rejoin the trackbed where it crosses the Rawthey. Turn left along it on an embankment as far as the Sedbergh to Kirkby Lonsdale road and turn right along it into Sedbergh.

It was at Brigflatts that the Society of Friends, inspired by the visit of George Fox, acquired land for a burial ground and a meeting house. They built it themselves in 1675 and it has been in continuous use ever since. The building is plain but pleasant and has become a place of pilgrimage, attracting many visitors.

Until 1974 when the county boundaries were re-drawn, Sedbergh was in Yorkshire. Today it belongs to Cumbria. It is a small, attractive town with a famous public school, well sited at a meeting of valleys at the southern end of the Howgills. How pleasant it is to amble along its narrow main street on a warm, sunny evening! The temptation to linger is strong.

IV   Cumbria

All of Lancashire's proud territorial possessions 'north of the sands', including Coniston Water, Lakeland's third largest lake, Esthwaite Water, the west bank of Windermere and the Old Man of Coniston, were lost to Cumbria in the local government re-organisation of 1974. This did not please Lancastrians; Cumbrians and Westmerians were none too happy about it either, for they saw the merger as a threat to their separate identities. However, it takes more than a piece of bureaucratic bumbledom to do that and visitors to Cumbria will quickly be made aware of the background to the area they are in. The locals will tell them.

They will also be quick to point out that all parts of Lakeland are superior to anywhere else in England. They will impart that people become 'lakers' for all sorts of reasons, walking, climbing, cycling, pony trekking, water-skiing, canoeing, or simply browsing, pottering or studying subjects with a strong local flavour like geology, the Lakeland poets and ornithology. They may mention the scenic appeal of Lakeland but, really, this won't be necessary: Lakeland scenery is quite capable of speaking for itself.

From the south the old market town of Kendal is regarded as the gateway to the Lakes although many people approach Windermere by way of Ulverston and Coniston. From Shap there is a first rate though little used track across the bleak Ralfland Forest into seldom visited Swindale. Also from the east the Eden Valley provides easy access; and Cockermouth near the southern limit of the Cumbrian plain is ideally situated for reaching the Lakes from the north.

The Lake District is shaped like a crude cartwheel with the larger lakes radiating from the hub, Sergeant Man, like spokes. It is these meres and the high ridges and mountains between them that, more than any factor, have attracted visitors in ever increasing numbers to this most lovely place for the past 200 years.

Today these lakes, Bassenthwaite, Coniston, Crummock Water, Derwentwater, Ennerdale, Ullswater, Wastwater and Windermere among them, are household words, as are the defined peaks, the steep sided ridges, the high passes, the arêtes, screes, ghylls, knotts and hollows, the tarns and the becks of the glaciated uplands between and around them. Enchanted places all, with names that stir the blood and make the feet itch: Crinkle Crags and Bowfell, Great Gable, Haystacks, Helvellyn, High Street, Pillar, St. Sunday Crag, Scafell Pikes: like Topsy, the illustrious list just grows and grows.

Sergeant Man may be the hub of the Lake District cartwheel but its heart lies a few miles away to where two small lakes, Grasmere and Rydal Water share an idyllic setting.

Unlike most rural areas in the country, where the social life of the countryside tends to flow to one central town, that of the Lake District valleys does not revolve around the hub of the cartwheel. From the dale heads it flows outwards along each valley, rarely crossing intervening ridges, to where there is a town or village serving that particular valley. Ambleside, Broughton-in-Furness, Cartmell, Coniston and Keswick are good examples of this type of place. Further out, where the Lakeland fells make contact with the surrounding lowlands is to be found a ring of places like Appleby, Cockermouth, Kendal, Penrith, Ulverston and Whitehaven, which are the market towns for the surrounding district. It is in these peripheral towns and villages, both the inner ring serving specific valleys and the outer ring of market towns that much of the social life of the Lake District valleys is to be found.

West Cumbria's coastal plain, slotted between the western fells and the sea, is the county's industrial belt. For many centuries, beginning during the Roman occupation, a saline industry prospered there, as did a fishing fleet. From the 12th century Egremont had an iron industry and coal was being worked in the coalfields around Whitehaven by the 13th century. By the mid-seventeenth century textiles, ropes, sail-cloth, pottery and clay pipes were all manufactured there. For the next 200 years industry expanded steadily and this attracted droves of workers into the area. But by the end of the nineteenth century a steady decline had begun. Now people in ever increasing numbers began to leave the area. Between the two World Wars West Cumberland's unemployment figures were among the highest in the country. The second World War revived the region's industry but this was short-lived. Today the coalfields, foundries and mines are closed and new light industries are being introduced into this depressed corner west of the Lakes.

From Crummock Water the River Cocker flows away from the mountains to join the Derwent by the quiet old town of Cockermouth, Wordsworth's birthplace. Though just outside the girdle of Lakeland, Cockermouth is set in delightful country which spreads northwards to Carlisle in a most pleasing manner, proving that outside Lakeland's cartwheel there is a lot of varied and impressive scenery, much of which is worthy of attention.

'Merrie Carlisle' is the very hub of border history and strife. It came into being when the Romans built a bridge head fort where Carlisle cathedral now stands. William Rufus captured Carlisle in 1092 and fortified it. He also built the city walls which, though heightened, strengthened and rebuilt many times, enclose the city for 700 years. It was not until 1810 that the demolition of the walls began. Part of the west wall remains to this day.

Carlisle has always been in the thick of the border's stirring past. When the Scots held it they strengthened it against the English and when the English held it they strengthened it against the Scots.

The River Irthing brings the Roman wall into Cumbria. It enters the county at Gilsland and continues to Willowford and so down the pleasant Irthing Valley. To the west of Carlisle it turns northwards to the Solway Estuary, beyond where there is nothing of it to be seen.

England's highest market town, windy Alston, perched on a hill above the South Tyne, is part of Cumbria, as is Cross Fell, the highest summit of the Pennines. Some of the most spectacular parts of the Pennines, including High Cup Nick, belong to Cumbria, as does the fertile Vale of Eden, which has so much to offer the discerning visitor.

From its birth on the lonely fells above Hell Gill the lovely River Eden plunges into the narrow defile of Mallerstang and on, through a delightful pastoral landscape and a thousand years of history to empty into the Solway Estuary north of Carlisle.

For company it has Wild Boar Fell, pele towers and castles, bustling market towns and proud villages. For much of its length it has, when it blows, the Helm Wind, the only wind in Britain to have a name. Every year, in June, gypsy horses, grois, are washed in it ready for sale at Appleby Fair, the largest Romany gathering in the country. In season wild flowers grow in profusion along its banks and boundless wildlife seeks sustenance from its clear waters.

Every bend of the river brings fresh delights, every mile of its length is an exciting adventure. So beware: for it is also possessive. In next to no time it will have thrown its spell around you; and when that happens you will be reluctant to leave it. The thing to do, therefore, is to enter Cumbria from the south, explore the county at leisure and leave the Eden Valley until last. The only snag is that, Cumbria being Cumbria and Lakeland being Lakeland, you may never get there.

22. KIRKBY STEPHEN - RAVENSTONEDALE

Length :   5¾ miles

Opened : for goods traffic - 4th July, 1861
for passenger traffic - 8th August, 1861
Closed : for passenger traffic - 1st December, 1952
for goods traffic - 22nd January, 1962
O/S : Sheet No.91; Series 1:50,000

> *... ewes sure-stepping the tarn*
> *in push-and-pilgrim style,*
> *or the blue where the valley turns*
> *down from sight (beneath*
> *that scrag settlement*
> *the Kirkby railway used to reach*
> *its sandstone viaduct) ...*
> *Michael Ffinch.*

For many years during the early development of the railways the Northern Pennines and adjoining moorland held no attraction for the railway promoters. In such wild and thinly populated an area the prospect of worthwhile local traffic was slim. So the early developers looked in other directions and an area of the Pennines covering some 2,800 square miles was, for the most part, ignored. Then in the mid 1840s, this previously uninviting upland began to be seen in a new light, as a suitable course for a through route linking east and west. Six tran-Pennine routes were proposed, four of which would join the Lancaster and Carlisle Railway, two at Clifton near Penrith and two at Tebay.

In order to avoid duplication of routes the Northern Counties Union Railway was formed. One of the branch lines it was authorised to build was from Barnard Castle via Kirkby Stephen to Tebay. But the N.C.U.R. carried a workload that proved impossible to fulfil because of lack of funds and it was this severe financial situation that brought about its downfall.

Its successor was the South Durham and Lancaster Union Railway whose prime interest was catering for the potential mineral traffic between the industrial areas of County Durham and Furness.

On 18th November 1856, at a meeting of interested people, mostly hard headed industrialists, held at Kirkby Stephen, a resolution was passed which stated 'that it was expedient that a railway be formed to connect the extensive Coal and Ironstone fields in the East part of the Island with the important Shipping Ports and Manufactories on the West side of the Island'.

The Lancaster and Carlisle Railway proved obdurate regarding

157

junction facilities at Tebay but otherwise the building of the line from Barnard Castle to Tebay was fast. There were several reasons for this. The line over Stainmore did not compete with any existing or suggested line: the locals wanted it: since its route was over uncultivated moorland no farmer was disturbed to any extent. Moreover the line had the backing of the Stockton and Darlington Railway of which the S.D.L.U.R. was really a part. It was the S. and D.R.'s usual practice to float a separate company for each of its branches and the Barnard Castle to Tebay line came into that category.

The first sod was cut at Kirkby Stephen by the Duke of Cleveland on 25th August 1857, by early 1860 most of the viaducts were nearing completion and the permanent way had been laid along 17 of the 34¾ miles between Barnard Castle and Tebay. By July 1861, the line was complete, had been inspected by the Board of Trade and passed for use by passenger traffic. This caused great rejoicing among all concerned because for the line to pass the Board of Trade inspection first time was a considerable feat considering its length and the engineering works involved. Mineral traffic had been using the line since 4th July: the passenger service was inaugurated on 8th August 1861.

When the service opened two passenger, four mineral and two combined mineral and goods trains travelled from Darlington to Tebay every weekday. Ten years later there were still only two through passenger trains running during the winter months; but they were increased to three during summer months. By the turn of the century there were four through passenger trains from Darlington to Tebay every weekday during the summer months and three during the winter months, along with an average of 21 mineral and goods trains booked to run between Kirkby Stephen and Tebay. A usual weekday's working from Tebay via Kirkby Stephen eastwards over Stainmore was four passenger, ten mineral and three goods trains.

When, in the early 1920's, the L.N.E.R. took control, most of the through trains were diverted from Tebay to Penrith. On 1st December 1952, the Kirkby Stephen to Tebay passenger services were withdrawn, the last train running on the evening of 29th November. The author, who at that time was a booking clerk at Kirkby Stephen, issued the very last ticket from there to Tebay.

The full length of the line from Kirkby Stephen to Tebay was originally built as a single track. But with steadily increasing traffic this proved inadequate and on 24th April 1872, authority was given for the line to be doubled between Gaisgill and Tebay. On 23rd April the following year authority was given to double the section from

Kelleth to Gaisgill and on 24th March 1875 that from Sandy Bank to Kelleth. Yet inexplicably the remaining 4¾ miles or so between Kirkby Stephen's west signal box and Sandy Bank remained single track although Smardale Viaduct, the only major engineering works on that length, had been built to take double track. Many years later, in 1931, for economic reasons, Sandy Bank box was abolished and one of the tracks between there and Ravenstonedale station, as Newbiggin had been renamed, was removed thus increasing the length of single track by a mile. That is how the line remained for the rest of its life.

The walk is administered by the Cumbrian Trust for Nature Conservation, Church Road, Ambleside, from where permission must be obtained before setting out. Guns are not allowed, collecting of plants is forbidden and dogs must be kept on a lead. Several notices along the route echo this message - needlessly, in my view, because walkers are responsible people whose love of things natural is strong.

Aesthetically Kirkby Stephen East station - that is the name it was given towards the end of its day to differentiate between it and Kirkby Stephen West on the Settle-Carlisle line - has gone downhill. There are weeds growing along the platform and on the permanent way. The industrial buildings now built on and alongside what used to be the covered part of the platform look incongruous; but they provide employment and that is all to the good. The engine sheds have gone but memories remain and it is much better to have memories, even sad ones, than none at all.

One far from sad reminiscence concerns a colleague. He was on duty in the booking office and had accepted a lurcher to be despatched on the next passenger train. The station had a regular traffic in lurchers and other breeds. The drill was, once the fare had been paid, for the dog to be tied to one of the platform seats by its chain. There it would remain until the train it was to travel on arrived.

On this occasion, as the train drew into the station, my colleague came out of the booking office to hand over the lurcher to the guard. Perhaps it was the noisy hiss of escaping steam that frightened the animal. At any rate, as my colleague bent to undo the chain, the lurcher broke free and sped up the platform. His face contorted with dismay, my colleague raced after it, shouting to anyone who would listen, 'somebody please stop that dog - it's a parcel'.

For about three quarters of a mile the disused Eden Valley line and the one to Ravenstonedale share the same way out of Kirkby Stephen. Then, at the west end of a cutting there is a parting of the ways, the track to Ravenstonedale station bearing to the left, uphill, through another cutting. It continues under a bridge carrying the road from

159

Kirkby Stephen to Waitby and on, in a great curve, along embankments and through another cutting to the site of Smardale station. It is uphill all the way. In fact the old line climbs for 4¾ miles from Kirkby to Sandy Bank then drops for seven miles to Tebay.

Uphill it may be, but the gradients are not severe and there is plenty to see. Foxgloves, wild pansies, primroses, forget-me-nots, cowslips, milk maids and dog roses all flourish on the green slopes of the cuttings, beyond which the hills of Westmorland spread out, fold upon glorious fold, to delight the eye of the beholder.

In the sky above 'dorps', or carrion crows, black-headed gulls, oystercatchers, herons and peewits are frequently seen.

Within the parishes of Waitby and Smardale and Ravenstonedale, through which the route cuts a fine swath, are to be found some of the most important prehistoric village settlements in what is still in the hearts of the local folk, north Westmorland. Most are on high ground because low lying land at that time would have been covered with forest, scrub and swamp infested with dangerous, wild animals. Also high ground, especially the summits of Knolls, was a favourite site for a settlement because such like places were easily defended.

Squatting on a cone-shaped hill on the right, close to the start of the walk, is an oval-shaped enclosure covering some two and half acres. It is surrounded by a moat with an embankment thrown up on the inside. It may have been a village surrounded by defense works or perhaps only an Ancient Briton's cattle fold where stock could more easily be defended from marauding humans and wild animals. But it has a proud name, Croglin Castle.

To the south of the course of the old railway just before it goes under the Kirkby Stephen to Waitby road-bridge there is a similar castle or fort and this is called Waitby Castle.

At Smardale, a little further along the track and again to the south of it, is an ancient hall built in the Scottish baronial style. It is a square building with a round tower at each corner. This is Smardale Hall, named after the de Smardales, whose residence it once was. The name Smardale is of Old Norse origin and means 'the valley with the clover pasture'. Like Alice's Cheshire cat Smardale hamlet, always somewhat isolated, has all but vanished leaving little more than the Hall itself.

Between the site of Smardale station and the half mile distant viaduct which carries the Settle-Carlisle line over Smardale Gill most of the way is along a narrow path running down the middle of an embankment top. Young trees grow in profusion on the embankments steep slope. They press close to the path, the ones on the right leaning inwards to the left, those on the left leaning to the right so that progress is made through a living arboreal tunnel. The effect, both in summer when lush greenery abounds and in winter when the bows are bare, is rather magical.

To approach Smardale viaduct from the east is not to see it at its magnificent best. You see ahead that part of the huge structure which spans the route you are on, the old line to Tebay. But in order to see it in relation to its setting it is best to pick some rather distant vantage point like the roadside close to the bungalow near the site of Smardale station. From there you can see just how well it fits into the surrounding countryside.

Work began on its construction in 1870 and five years later it was completed. It stands on a bed of red shale which lies beneath 40 feet of clay. The sinking of the foundations to that depth without the availability of the sophisticated machinery we have today was in itself a commendable achievement. The viaduct spans Scandal Beck at a height of 130 feet, it is 700 feet long, has twelve arches, each of 45 feet and contains more than 60,000 tons of stone. It was built to last and I hope it will long continue to do so; for the Settle-Carlisle line, the most scenic in England, could, if properly administered, become a tremendous asset to our tourist industry.

Leaving the viaduct behind, the route continues for one almost level mile along a contour midway up steep sided, heavily wooded Smardale Gill, on top of which are to be found strip lynchets or cultivated terraces, the sites of three settlements, three tumuli and the foundation of a circular hut. In the valley bottom Scandal Beck flows merrily along, half hidden from our route, during the summer months by a profusion of greenery.

Smardale Gill, now a nature reserve, is home to a rich variety of fauna, including the otter and the badger, both of which are nocturnal and therefore rarely seen. You have a far greater chance of seeing foxes, stoats, weasels, rabbits and hares.

The flora is pretty good, too.

One or two paths lead up and down the valley side from the old rail track but otherwise Smardale Gill makes few allowances to man. The Cumbrian Trust for Nature Conservancy appears to take the view, quite correctly in my opinion, that man is the intruder and that in this wild valley the interest of the flora and fauna must take precedence over the demands of *homo sapiens*. When you create a nature reserve you have to known what is there before you can begin to conserve it. The Trust has done its homework well and acted on its findings to the benefit of the wild creatures and plants whose home it is. So, congratulation, Trust, in getting your priorities right.

Quite unexpectedly the route swings to the right and soars diagonally across this unspoiled and beautiful valley on a magnificent stone viaduct. This imposing structure, built to carry a double track which, in fact, it never did, has fourteen spans, each thirty feet wide and the tallest of which is to be found close to the eastern side of the gill. It is 353 feet long, has a maximum height of 90 feet and cost £11,289 to build. Far from symmetrical, it had to be constructed that way because of the lie of the land.

Once across the gill the track continues along the valley side, passing over more buttress walls, before turning away from the confines of Scandal Beck.

Smardale bridge leaps Scandal Beck close to where river and disused railway part company. A slight detour here along an ancient pack-horse road is very rewarding because just beyond where the pack-horse road begins to climb Smardale Fell are some mounds about 15 yards long and 5 yards wide. They are known as 'Giants' Graves'. They look like ancient tumuli and since they are in a locality known to contain about thirty such mounds some archaeologists doubt that they are. They suggest that the 'Giants' Graves' were constructed as platforms for stacking bracken.

Looking back, across the route of the old line to above the limestone scar running parallel to it, a most important ancient settlement with its dykes and tumuli can clearly be seen. But you have to know what to look for; and to do a bit on converting. The sunken ways used to be farm tracks: the small patterned areas are the remains of stone huts: the long banks are the foundations of walls marking boundaries and enclosing fields. They cover one hundred and sixty acres divided into three villages which together become the prehistoric Severals village settlement. The name comes from Severals village, the largest of the three and the one closest to our route. It is bounded on the west by Severals Gill, on the south by the limestone scar so clearly seen from the pack-horse road above those 'Giants' Graves' near our route, on the east by the very steep sided Smardale Gill and on the north by another limestone scar.

Connected to the settlement on its southern side is an irregular shaped area of about one hundred acres enclosed by two miles of dykes. This was probably used mainly as an enclosure for captive wild sheep or cattle. Here they could be kept safely as a food supply. Oats, peas, beans and barley were grown within this huge enclosure in strip lynchets or ranes, to provide frugal fare for the villages. More 'Giants' Graves' can be seen near the enclosure's southern extremity together with some tumuli.

Our route cuts right through the middle of this complex, effectively separating village settlement and cattle and sheep enclosure.

Over to the right as Ravenstonedale station is approached lies a rather splendid dwelling, Brownber, for a great many years the home of the Fothergill family.

During the latter half of the 17th century one Anthony Fothergill was living there. His daughter, Elizabeth Gaunt, a kind-hearted lady, lived at nearby Tower House. She inadvertently made history by coming to the aid of one James Burton, a man implicated in the Rye House Plot. Later this detestable object turned King's evidence for a bribe, denounced Elizabeth and appeared as principal witness against her at her trial before the notorious Judge Jeffreys. The charge was harbouring a rebel. She was sentenced to death and became the last woman to be burned at the stake at Tyburn. There is a lovely stained glass window to her memory in Ravenstonedale church.

Sunbiggin Tarn, a marvellous centre for ornithologists and less than two miles from Ravenstonedale station is home to a very large gullery of black-headed gulls. Also found there are teal, mallard, water hens, snipe, peewits and so many others.

Ravenstonedale station, in Newbiggin village, marks the end of this exciting and most interesting walk, the remaining six miles to Tebay having become part of the A685. But for anyone wishing to continue to Tebay the walk is a very pleasant one, on level ground, through superb country. On the left or south side of it the lonely Howgill Fells rise, smooth and rounded as basking seals and Ravenstonedale Moor, to the north, looks down invitingly. For company the infant Lune, having departed its birthplace on the northern flank of the Howgills close to Newbiggin, is with you all the way.

Should you decide to walk the full twelve miles to Tebay, refreshments are available at the Cross Keys Inn. If you call it a day at Ravenstonedale station, Newbiggin has a pub and there are two more in nearby Ravenstonedale village.

23. KIRKBY STEPHEN - WARCOP

Length :	5 miles 68 chains
Opened :	for goods traffic - 8th April, 1862
	for passenger traffic - 9th June, 1862
Closed :	for goods and passenger traffic - 22nd January, 1962
O/S :	Sheet No.91; Series 1:50,000

> *God gave to men all earth to love,*
> *But since men's hearts are small,*
> *Ordained for each one spot should prove*
> *Beloved over all.*
> *Rudyard Kipling.*

Of all the walks along disused railways none is more evocative to me than this short section of the Eden Valley line: none holds more memories. For I travelled along it daily from Kirkby Stephen to school at Appleby during term time in the salad days of my youth. It was the strangers on these journeys with whom, briefly, I shared a compartment that stirred within me a wonder as to who or what these fellow travellers were and where they might be going. Sometimes, if the traveller was alone, settled in his or her corner, fending off any attempt at conversation, the mystery would deepen. If this happened in wartime or mid-winter, with the compartment lights dimmed to comply with strict blackout regulations, the fellow travellers's dim figure would become, for me, the very essence of intrigue. There I would be hurtling through a darkened rural landscape pulled by an iron monster that belched smoke and sparks as it thundered along, probably sharing a compartment with a German spy! So a stranger on a train could, and frequently did, make the adrenalin flow.

On one occasion, returning home from school, our gang - school boys, where possible, travelled in gangs in the charge of a prefect - shared the compartment with a soldier. He was a wonderful character who, even as the train began to draw out of Appleby station, handed out cigarettes. Soon, with all of our gang puffing away at the forbidden weed, this remarkable man had us roaring with laughter at his outrageous tales, one of which was a fine and very short railway mystery story. It went like this:-

'The compartment I was travelling in was shared with another person who suddenly asked me if I believed in ghosts.

'Well-er-no', I replied.

'Neither do I', he chuckled - and vanished'.

Well now the line has vanished, at least as far as Warcop and from west of Appleby to Clifton Moor Junction, but the ghosts remain. In just one century of operating the Eden Valley line has produced plenty of those.

The first sod was cut at Appleby by Lord Brougham and Vaux on 4th August 1858, the Eden Valley Railway Act having received Royal Assent on 21st May of that year. There had always been some opposition to Tebay being the point of contact between the S.D.L.U.R. and the Lancaster and Carlisle Railway. So almost as soon as it was chosen, steps were taken to form another company to build a connecting line from Kirkby Stephen to Clifton - renamed Clifton Moor in 1927 - some 4½ miles south of Penrith.

The 22 miles long line was much easier to construct than the S.D.L.U.R. had been because throughout its length there were no major engineering works. Three viaducts had to be built but they were not very tall, the highest, at Skygarth, half a mile west of Temple Sowerby, being only 35 feet high. Two, at Musgrave and Skygarth, crossed the Eden, were of stone and iron and looked more like bridges than viaducts. The third was built completely of stone and spanned Hilton Beck and Coupland, 2 miles south-east of Appleby station. This one did look like a viaduct.

At the Clifton end of the line the junction was so constructed that traffic for Penrith had to do a reversal to get there. The unsuitability of this arrangement was so obvious that even before the line was opened a Bill was put before Parliament seeking powers to make a second connection with the Lancaster and Carlisle a mile further north and facing so as to allow a through run to Penrith. Royal Assent was granted on 7th July 1862, and the extension was opened on 1st August 1863.

It was in 1863 that both the S.D.L.U.R. and the Eden Valley line came under the ownership of the N.E.R.

Except for the short section from Clifton station to the Eden Valley Junction and from Appleby station to the junction with the Midland line the Eden Valley line was single track only.

Leaving Kirkby Stephen, the line fell all the way to where it crossed the River Eden at Musgrave, a distance of four miles, 2½ of which were on a gradient of 1 in 100. Then it was fairly level going until 1½ miles east of Appleby, which was reached on a climb of 1 in 100. From Appleby to just beyond Kirkby Thore it was downhill all the way. Between Kirkby Thore and Temply Sowerby the line climbed over a hill and down the other side to reach, at Skygarth viaduct, the line's lowest point, 351 feet above sea level. Then it climbed to Eden Valley Junction from where it ran gently downhill for the remaining 3¼ miles into Penrith.

By leaving your transport in Kirkby Stephen market square an interesting alternative start to the walk presents itself. Instead of walking southwards along Market Street and its continuation, South Road, to the site of Kirkby Stephen East station, take any of the side alleys on your right to join Faraday Road, which runs parallel to it, and turn left along it. At first there are the backs of houses on your left and fields on your right. But soon the dwellings end and Faraday Road, now a lane, continues between fields to Green Riggs, a farm lying alongside the track.

Alternatively you can start at the bobbin factory on the site of Kirkby Stephen East station and, walking north-westerly along the trackbed, Green Riggs Farm soon comes into view on your right.

Continue through the cutting immediately ahead and, at its far end, along an embankment, still in a northerly direction. Ignore the cutting climbing away on your left because this is the way to Ravenstonedale.

The going is easy, downhill, through a pastoral countryside lush with a plethora of bird and animal life. It is a nature lover's delight, this rolling countryside with its patchwork of coppices, lush pastures and meadows stitched together with well cared for fences. For in this tidy farmland hedgers still bend, twist and weave the living wood into neat, strong hedges, as pleasing to the eye as they are effective in confining and sheltering sheep and cattle. This is good news for all those creatures who make their homes in and under these vital, living boundaries, for good hedging means that their habitat is secure and therefore their chance to live is so much stronger. Fortunately the monstrous 'buzz saw' has not yet been used here to any degree. I hope it never will be and that these same hedges, so well tended by generations of caring Westmorland farmers will continue to be maintained in the traditional way to the benefit of farm husbandry and wildlife alike.

Appearances can be deceptive. Within the fields themselves, so fresh and green and inviting, the changing habits of farming are having a marked effect on the wildlife population. Once meadows were left until high summer before haytime, when they were cut and by then most of the ground nesting birds had raised their young and were safe. Now many of the fields are cut for silage - cattle food produced from grass by fermentation - much earlier in the year when the ground nesting birds are still nesting and many of their nests and young are destroyed. Skylarks' nests are frequently destroyed by early grass cutting and consequently their joyful song is heard less and less. Yet so invidious is this environmental change that it is quite likely the farmers themselves do not appreciate the damage they are inadvertently perpetrating.

More and more the disused line is becoming a haven for an increasing number of wild creature and this is all to the good. Even the grass edging the bed of the old line is allowed to grow and seed and die so that in late summer and autumn on each side of the track you have hay on the hoof! In a small way this helps redress the balance.

About half-way between Kirkby Stephen East and Musgrave

stations the track crosses Scandal Beck and, briefly, the two run side by side, the track along an embankment with, to eastwards the beck at its foot.

Herons frequent this stretch of water and if you approach the embankment quietly and have your eyes peeled, the chances are that you might see one. Over the years I have observed herons hereabouts many times and not once has the thrill diminished. Should you be lucky enough to glimpse a heron before it spots you, do not make the mistake of standing behind a handy tree trunk. Stand in front of it. That way you do not have to move to peer round it and therefore, because movement causes noise, the heron - or any other bird or animal for that matter - will be less likely to hear you. Should you be wearing a hat, pull it forward to hide your forehead but do not attempt to camouflage it with leaves or grass because these shudder at the slightest movement and could give you away.

There is something rather special about Scandal Beck as seen from on top of this embankment. For no matter what the season it always looks enticing. Maybe its eastern backcloth, the Pennines, has something to do with it: perhaps it is the lively beck itself: or it might be the symmetry of the countryside through which it flows. Whatever the reason, when it bends away from the track to flow eastwards, soon to feed that fairest of rivers, the Eden, the temptation to follow it downstream is strong. I have seen it when wisps of autumn mist still lingered in the hollows, when Maytime birdsong poured out on every side, when midsummer sunshine enamelled the green banks and when the ice-edged beck flowed darkly through a snowy wonderland that sparkled like crushed diamonds beneath a wan, winter sky; and it still remains a favourite with me.

One and a half miles further on, just north of a cutting, the old line crossed first a road then the River Eden on the first of the line's viaducts. Now both the bridge over the road and the viaduct have been demolished. The way ahead is down from the trackbed onto the road and right along it to a T junction then left, over the Eden and up a gentle slope, passing Musgrave station on the left. At a T junction turn left and immediately cross the bridge over the track and return to the old line down the cutting side.

Musgrave station used to be a dismal place. The strongest memory I hold of it is waiting for the last train home on a cold and rainy November night. It presented an appearance of unmitigated gloom such as only a wayside station in the heart of an English countryside could do. Its waiting room was cheerless, the oil lamps on the platform swung forlornly in the wind and the wet rails shone now and then as the moving lamplight caught them.

In daylight and under a warming sun the station looks better; but the memory remains.

Musgrave station served Musgrave parish which is divided into the two townships of Great and Little Musgrave. The Musgrave family held this manor until just before World War I and resided there for several centuries until about the middle of the fourteenth century when they moved to Hartley Castle. There they lived until 1735 when they built Eden Hall near Langwathby, using stone from Hartley Castle, and went to live there.

In the middle of a field at the west end of Hall Garth Farmstead, less than a mile east of Great Musgrave is an almost square mound. It marks the site of the Musgrave's old feudal castle or manorial hall.

On the hillsides to the east and west of Hall Garth can be seen some of the finest examples of strip lynchets to be found in all Cumbria.

The beautiful low hills of the valley floor along which the track forges its merry way from Kirkby Stephen to Musgrave are ever present all the way to Warcop and beyond. On all sides its rich farmland famed for its lush appearance and its abstruse blend of good husbandry and naturalness. 'Look after the habitat and the animals will look after themselves', goes a profound conservationist's saying; and to a large extent this has been allowed to happen in the Upper Eden Valley where man and wild creature have learned to live and let live.

There is a wealth of wildlife to be found in the cuttings and down the embankments but you will usually need more than luck if you want to make a study of the little creatures who have their homes beside the track. For the chances are that your presence will be detected by them long before you know where they are; and that will be the end of it. What you need to supplement luck are a bit of forward-planning, stealth, cunning and attention to details.

The trouble with us humans is that we appear to have lost our sensitivity. We can neither hear the high notes a dog can nor pick up a scent over a distance. In certain respects we see, hear, sense and understand less than birds and animals. Yet we rank ourselves as the all-knowledgeable creature who believes that what we cannot see, hear or sense does not exist.

So, as we walk along the track we look around and wonder. This is good for wonder is the beginning of wisdom while the reverse side of wonder is negativism.

To the north side of Warcop that part of the Pennines which includes Musgrave Fell, Warcop or Middle Fell, Long, Roman and

Mickle Fells is now an important R.A.C. range covering some forty thousand acres. It was built during World War II at a cost of some millions of pounds and is a training centre for tank crews, artillery and commando units.

A permanent army camp is sited close to Warcop Hall Park which is famed for its wild cherry trees which, in full bloom, are absolutely glorious.

The walk ends at Warcop station because the line between there and the junction with the Settle-Carlisle line at Appleby is still in use.

From Warcop station a road heads eastwards, then bends to the left to join the A66. A large field to the right of this road is the site of one of the most famous fairs in northern England. It dates from 1329 when a Charter to hold it was granted to Robert de Clifford by Edward III and is called Brough Hill Fair. Primarily a great centre for trade in horses, cattle and sheep, much business was also done there in woollen goods, hardware and rubbishy articles or kelter which cheap-jacks, tinkers, quacks and charlatans had for disposal to the unwary.

The fair is still held annually on 30th September and 1st October, by which time winter weather has usually set in: hence the local name for a cold, wet spell is Brough Hill weather.

Having arrived at Warcop, an exploration of this beautiful village is most rewarding. Leaving the station, follow the road past the front of the station buildings and downhill to a T junction where turn left and immediately go under the railway bridge. The road, bounded on both sides by lovely, shallow woods, leads directly into the village where soon, on the right, the Chambley Arms comes into view. On a hot day, following a good walk, this hostelry is a most welcome sight.

So, for a more uplifting reason, are the humpback bridge in the middle of the village and the gentle stream gliding beneath it, the splendid weather-cock on the green, the few lovely mansions, each set in its own well laid out grounds and the fine old sixteenth century bridge over the River Eden which flows past the edge of the village.

Warcop is on a Ribble bus route and a timetable at the village bus stop shows current bus times from there to Kirkby Stephen and other destinations up and down the valley.

As Warcop station is approached the track goes under a bridge carrying a lane. This lane links Flitholme hamlet to the east with the B6259, a third of a mile away to the west. Anyone wishing to do so can leave the track here, take the lane to the B6259 and go right along it into the village.

This grand walk is not open to the public, so permission should be obtained from the present owners whose names can be obtained from

B.R. Should you forget to do this, please take care to respect the countryside, do no damage and avoid anything that is obviously private. If you consider the owner of the track, usually a farmer, as you would have him consider you, all should be well and usually is.

This walk is a memory maker; and God gave us memories that we might have roses in November.

24. ARNSIDE - HINCASTER JUNCTION

Length	:	5¼ miles
Opened	:	26th June, 1876
Closed	:	4th May, 1942 for passenger traffic
		9th September, 1963 - Sandside-Hincaster for all traffic
		17th June, 1968 - Sandside goods station
		1st January, 1972 - Arnside-Sandside for all traffic
O/S	:	Sheet No.97; Series 1:50,000

> *How still it is; the signal light*
> *At set of sun shines palely green;*
> *A thrush sings: other sound there's none,*
> *Nor traveller to be seen ...*
> *Walter de la Mare.*

Arnside, where Old Westmorland once met the sea, is a place of steep and narrow streets, culs-de-sac and narrow, inter-connecting passages. It sits on a hillside overlooking the beautiful Kent Estuary and because the underlying rock is limestone, a wealth of plants bloom. The air is pure and the environment breeds contentment. But above all, Arnside is a place for loitering, looking, listening and talking to the homely folk who were born and bred there and were lucky enough not to have to leave this enchanted spot.

Earnwulf the Viking made his home on a headland called it *Arnulvesheved* and so Arnside came into being. Later the hamlet of Arnside became part of the Manor of Beetham, it was to the Lord of the Manor of Beetham that Arnside people paid their dues and it was to Beetham that they carried their dead for burial along a corpse road by Fairy Steps woods.

Morecambe Bay was, and remains to this day, difficult to cross on foot. There are only two relatively safe routes, a long one from Hest Bank to Grange-over-Sands and a shorter one from Arnside to Grange-over-Sands. The routes are never constant since the channels cut by the River Kent shift almost daily and quicksands abound. The estuary is so flat that when the incoming tide flows it rushes upstream as a bore, often three feet high. Local fishermen will tell you that on the highest tides, 'on top of the flood', the tide travels as fast as a good horse can run. A strong tide can flood the whole of the Kent Estuary in less than half an hour.

For 2,000 years Lakeland's alternative southern approach to the oversands journey was a long and wearisome overland trip. Many travellers would prefer to risk the sands crossing, setting off at low tide on foot, on horseback or by coach or similar equipage; and quite a few fell foul of the quicksands and were sucked under while others failed to beat the fast flowing tide and drowned. Then came the building of the railways and the oversands route ended when, in 1857, the Carnforth to Furness line was built and crossed the Kent Estuary on a viaduct.

Today a completely re-built fifty-arch viaduct, 522 yards long, carries the Furness line; and special oversands walks, led by Cedric Robinson, Morecambe Bay's only official sand pilot, take place regularly during the summer months.

When Hindpool ironworks, on the Furness coast, was opened in 1859 it created a demand for coke for smelting the iron and since Cumberland coal did not produce good coke, supplies had to be brought from County Durham. The North Eastern Railway conveyed the coke over Stainmore to Tebay from where it was moved south along the L.N.W.R. to Carnforth. There the coke wagons were reversed to travel along the Furness Railway to their destination.

Already very much involved with haematite iron ore traffic from west Cumberland and with the exchange of mails between a succession of night postal trains, Carnforth's facilities became fully stretched dealing with the coke trains from south Durham.

In 1867 the Furness Railway obtained powers for a line to be built from Arnside to join with the L.N.W.R. at Hincaster in order to cut out the reversal from Carnforth along the Furness Railway. The new route was opened on 26th June 1876; but the venture was short-lived and the coke trains soon returned to their original route. This state of affairs continued until World War I when the volume of traffic became too much for the exchange sidings at Carnforth and the need arose for a more efficient use of motive power.

A powerful local man with a lot of influence in Parliament, George Wilson of Dallam Tower, had several clauses included in the Acts of 1865 and 1867 that gave authority for the building of the Arnside to Hincaster Junction branch. One compelled a diversion of part of the line across the River Bela on 'arches and pillars' so as to obstruct the view from this estate as little as possible. He also demanded and got a weir erected across the Bela and a station built near Dallam Tower at which at least one train a day would stop.

The Bela viaduct, sadly no longer there, was an imposing twenty six arch affair and the station, Sandside, now an ugly block of flats, was very well proportioned with an overhanging chalet-type roof.

On 1st July 1890, a second intermediate station was opened at Heversham, two miles north-east of Sandside and some 200 feet above it. Sandside station was at sea level.

When the line was opened the F.R. began a weekday passenger service of five passenger trains each way between Grange-over-Sands and Kendal, using running powers over the L.N.W.R. The journey was a very pleasant one, first crossing the viaduct over the Kent Estuary, then running alongside it almost to Hincaster and continuing northwards, first to Oxenholme, then down the branch to Kendal. Not only was the service a colourful one, never far away from hills, it also had among the locals at any rate, a rather splendid, enigmatic name, 'Kendal Tommy'. The line ceased to operate on 4th May 1942.

The first time I travelled on 'Kendal Tommy' was as a school boy en route to a holiday, the first of many wonderful ones along the Kent Estuary, *en famille* at Storth, just up the hill from Sandside. In those days Sandside had one wooden shop that sold everything a holidaying youngster would wish for.

The Ship Inn, Sandside

Arnside-Hincaster Junction Line

What also captured my attention, and still holds it after all these years, was the wealth of bird life to be found along the Kent Estuary, particularly waders. Today, at midwinter peak, more than 200,000 of them are to be found in this ornithological paradise. Nowhere else in the country can claim such large numbers of knot, dunlin, sanderling, ringed plover and oystercatcher as are to be found in what surely must be the most beautiful bird sanctuary in England. Happily the old Arnside to Hincaster Junction line runs right alongside it so there is ample scope for wader watching. Binoculars come into their own on this walk and a bird recognition book is another useful adjunct. *(Birds of Morecambe Bay* by John Wilson. Cicerone Press.) However, with such an abundance of varied bird life available, watches tend to loose their importance because time itself ceases to matter.

Since a viaduct no longer spans the Bela, a small detour is necessary. The way is upstream to join the nearby B5282 where it crosses the river, then back down the other bank to rejoin the disused track, which now turns inland, away from the Kent Estuary. It passes through a gentle, hilly landscape for some 2½ miles to Hincaster Junction where a few houses and a telephone kiosk mark the end of a most interesting walk.

As several of the walks presented in this book testify, a walk along a disused railway line need not have two separate ends: some really first class ones are circular with the defunct railway line forming a segment of the circle. The Arnside to Hincaster Junction line offers such a walk.

It begins at Arnside, is about 8½ miles long and takes in the limestone uplands which lie between the perilous Milnthorpe sands and the pretty village of Beetham, whose church is reached along an avenue of rambler roses.

Leave Arnside along a secondary road to Hazelslack from where take the old corpse road which climbs across the weathered limestone of Underlaid Wood to where, on the ridge above Fairy Steps, a broad track leads off to the north. Take it and after about a mile it meets at a right angle the road from Storth to Beetham. Turn right along the road for half a mile to a T junction where turn left to Haverbrack and continue through a deer park to the B5282 where it crosses the Bela. Turn left for ⅓ mile and where the road crosses the Arnside to Hincaster Junction line to join it and stay with it back to Arnside, making a detour to pass what used to be Sandside station. The variations on this circular walk are manifold. The route given here is not the most spectacular but it has the saving grace of being easy to follow and furthermore, in this instance, the circle is superior to the straight line.

Fairy Steps is a narrow staircase ascending a fissure in a limestone outcrop. Fashioned by nature with a little help from man, this bewitching spot has become somewhat overgrown with trees. True, exquisite ferns still thrive there in cracks in the rock and gentians, rock roses, wild strawberries and other limestone lovers still garland its approaches; but oh, those constricting trees! Fairy Steps today look rather like sleeping beauty's castle just before the prince hacked his way through the dense thicket to kiss her awake. It could use a prince right now.

25. LAKESIDE AND HAVERTHWAITE RAILWAY

Length :   3¼ miles
Opened :   for goods traffic - 23rd April, 1869 from Greenodd
            Junction to Newby Bridge
            1st June, 1869 from Newby Bridge to Lakeside
            for passenger traffic - 1st June, 1869 from Greenodd
            Junction
Closed :   for goods traffic - 6th April, 1964 from Haverthwaite

174

for passenger traffic - 6th September, 1965 for the whole Lakeside branch
complete closure of the Lakeside branch 24th april, 1967
officially re-opened - 2nd May, 1973

O/S   :   Sheet No.96; Series 1:50,000

> *With a shriek, a bound, a shiver,*
> *With a wild, unearthly scream,*
> *Tunnelled, rumbling, rolling round us,*
> *Clouds of smoke and blinding steam.*
> *Francis Bennoch.*

When in 1864, the Furness Railway was opened, passengers wishing to travel on the Windermere steamers sailing from Newby Bridge to Bowness and Ambleside had to take coaches from Dalton to make their connections, there being no rail link available. Being fully aware of this omission the Furness Railway Company contemplated building a branch to the southern end of the lake; but nothing was done. Not until 26th October 1865, was a decision taken to extend a link from Greenodd to Newby Bridge. By an Act of Parliament of 16th July 1866, authorisation was given for a seven miles long branch to be built from Plumpton Junction, 1½ miles east of Ulverston to Newby Bridge. The Act also provided for the construction of a quarter of a mile long curve from Leven Junction, on the main line, to Greenodd Junction to allow trains to run onto the new branch from the east.

The branch, which was of single track apart from the triangular junction with the main line, which was double, was opened for goods traffic as far as Greenodd on 18th March 1869, and from there to Newby Bridge on 23rd April.

Newby Bridge is not sited on Windermere. It lies south of the lake on the headwaters of the River Leven. This made it unsuitable as a berth for the lake steamers because to get there they had to cope with strong currents in a confined area. The Furness Railway Company, therefore, decided to extend the branch half a mile further upstream to Lakeside on Windermere itself, where a purpose-built quay was erected. The extension was opened on 1st June 1869, to coincide with the introduction of passenger services.

Greenodd station stood so close to the tidal Leven that a high tide water came close to lapping the up platform. Taking advantage of this phenomenon the Company had windows placed on all sides of the waiting room to enable passengers to enjoy the view while waiting for their trains.

Between Greenodd and Haverthwaite the line crossed the Leven on bridges broad enough to take double track. At Haverthwaite there was a passing loop which began inside a short tunnel to the south of the station. Beyond a further small tunnel on the other side of the station the line ran through a beautiful, wooded landscape all the way to Lakeside.

Eager to exploit the line's tourist potential, the Company spent so much money on its station buildings that shareholders began to complain about unwarranted extravagance.

At Lakeside a large ridge and furrow roof covered the combined railway terminus and steamer pier. On a long veranda that ran parallel to the lake and the platform an orchestra enchanted tourists as they dined in the restaurant and refreshment rooms. What a pity, then, that with so much thought having gone into planning these rather splendid buildings, the coal dump for the steamers was placed right in front of them!

Probably the most famous vessel to use Lakeside pier was the steam yacht *Esperance*. It belonged to the Furness ironmaster H.W. Schneider who lived in Bowness. Every morning he would leave his house preceded by his butler carrying an extravagant breakfast in a covered and heated salver. This the butler would serve to him during the six miles long journey to Lakeside where he would disembark to enter a reserved first class compartment to complete his journey to his Barrow office. The *Esperance*, which is now in the Windermere Steam Boat Museum; is better remembered than its owner as the houseboat in *Swallows and Amazons*, Arthur Ransome's glorious adventure story.

In the summer of 1869 a screw driven steamer, *Swan*, joined the three existing paddle-steamers, *Fire Fly*, *Dragon Fly* and *Rothay*. Then, in 1871, a freight carrier, *Raven*, came into service as a waterborne delivery van. In 1879 two more passenger steamers, *Teal* and *Cygnet*, were added to the fleet, followed in 1891 by *Tern* and in 1900 by *Swift*. But the pride and joy of the Furness Company was a luxury steam yacht, *Britannia*. By 1920 the three paddle-steamers and the steam yacht had been scrapped. Then *Cygnet* and *Raven* were sold and, in 1936, motor vessels of the same name replaced *Teal* and *Swan*. Finally, in the post- World War II years *Swift* and *Tern* were converted to diesel, thus bringing to an end Windermere's age of steam.

From the outset the branch did well, attracting an increasing volume of tourists as the years passed. Special trains were run throughout the year, skater's specials being particularly popular whenever Windermere was frozen. These were the line's halcyon days and they were beginning to fade when, in 1920, because of mounting losses, the winter steamer sailings were withdrawn in favour of a bus link between Newby Bridge and Ambleside.

The rot having set in, local traffic gradually shrank until, on 26th September 1938, the all-year round passenger service was reduced to a summer service only. In 1941, having been reduced to only one Millom-Lakeside train on alternate Sundays, all passenger traffic ceased; but on 3rd June 1946 it was restored on a seasonal basis.

By 1960 the line was once more under the threat of closure. Then B.R. decided to expand the Windermere steamer service and in conjunction with the decision, most of the line was re-laid, using experimental concrete sleepers. Things were looking up.

On 6th September 1965, passenger services were withdrawn.

Freight traffic which had already ended beyond Haverthwaite on 6th April 1964, survived to that point until 24th April 1967, when as a direct consequence of Backbarrow Ironworks closing down, the branch closed completely.

Following the closure of the line, enthusiasts made moves to reverse the situation. They formed themselves into the Lakeside Railway Society in 1968 and as such, proposed re-opening the branch from Plumpton Junction. A depot had been established at Carnforth and it was hoped that engines based there would supply the branch's motive power. Sadly, due to lack of funds and other problems the whole length could not be re-established. In 1969 the section to the south of Haverthwaite was sequestered for road improvements. But before the rail link was broken steam locomotives and rolling stock were moved to Haverthwaite for use on the remaining 3¼ miles between Haverthwaite station and Lakeside via Newby Bridge.

On 13th October 1972, a Light Railway Order was granted and, on 2nd May 1973, the Lakeside and Haverthwaite Railway was officially opened by Bishop Eric Treacy.

Public services began three days later.

Today the Lakeside and Haverthwaite Railway Co. Ltd., supported by the Lakeside Railway Society, carries large numbers of tourists to the cruise vessels on Windermere. Combined rail and boat tickets are available and the trains are usually steam hauled. The Company owns twelve steam locomotives and two diesels which are used mainly for maintenance work.

The best motive power consists of two Fairburn 2-6-4 tank engines which were built in 1950 and 1951 to former L.M.S. designs. What a marvellous sight they make as they pass along this single track through leafy, hilly country hauling B.R. mark 1 coaches, also from the early

1950s. They combine all the best features you would expect of a branch train.

A ride along this very pleasant, little line takes about fifteen minutes and recaptures the atmosphere of the late 1940s and early 1950s. It is open at Easter, from then until May, Sundays only, daily from May to the end of September and at weekends only throughout October.

This walk incorporates a ride on this delightful line and can be done at any time of year. Anyone so doing between the end of October and Easter must walk both ways. But this is a real pleasure, I assure you.

Haverthwaite village, 'the clearing where oats are grown', is a huddle of houses and farms south of the A590. Haverthwaite station lies some distance away, to the north of the A590. A path across a field is their umbilical cord.

We decided to leave the car in Haverthwaite station car park, walk to Lakeside and return by train. It was a lovely, soft morning and the sun's rays, pouring through the trees were so beautiful that it was easy to understand why, in the old days people believed in heavenly visitations.

Leaving the station, the way is along the A590, eastwards towards Backbarrow for a short distance before taking the inviting secondary road on the left. Sandwiched between the track and the Leven on its right, this quiet road wanders pleasantly through a delightful, sylvan landscape.

The deep green of late summer looked lovely against a clear blue sky the day we took this enchanted saunter. With so much to admire en route, warming sunshine, convivial company and all day before us, we considered ourselves thrice blessed.

Although trees predominate, they enhance rather than detract from the splendour of the walk. No rigid ranks of conifers, standing shoulder to shoulder, plague this lovely area, shutting out the light and plunging everything into Stygian gloom. On the contrary, it is from the surrounding woods that this lovely little walk receives much of its charm.

Where, after about half a mile, the road bifurcates, do not take the right fork across the river. Instead keep to the left, close to the track; and half a mile further on, immediately after going under the railway, where a road leads off to the left, ignore it and continue straight ahead. After another half mile of pleasant walking where, on a right-hand bend a road from the left cuts across it from the left, follow the bend which ends at a T junction. Turn right here and the road will bring you to Newby Bridge.

Newby Bridge is a little village that spends much of its time catering for tourists. Most of it is on the right bank of the Leven but the Swan Hotel, its eighteenth century hostelry, is on the left bank. A rather nice seventeenth century bridge spans the river near the hotel which is useful if you live on the right bank and feel a thirst coming on.

How easy it was to wax lyrical on this gentle walk with the sun's heat warming both earth and heart. I looked over the bridge at the wind-ruffled water and followed the straight flight of a swallow. Soon it would depart and with it the summer. Already the chestnuts were beginning to turn. Soon autumn would be here, daubing the trees in rich reds, russets and gold. If the fine weather held, dead leaves would fall to circle and eddy on the pavement and rattle across the road. And still the walk would hold its charm because it is a walk for all seasons.

On leaving the Swan we took the first right, crossed the railway and after a very pleasant mile, this time with both rail and river on our right, arrived at Lakeside, there to await the next train back to Haverthwaite.

26. FOXFIELD - CONISTON

Length   :   10 miles
Opened :   From Kirkby-in-Furness to Broughton-in-Furness -
February, 1848
From Broughton-in-Furness to Coniston -
18th June, 1859
Closed   :   From Foxfield - 6th October, 1958 for passenger traffic
30th April, 1962 for goods traffic
O/S   :   Sheet Nos.96 and 97; Series 1:50,000

> *What have these lovely mountains*
> *worth revealing?*
> *More glory and more grief*
> *than I can tell.*
> *Charlotte Bronte.*

Coniston village, 'the King's manor', came into being not because of farming but because of copper ore which has been mined there for two thousand years. Large-scale working of the ore began in 1599 and continued for two hundred and fifty years until the decline began.

Miners working in dangerous conditions in darkness relieved only by candle-light bored into the rock, laid the gunpowder charges, fired them and, after the blast, put the ore into kibbles or buckets which, when full, they carried to wagons on the upper levels. The loaded wagons were taken to the mine entrance where the ore was washed and sorted by little boys. The ore was then crushed in mills, washed a second time in jigging troughs, pounded and washed again. The scene of all this activity was aptly named Copper Mines Valley down which Church Beck still tumbles from square shaped Levers Water.

Some of the copper ore was carried by pack-horse over Dunmail Raise to Keswick to be smelted but most was hauled south, at first solely by pack-horse and later, increasingly by boat down Coniston Water to Nibthwaite then overland to Greenodd or Ulverston for onward shipment to Wales.

These means of transport presented many long-standing difficulties which, in turn, restricted expansion at the mines; and it was in an attempt to solve these transport problems that in 1849 it was proposed to build a 3ft.3ins. gauge line from Broughton to Coniston.

Prior to that, when the original Furness Railway was opened in 1846 it included a line leaving the main line at Millwood Junction, a little north of Furness Abbey, and going north to Kirkby-in-Furness. More or less coinciding with its opening further powers were obtained to extend it to Broughton-in-Furness, to provide an outlet for the copper ore from the Coniston mines, some nine miles away. This extension was opened in 1848 and in 1850 the Whitehaven and Furness Junction Railway joined it at Foxfield. Thus the section from Foxfield to Broughton-in-Furness became a branch line.

The 1849 proposal to extend the branch from Broughton-in-Furness to Coniston came to nothing but seven years later it was proposed that a standard gauge line be built following the originally proposed route. This time the line was built and on 18th June 1859, it was opened to passenger traffic.

The branch was not used for goods and mineral traffic until 1860; and this coincided with the opening at Coniston village terminus of a short extension to Copper Mines Wharf. From the beginning the line was worked by the Furness Railway which became vested in it by an Act of Parliament of 7th July 1862.

The coming of the Foxfield to Coniston branch line was rather too late to be of great benefit to the copper mines, for soon after its opening came the decline in copper ore production. Slowly at first, beginning in the mid-1860s and increasing steadily as one by one the mines became worked out, came the inevitable shrinking of mineral traffic receipts.

More and more the branch came to depend on tourism. Unfortunately, it had the serious disadvantage of facing westwards, away from both central Lakeland and large centres of population. Moreover, Coniston terminus had been sited high above the village and the lake in order to give easy access to the mines. Yet despite these setbacks the branch became an attractive tourist line to a part of Lakeland that had hitherto been difficult to reach.

Almost as soon as the line opened some of the Furness Railway directors established steamer services on Coniston Water. In October, 1859, the famous *Gondola* was launched and in June 1860, began regular summer services. This remarkable vessel, a cross between a Venetian gondola and an English steam yacht, became a real crowd puller. So much so that when a replacement, *Lady of the Lake* was launched in May 1908, sentiment for the *Goldola* proved so strong that both vessels remained in service until sailings ceased in 1914. The *Lady of the Lake* was broken up in 1950 but the *Gondola* was spared that fate. It was converted into a houseboat and later sank. But that was not the end. The National Trust acquired it and, following a £100,000 appeal, the vessel was restored by Vickers of Barrow, who did a first class job. In July 1980, the *Gondola* recommenced public sailings, and a link with the past has been restored.

The branch line itself, being unobtrusive and passing through delightful scenery became very popular with tourists. It provided so pleasant a way of getting into the heart of Lakeland that it is difficult to appreciate why John Ruskin, 'the greatest master of English descriptive prose' was so bombastic about it. Perhaps being an environmentalist as well as an artist and writer has something to do with it. He fought the coming of the railway to the Lakes just as earlier William Wordsworth had, for he did not relish a mass influx of visitors to the area.

In 1871 John Ruskin bought Brantwood on the eastern shore of Coniston Water and lived there until his death in 1900. He was a major influence in the founding of the Lake District Defence Association which was established in 1883. Sadly from that date he spent the rest of his life in 'a state of clouded peace'. It was during this period that he would poignantly and punctiliously go outside to watch the crimson streaked evening sky over Coniston Water whenever his servant called, 'The sunset, Mr. Ruskin'.

For a short period a Furness Railway steam rail motor, one of two built in 1905, worked the branch, pulling a four-wheeled trailer coach. Both were withdrawn in 1918.

During the L.M.S. and B.R. days there were eight trains daily between Broughton-in-Furness and Coniston and one between Fox-

Site of Coniston Station

field and Broughton-in-Furness. They were well patronised by locals and, in summer, by tourists.

In 1958 B.R. announced that, since the line was making an annual loss of £16,000, the service would be withdrawn. The neighbourhood was shocked because B.R. had made no effort to economise on the excessive operating costs. It was an arbitrary decision, protests were spurned and there was a strong suspicion that the accounts had been falsified. On 6th October 1958, passenger services were withdrawn. To make matter worse the closure almost coincided with the opening of a central secondary school at Coniston which had a large pupil catchment area. B.R. provided a bus service which ran to connect with some of the trains at Foxfield but, unbelievably, this service was not mentioned in the railway timetable. Furthermore the cost of burdening an already inadequate road system with another bus service along with the necessary road improvements was almost as much as would have been required to run a light diesel service along the line. So in an atmosphere of acrimony and bitterness the Foxfield to Coniston branch became the first Lake District line to be closed to passengers.

A thrice weekly goods service continued until 30th April 1962, when the branch closed completely.

The narrow road northwards from Foxfield to Broughton-in-Furness follows closely the route of the old line; but it is not until Broughton station, now a private dwelling, is passed that the walk along the line begins proper.

Broughton-in-Furness, where the Silurian rocks of southern Lakeland meet the flatlands of the Duddon Estuary head, has been there for a long time. It was a chapelry under Kirkby Ireleth in pre-Norman times and has had a market since the mid-thirteenth century. Mostly it is quiet but on high days and fair days it becomes very lively. It has weekly auctions and fairs in April and October. The Lammas Fair, which was held in the market place every August 1st is no more, but the old proclamation is still made by the bailiff and the ceremony is marked by the distribution of coppers for the children.

A cutting marks the start of the walk along the trackbed proper and throughout its very pleasant length the old line keeps a very low profile.

At Torver a grand opportunity to walk along the western shore of Coniston Water presents itself and this refreshing circular round of Torver Common is too good to miss. About 200 yards beyond the village take the path on your right by Grass Guards and so down to the lake by way of Torver Common woods. At the shore-line turn right and walk along the water's edge for almost two miles to the road at Sunny Bank and go right along it to Mill Bridge where a track on the left follows Torver Beck into Torver village. This captivating departure is 4½ miles long and you should allow about two hours to walk it.

Coniston is a sheltered water, straight and long, making it an ideal place for attempting water speed records. The late Donald Campbell in Bluebird tragically lost his life there when his boat somersaulted after either hitting a submerged log at speed or becoming airborne. The accident has never been explained satisfactorily.

Yes, Coniston is well suited to the excitement of high speed trials.

But my thoughts were of a richer, more wonderful world in which adventure without evil evolves through the straightforward, practical plot of Arthur Ransome's classic *Swallows and Amazons*. Coniston Water is synonymous with Arthur Ransome whom fellow novelist Hugh Walpole called 'the best writer for boys and girls in England today'.

The Old Man of Coniston overlooks the slate-built village of Torver, the peat shieling, with its church, its school and, between them, its pub, The Church House Inn. A twelfth century chapel originally stood on the site of the present church but it was not until 1538 when Archbishop Cranmer granted a deed of consecration which allowed burials in the chapel grounds. Prior to 1538 the dead had to be taken to sixteen miles distant Ulverston for burial.

If the walk is any criterion, travelling along the Foxfield to Coniston branch in a swaying railway carriage must have been fun, for along it interest and lovely varied scenery go hand in hand; and at the end of it was, in its heyday, this jewel of a station in a superb mountain setting.

Coniston, 'the King's manor', is quite large for a village. It puts the seal on this grand walk by offering more than a hint of goodies to come - provided you can spare the time. For towering over it to the west is the same Old Man that has been our companion for so many miles and which from Coniston looks particularly inviting.

The usual ascent from Coniston is along the Walna Scar and quarry roads from beyond the old railway station. A better way is from the Sun Hotel on a path along the south bank of Church Beck and continuing past Miner's Bridge, not over it, until the quarry road is met at a bend. The way is now through the quarry, climbing steeply to join a well used path to the summit at 2,633ft. An even better way, lesser used but more exciting, is via Boo Tarn.

Whichever way you choose, the views from the top will make the slog worthwhile. From the summit cairn the whole of Morecambe Bay can be seen as, on a clear day, can parts of Ulster and Scotland. To the north and east the Lakeland fells are spread out in breathtaking grandeur.

As the most favoured route up the Old Man begins at the Sun Hotel this hostelry makes a fine overnight stopping place. But there are others, like The Black Bull, a former coaching inn. Turner stayed there in 1797 since when the plumbing has been much improved.

Should the prospect of climbing the Old Man be altogether too much on top of your walk from Foxfield why not take the opportunity to explore at a slightly lower level?

Brantwood, John Ruskin's lovely home, is only a mile and a half

184

away to the south-east; and the Anglican church of St. Andrew, where he chose to be buried in preference to having a national grave in Westminster Abbey, is very close, in Coniston itself.

If Coniston is a Lakeland honey pot, I mused, surely it is right and proper to call the disused line leading so pleasantly to it from Foxfield an absolute honey. For that is precisely what it is.

27. PIEL PIER BRANCH

Length : 3 miles
Opened : Roose Junction-Piel Pier - 24th August, 1846
            Salthouse Junction-Parrock Junction - 1873
            Piel station, Roa Island - October, 1881
Closed : Roose Junction-Parrock Hall Junction and Piel Pier - 1st October, 1881
            Salthouse Junction-Piel - 6th July, 1936
O/S   : Sheet No.96; Series 1:50,000

Professing loud energy, out of its junction departed
The branch line engine. The small train rounded the bend
Watched by us pilgrims of summer, and most by me:-
Edmund Blunden.

Broad sands, divided by the Piel Channel, lie between the mainland to the south-east of Barrow-in-Furness and the north-eastern tip of Walney Island; and two thirds of the way across them, south of the mainlands's southernmost point lies Piel Island, originally called Fouldra or Fotheray.

In the 12th century Fouldra was held by the Abbots of Furness who found its sheltered harbour and its isolation well suited to the un-monk-like trade of smuggling and the import of restricted commodities like corn and the export of fleeces.

As a direct consequence of Scots raids on the mainland in the 1320s the Abbots were granted permission to crenelate the dwelling house they had built on Fouldra.

A large body of Irish and Flemish soldiers brought the young imposter Lambert Simnel to Piel in 1487 to claim the throne of Henry VII. The Abbots of Furness kept aloof from this uprising but in 1536 they became involved in some dubious dealings with the leaders of the Pilgrimage of Grace. As with other monastic establishments the community at Furness Abbey was dissolved by the King's Commisssioners.

Smuggling continued on Piel Island and in the 18th century the King's Boat was based there to keep an eye on contraband landings.

In 1840 John Abel Smith, a prominent London builder, purchased Roa Island, sited on the north side of the Piel Channel, midway between Piel Island and the mainland. It covered an area of five acres and he paid £500 for it with the intention of building an embankment connecting it with the 'neighbouring island of Great Britain' along a causeway across which a train would run to connect with a train ferry. This ferry would ply from Piel Island to connect with the Preston and Wyre Railway in which he had a large financial interest and the London-Glasgow trains. To reach this ferry on Piel Island, Smith also intended building a pier linking Piel and Roa Islands.

The Bill for the pier's construction failed in 1841 but in 1843 a revised one succeeded. This second Bill was for a pier turning westwards into deep water and the Piel Channel and it gave Smith authority to build both pier and embankment at his own expense.

The Furness Railway agreed to extend its Rampside branch along the embankment to Roa Island, from where Smith was to construct the 810ft. long Piel Pier, which would have the advantage over Barrow of offering deep water facilities at all states of the tide. It had little option, for had it not agreed to build the branch to Rampside and along the causeway, Smith would have built a competing line.

The agreement between the Furness Railway Co. and Smith stated that it would extend the railway along the embankment and onto the pier if Smith would complete the pier. There was nothing in the agreement about opening the pier for traffic. Smith undertook to have the pier ready for the opening of the railway in 1846 but the undertaking was not fulfilled. Therefore the Furness Railway took their slate and iron ore trains to a jetty at Barrow.

The Piel branch left the Furness Railway at Roose and joined the embankment south of Rampside station, reaching it along a wooden trestle of sixteen twelve feet long spans. At Roa Island the 3,000ft. long embankment turned west onto the pier.

And what a pier! It was a timber trestle structure built on three levels. The bottom level was a low water pier 100ft. long, the middle level was 370ft. long and the top level, the one that carried the rails, was 810ft. long. The top level was used for carrying slate and iron traffic at high water.

The opening date for passengers was 24th August 1846, but it was withdrawn at the end of the summer season because of difficulties in working both passenger and mineral traffic over a single line.

Following the completion of a station at Furness Abbey alongside the Manor House, which was bought by the Furness Railway and converted into an hotel, the line between Roose and Millwood Junction was doubled in 1847.

Unfortunately the expected increase in passenger traffic was hampered by more problems at Piel pier. The Furness Railway purchased the steamer *Helvellyn*, formerly *Windermere*, to operate a cross-bay service between Fleetwood and Piel to compete with existing sailings from Fleetwood to Bardsea. It was advertised to begin on 24th May 1847, but Smith's conditions for landing passengers at the pier were unacceptable and the steamer was diverted to Barrow where the fluctuating tides caused great inconvenience. The timetable had to be varied to fit in with the tides and this made the service unpopular.

In May 1848, following agreement between Smith and the Furness Railway, sailings reverted to Piel until the end of that summer but there was no winter service to follow and Piel branch was closed because it could not cover its expenses.

Smith wanted to sell out to the Furness Railway and in 1851 tried to force the issue by bringing out a Bill for a direct line from the pier to Lindal. This was successfully blocked by the Furness Railway and the Bill was withdrawn.

Negotiations were now opened between Smith and the Furness Railway and it was agreed that the Furness Railway would lease the embankment, Roa Island and the pier for 999 years. But before this could be confirmed a severe storm on 27th December 1852, destroyed a third of the pier, a wooden goods shed on Roa Island and damaged the embankments. Smith tried to hold the Furness Railway to the terms of the agreement but failed.

The Furness Railway bought all his rights and property for £15,000 and spent a further £1,645 repairing the pier and the embankment.

In 1867 the Furness and Midland joint line was opened from Carnforth to Wennington on the former North Western line from Skipton to Lancaster. To accommodate the Midland trains the Furness Railway re-built Piel pier with a station at the end.

The Furness Railway, Midland and James Little & Co. jointly owned the Barrow Steam Navigation Co., which on 1st July 1867, began a service using the steamer *Herald* to Douglas, Isle of Man. On 1st September 1867, they inaugurated a service to Belfast, using three small paddle steamers.

In 1878 the Ramsden dock at Barrow was completed and in 1881 the Furness Railway opened a station adjacent to it. This marked the end of more than a decade of successful operating from Piel pier. The Isle of Man steamers were transferred to Ramsden dock from 1st June 1881, and the Belfast service followed suit in October of that year.

On 1st October 1881 Piel pier was closed and the connection from Roose Junction to Parrock Hall Junction was abandoned on 27th March 1882.

A new station, using the old name Piel was built on Roa Island and the service from Barrow to the new Piel station survived until 6th July 1936.

Piel pier was left to rot until 1891 when it was dismantled. Now a few stumps of the pier remain near the shore together with a few buildings on Roa Island. The embankment is a road. Only the restless waters remain the same.

Today, thanks to positive thought put to good use by Barrow-in-Furness Borough Council and the Cumbrian Trust for Nature Conservation in co-operation with British Gas and the C.E.G.B. the Piel pier branch has become an important part of the excellent Westfield Nature Trails quartering the coastal belt between Barrow and the village of Rampside.

Our walk begins at Salthouse Junction from where, having curved initially to Parrock Hall Junction it follows an almost straight line as far as Barrow on-shore terminal where it bifurcates. It is along this stretch that the line was built on an embankment high enough to withstand the highest tides. The embankment enclosed a large saltmarsh which, when filled with sand and gravel, became the site of Roosecote Power Station.

Over to the right as the route straightens after coming out of the initial bend is an interesting pool fringed with reed beds. It lies, with others, on land owned by the North West Water Authority and attracts several species of duck including mallard, teal and wigeon. Moorhens thrive there and it is home to sedge warblers for whom the reed beds are their natural habitat.

Roosecote Power Station uses Cavendish dock, which lies just beyond Salthouse pool, as a cooling reservoir and partly because of this and partly because of its size, the water is 2 to 3 degrees warmer than in any of the other Barrow docks. For this reason great numbers of birds are attracted to it. There you will find mute swans, coots, cormorants and great, white drifts of gulls sitting on the warm water.

Anyone wanting a closer look can take a bridleway along the eastern side of this reservoir which runs between it and the aforementioned Salthouse pool. It is a must for ornithologists.

This is a landscape of low, rounded hills, drumlins which are heaps of moraine left behind when the glaciers of the last ice age retreated.

The hollows between them tend to be marshy and many have been drained. The feathery plumes of the common reed mark these drainage ditches which are often to be found close to hedges. The hedges, sitting on cobbled-faced earth banks, play a very important part in this area because apart from keeping sheep and cattle in and serving as sanctuaries for wildlife they act as wind-breaks. The prevailing winds are strong, salt-laden south westerlies as many lopsided bushes testify. Foliage clusters on the less exposed sides, away from the wind and so growth is strongly one sided.

The farmland near the coast is mainly good quality grazing land.

The long stretch of Roosecote Sands, to the right, has been designated by the Nature Conservancy as an area of special scientific interest because of its importance as a feeding ground for waders.

In direct contrast the lagoon to the left is dangerous. It is there that pulverised fuel ash is stored for the construction industry. P.F.A. is a by-product of the burning of coal in a power station. When the A590 in south Cumbria was built 30,000 tons of P.F.A. were used in its construction. Two previous lagoons have been filled with P.F.A. and landscaped.

Where Barrow on-shore terminal blocks the way ahead there is a choice of routes but for the purist the right-hand one is the one to take because it eventually returns to the disused track while the other equally good one doesn't.

A great deal of thought has gone into the building of Barrow on-shore terminal. It sits in a natural hollow surrounded by low hills and has been extensively landscaped, several thousand trees and shrubs being used to make it as unobtrusive as possible. Built on the best location between North Wales and St. Bees Head for a pipeline landfall from the drilling platforms of the Morecambe Bay gas field, it is British Gas' newest gas treatment terminal. Its facilities, spread over twenty hectares of land, receive, treat and meter the gas before passing it into the national gas grid. On entering the terminal the gas passes through a series of pipes called a slug catcher in which slugs of oily liquid called condensate are caught. The condensate is piped separately to Barrow docks where it is taken by tanker to be used as a feedstock in the chemical industry.

The terminal also dries gas by refrigeration and adds odorant to give the gas its characteristic smell. This is done as a safety measure because Morecambe Bay gas has no natural smell. Then the quality of the gas is checked together with its pressure and temperature before it enters the on-shore pipelines.

Ridding Head Scar, seen ahead as the right-hand fork takes you westwards, is a shingle bank bordering the southern end of Roosecote Sands. It is one of the last areas to be sumberged by the rising tide and sometimes during neap tides remains exposed even at high water. For this reason waders like oystercatchers and curlews roost there.

Rounding the corner of the on-shore terminal brings Westfield Point into view. It is a clifftop viewing point giving very good views over Walney Channel from the cranes of Barrow in the north to Walney lighthouse and beyond in the south. And that's not all: at low tide shelduck gather on the glutinous mud spreading from the foot of the cliffs to feed on the thousands of small snails, hydrobia, that live there.

The cliffs are low and composed of glacial sand topped with a thin layer of glacial till or boulder clay. Being sandy they are fairly unstable and are being eroded steadily at the rate of 0-1 meters a year. Wind, not the sea, is the culprit for only the very highest tides touch them. The holes with which the cliffs are riddled provide nest sites for sand martins and shelter for toads in the breeding season.

A little beyond Westfield Point viewing station the way splits again, one path continuing along the clifftop, the other turning left to return to the disused line. There a right turn along it will bring you, via a narrow cutting, to Rampside station at the west end of Rampside and so out onto the causeway.

From the causeway, now a road, Foulney and South Walney can be seen. Both are reserves of the Cumbrian Trust for Nature Conservation and contain large populations of gulls and terns.

The vast area of mud, sand and saltmarshes fringing the Walney Channel into which the causeway thrusts appears to be devoid of life; but nothing could be further from the truth. The place simply teams with life. Cockles, lugworms, crabs, snails and many invertebrates lie buried in the clinging mud waiting for the twice daily tides to bring them their food. In turn they provide food for the many kinds of birds whose feeding ground this is. It is all part of Nature's delicate balance.

28. T'LA-AL RATTY

Length	:	7 miles
Opened	:	for mineral traffic - 24th May, 1875
		for passenger traffic - 1876
Closed	:	for passenger traffic - 1908
		for mineral traffic - 1912
Re-opened	:	as 15″ gauge - 1916

190

Closed	:	for passenger traffic - between 1939 and 1946 Put up for sale - 1958. Purchased by the Ravenglass and Eskdale Railway Preservation Society - 1961. Still operating. Full length of circular walk from the Woolpack Inn via the River Esk and Muncaster Fell, including the 7 miles long ride on t'la-al Ratty, is 13½ miles.
O/S	:	Lake District Tourist Map. 1″ = 1ml or Lake District West 1:25,000

> *The earth has pleasures all our senses share:*
> *The music of a stream, the scented air.*
> *The clouds, the hills, the trees that greet our eyes,*
> *Contribute to the memories we prize.*
> *Francis Gray.*

The rising sun had steamed out the morning mist clinging to low lying hollows and dips. Hardknott Pass and, at its western foot, the well sited Roman fort of Mediobogdum, or Hardknott Castle as it is better known, were to our backs. With mounting excitement we drove down Eskdale, eager to explore 'the valley of the trains'. Our destination was the Woolpack Inn, a mile east of Dalegarth station and the start of one of the most beautiful, varied and exciting railway-connected walks I have ever come across.

Eskdale, one of the loveliest of Lakeland's valleys, has its head in the clouds where Scafell, Scafell Pike, Bowfell, Crinkle Crags and Harter Fell form the English Alps and the Esk is born among bleak and craggy ridges. As the clear waters fall from the high fells they flow through a verdant land of woodlands and pastures to where, at Ravenglass, Eskdale dips its feet into the Irish Sea.

Between the lower reaches of the River Esk and the flat pastures of Miterdale the broad mass of Muncaster Fell rises to the 600ft. contour, reaching 757ft. at its summit on Hooker Crag. Running along the northern flank of this miniature mountain is the Ravenglass and Eskdale Railway, 't'la-al Ratty', a most important ingredient in this blue ribbon of a walk.

'T'la-al Ratty' is a small gauge railway running between Ravenglass and Dalegarth. La-al is Cumbrian for little, but nobody knows where the name Ratty originated. It was built originally on a track gauge of thirty three inches to carry iron ore from the Nab Gill mines, near Boot, to the main line at Ravenglass. Within two years of its opening, on 24th May 1875, the mining company had failed although the mines were still working on a limited scale and the line continued to carry goods and passengers. Never a commercial proposition, the line was closed to passenger traffic in 1908 and completely in 1912.

In 1915 Mr. W.J.Bassett-Lowke, the famous model engineer, took over the line and, at a cost of £11,000, converted it to the fifteen inch gauge it is today. The cost included five quarter scale locomotives, three steam and two petrol. The new small gauge railway was opened in 1916, mainly as a testing line for his model steam locomotives. Early on in its life as a narrow gauge line, attempts were made to provide an attractive and commercial service.

For the next forty two years the line survived mixed fortunes, including its complete closure for passenger traffic throughout World War II.

In 1958 the line was put up for sale. In 1959 a Preservation Society was formed and the line was saved. In 1961 the Ravenglass and Eskdale Railway Co. Ltd. took over and began to build up a rolling stock of steam and diesel locomotives and both open and saloon coaches. Today it is Eskdale's most popular attraction and provides a novel means of transport at the beginning or the end of walks in Eskdale. Riding on Ratty, particularly in one of the open carriages, is great fun.

The Woolpack Inn looks like what it used to be, a resting place in days long gone for pack ponies and their leaders en route to the port of Whitehaven with loads of wool. It was from close to this old hostelry that we made a most pleasant start to our walk, along a short farm road to the left of and slightly down the valley to it. We soon arrived at a most interesting humpback bridge, Doctor Bridge, which carries a farm road across the Esk and on, to Penny Hill Farm, which was once an inn. Our route, however, remained on the right bank of the river and followed a path which weaves in a delightful way between gorse and bracken with the river on the left all the way. No sooner had we left Doctor Bridge behind than Birker Force could be seen spilling over a cliff to our left. It is a splendid sight.

After about three quarters of a mile we made a slight detour to inspect two girders spanning a rocky gorge. They once supported a bridge that carried a branch of the mineral railway from Dalegarth to mines on the south side of the Esk.

At the western end of a wall on our right and with the gin clear Esk sparkling on our left, we turned right into another lane which led north. At the entrance to this lane and on our left as we entered it, stands the 17th century, simple, granite church of St. Catherine's, Eskdale's parish church. In the churchyard there is a rather splendid

Tommy Dobson's grave near the River Esk.

memorial to Tommy Dobson, a local master of Foxhounds, whose whole life was devoted to foxhunting. On his headstone are carved his likeness, a fox's head, a hound's head, a whip, a horn and a fox's brush. Locally his reputation was far greater than that of John Peel.

Leaving the church, we walked up the lane, northwards, away from the Esk, for a short distance to where another narrower lane on our left meandered away between dry stone walls. We took this left-hand path and it brought us not to the devil but to the river again and then away from it, in arboreal splendour to a narrow tarmac road where we turned left along it, back to the Esk. We crossed the river and continued along the road to a junction of lanes with Dalegarth Hall in view ahead. Taking the left-hand fork we continued uphill along a way that curved to the left to where a signpost pointed along a bridleway on the right, leading to a deep wood with Dalegarth Hall on our right. The way snaked pleasantly through the wood to emerge in heathland with the river nearby on the right. Cotton grass abounded and gorse and broom threw great yellow blotches of colour across the summer landscape.

193

An unseen cuckoo mocked us: a buzzard flew, proud as a galleon, beating the still air with large unhurried flaps of its broad wings.

We continued along the riverside, passing a footbridge, to the good looking Forge Bridge, which we crossed on a pleasant country road which brought us nicely to the George IV where, in the interest of avoiding dehydration, we sampled the juice of enlightenment.

The George IV is pleasantly sited at a road junction near the bottom of a hill, which, on leaving the inn, we climbed to join a narrow lane at The Green Station. We went left, along it, keeping parallel to and alongside the railway permanent way for a little while. Then line and lane parted company, the lane leading into a field where it became indistinct. However, to our right, diagonally across this field, we spotted a stile, beyond which, at the far side of a pasture, Muncaster Fell beckoned.

Now the way ahead was particularly clear for triangular, yellow flags marked it. These, we later discovered, had been placed there to guide those members of the Cumbrian Fell Runner's Association who were participating in the annual Muncaster Fell Race. Had the flags not been there it would not have mattered to us because the way ahead, climbing the shoulder of Silver Knott, was broad enough to follow without difficulty.

As we reached a gate where two walls met at right angles slightly west of Silver Knott the first of the fell runners came into view ahead of us. Others followed, perspiring groups of them, with peat splashed legs and hot bodies. Their immediate destination was the check-point at the top of Silver Knott up which they slowly snaked like a grotesque caterpillar.

Once through the gate we bore left and soon reached Ross's camp, a flat slab of rock supported by three others. It was built by members of a Victorian shooting party, *circa* 1883, the date inscribed on it, to serve as a table for the shooters. Today it serves a much better purpose as an observation platform. From it the views, particularly up the valley, are very good. We were on the 600ft. contour and would stay on it for a mile and a bit before losing height in a profusion of rhododendrons at a gate in a fence.

We made a detour to climb Hooker Crag which, at 757ft. is the fell's summit. It has a trig column and a cairn and offers superb views in all directions. To the west the Isle of Man sits in a shimmering sea: Scafell, Bowfell and other equally impressive peaks form the mountainous skyline to the north-east: Hardknott Pass and Harter Fell lie to the east while to the south-east is Birker Fell. From up on Hooker Crag sea and mountain, salt marsh, fell and valley, woodland and open

Ravenglass terminus of t'La-al Ratty

heath spread in fine array for the eye to behold simply by turning the head. Glorious!

At the gate in the fence the path begins its descent to the south of a tarn half hidden by trees. It enters a walled lane at the bottom of which we turned right along the road from Millom and thus arrived at Ravenglass.

The Romans built Glannaventa as an estuary port just outside modern Ravenglass close to where the rivers, Irt, Mite and Esk reach the sea. It was, in those days, the most important port in the north-west. Agricola used it as a naval base and salt from Cheshire was unloaded there. Today the badly silted harbour attracts great numbers of amateur yachtsment and boat enthusiasts. Apart from one well-preserved building that was part of the bath house, little remains of the Roman town.

Ravenglass sits neatly at the foot of Muncaster Fell between the sand dunes and the sea-shore. In 1209 it was granted a charter by King John to hold a market and for a fair to be held annually in early August. Horse racing was an important part of this fair until *circa* 1813 when it ceased; and today both market and fair are no more, which is a pity.

Lakeland's famous Herdwick sheep were most likely introduced to

195

Cumbria's fells by Norse settlers. But tradition has it that they came ashore at Ravenglass from a wrecked Spanish galleon.

A nearby gullery harbours one of the largest colonies of black-headed gulls in Europe. More than 12,000 pairs are known to nest there. The gullery is closed from 14th May to 1st June but permits to visit at other times can be obtained from Cumbrian County Council at Carlisle. A sand bar prevents access by anything other than small craft but arrangements can be made with local boatmen to ferry small parties to the sanctuary.

The pride and joy of Ravenglass is 't'la-al Ratty' and we savoured the happy prospect of travelling on it to seven miles distant Dalegarth over a pint in the Ratty Arms, the railway's own pub. This delectable tavern is situated in that part of the old station building which once housed the booking office for the Furness line.

The railway museum is on the other side of the car park on the Ratty side of the station. There you can see the remarkable history of the Ravenglass and Eskdale Railway come to life through photos, models, relics and a slide show.

Twelve very smart quarter scale locomotives, some steam, some diesel, pull specially designed open or closed carriages along the seven miles of line, taking forty minutes to complete the journey. We paid our £1.85p single fares, climbed aboard a train of covered carriages pulled by a diesel engine and were on our way.

The line begins in Miterdale, not Eskdale. It does not follow the wide, marshy valley of the Esk. Instead it takes the smaller, slightly higher and less marshy valley of the Mite to the north, tracking first along the edge of the estuary and then across the foot of Muncaster Fell. The view to our left as we skirted the shore line was dominated by the salt marshes of the Mite with, behind, the sand dunes that line the coast as far north as Sellafield.

Five minutes and one mile after leaving Ravenglass we reached Muncaster Mill, a request stop, where there is a beautiful old water-driven corn mill which has been renovated by the Ravenglass and Eskdale Railway Co. for the Eskdale (Cumbria) Trust. In season, 1st April to 31st August, it is open daily except Saturdays and produces a range of traditional stone-ground flours which are available for sale. The mill is not powered by water falling from the fells because that source of supply is poor and unreliable. Its water supply comes along an artificial channel called a leat from a much more dependable lowland river. A clematis montana climbs one of the mill's walls and spreads across a roof to great effect.

The difference in altitude between Ravenglass and Dalegarth is

Cumbrian farmhouse with unusual round chimneys seen from the route of t'La-al Ratty walk

150ft. When the line was built, engineers designed the route to gain height as gradually as possible while keeping it on the narrow strip of land between the boulder clay of the plain, which was unsuitable foundation material, and the steep and craggy side of Muncaster Fell.

During the Ice Age, glaciers scarred and polished Muncaster Fell leaving it barren. When the ice retreated, huge blocks of granite were prised free from the fell and today they litter its lower slopes. It has taken many centuries for the fellside to gain soil and plant over. Even today only a few trees have managed to establish themselves on the upper slopes; and it is left to the bracken to soften the scene.

The old familiar patchwork of stone walls we passed was not built solely for confining cattle. Granite boulders by the hundred thousand had been brought down from the Lakeland fells and deposited randomly along the valley bottoms. When people first began to populate and farm these valleys, including those of the Mite and the Esk, they set about clearing the ground and soon found that making dry stone walls was a very good way of disposing of the unwanted stones.

Irton Road station serves the hamlet of Eskdale Green. As the train approaches it the first view of the Esk Valley is seen ahead. Eskdale Green, like the railway that serves it, is sited on dry ground well above the valley bottom.

Beyond Irton Road station the line rounds the eastern end of Muncaster Fell and keeping to high ground, swings across the gap between it and the high fell that is Miterdale's eastern boundary where it hugs its granite sides. We are now in typical Lakeland scenery which is much more dramatic than anything we have seen since leaving Ravenglass; for now we have steep granite crags towering over us on both sides. Then, suddenly, the River Esk comes into view on our right while to our left a granite quarry hides behind trees and shrubs.

The glacier which pushed down Eskdale all those centuries ago has left much evidence of its journey on the tough granite of Muncaster Fell against which it pressed. Those parts of the rock which faced directly into its path have been polished and smoothed by the tremendous pressure of the ice, while the sheltered parts have retained their roughness. This dramatic testimony was easy to see as we were transported along this final stretch of track to Dalegarth, the end of the line.

The approach to Dalegarth is delightful arboreal and all too soon our sturdy little locomotive, having done its job, sighed to a stop and we all alighted having thoroughly enjoyed our ride in 't'la-al Ratty'.

A pleasant road walk, eastwards from Dalegarth station would have brought us back to our car, near the one mile distant Woolpack: but the witchery of the soft blue sky with its tendrils of high flying cirrus was too much. We set off along the road to Hardknott but turned right at the first crossroads and took the quiet road to St. Catherine's church beside the Esk. From there we retraced our steps by the riverside to the car.

I can describe this walk in two words, *sui generis*, for, truely, this railway associated walk is unique.

29. ROWRAH TO CLEATOR MOOR

Length : 4 miles
Opened : Moor Row to Frizington: for goods traffic -
11th January, 1857
for passenger traffic - 1st July, 1857
Frizington to Lamplugh: for goods traffic -
November, 1862
Frizington to Rowrah: for passenger traffic -
12th February, 1864
Closed : Cleator Moor to Yeathouse: for goods traffic -
4th November, 1963

Yeathouse to Rowrah: for goods traffic -
21st August, 1967
Moor Row to Marron Junction: for passenger traffic -
13th April, 1931

O/S   :   Sheet No.89; Series 1:50,000

> *Tapping the rails as he went by*
> *And driving the slack wedges tight,*
> *He walked towards the morning sky*
> *Between two golden lines of light*
> *That dwindled slowly into one*
> *Sheer golden rail that ran right on*
> *Over the fells into the sun.*
> Wilfrid Gibson.

In the very early days of steam when the only lines were wooden ones found in collieries, men were employed to lay metal plates on them to given them greater durability. These men were called platelayers and were the forerunners of those railway men whose job it was, and is, to lay, fix and maintain the track.

The track was set down on a permanent way, which was so-called to distinguish it from the impermanent way laid during the construction of a new stretch of line.

In order to construct a permanent way large quantities of soil and rock had to be moved simply to neutralise the natural lie of the land and make level what seldom was level. It was largely a matter of digging out and building up, using what were, by our standards, very primitive methods. There were spectacular parts like tunnels and viaducts but the day to day work was usually a progression from embankment to cutting.

Soil brought from a cutting further back down the line was tipped over the end of the slowly growing artificial ridge that was to become the embankment. A tramline was laid from the cutting to the extreme edge of the embankment at which point a strong wooden baulk was fixed across it. Train loads of trucks filled with soil were carried along the tramline to a point some fifty yards back from the baulk where, one by one, the trucks would be detached from the train. Singly, each truck load of soil would be pulled forward by a horse walking not between the rails but alongside them in the manner of a barge horse on a tow path pulling a canal barge. As it came closer to the baulk the horse was made to increase its speed until the truck it was pulling had gained sufficient speed to carry it forward by its own momentum.

199

Then the horse was unhitched and the truck would hurtle forward to the limit of the growing ridge where the baulk would stop it and tip it forward so that the soil was flung over the end of the embankment.

Excavating a cutting, heavier work than building an embankment, was done almost entirely by rows of navvies using pick and shovel. The route of the intended line was marked across the face of the hill through which the cutting was to pass. Once the top soil had been removed a little cutting or gullett, just large enough to accommodate a row of wagons used for earth removal, was dug. These wagons were brought up the gullett for filling by the navvies who were working on the cutting sides just above the temporary line. Once full, the wagons were moved away in horse-drawn trains along the tramlines for use on embankment constructions. Meanwhile as the navvies loaded the wagons with soil the gullett was extended into the hill by more navvies working ahead of the tramlines.

A different and far more dangerous method was used if, because no embankments were being built nearby, there was no use for the soil. It was lifted up the slope cutting walls and dumped at the sides. This was achieved in a dangerous and most spectacular way called 'making the running'. Planks were placed up the sides of the cutting and the strongest of the workmen wheeled barrows of soil along them up the cutting sides. Long ropes were used, one being attached to the wheelbarrow and another to the belt of the man pushing it. Both ropes ran up the cutting side and round a pully at the top before being attached to a horse. When the barrow was loaded a signal was given to the horse driver at the top. The horse moved forward and the man with the loaded wheelbarrow was pulled up the side of the cutting, balancing the barrow ahead of him. All would be well as long as the horse pulled steadily and the man kept his balance. When he reached the cutting top he would tip his load, turn around and return down the plank to the cutting bottom pulling the barrow after him with his back to it while the horse took its weight and kept the rope taut.

However, should the horse slip or falter while the man was climbing the cutting side with his barrow full of soil or if he lost his balance on the muddy plank, he had to throw the loaded barrow to one side of the plank and himself to the other side. This was the best method he had of saving himself. Should barrow and man topple the same way there was a serious risk of the barrow's contents falling on him. It was quite common for a navvy to be thrown down the slope several times but these tough workmen got used to it and quickly became sure footed on the slippery planks.

Apart from the pick and shovel, gunpowder, which was used for

West Cumbria has a complicated network of old railways and this is typified by these two unconnected lines crossing at Rowrah

blasting, was about the only aid the navvies had. By the middle of the 19th century mechanical diggers were known and frequently used on the construction of the American and Canadian railways. But their cost was prohibitive: manpower was much cheaper.

Tunnelling was the most hazardous of all the railway construction jobs and building viaducts, especially in open country was the most spectacular.

There are no tunnels or viaducts between Rowrah and Cleator Moor but the line has some good examples of embankments and cuttings.

Although the word 'navvy', an abbreviation of navigator, was given to the canal builders of the 18th century, it was inherited by the railway men. It was used to describe someone who worked with a pick and shovel as opposed to a bricklayer or a mason. It was slang for railway labourer although some navvies also worked on the road, the docks and reservoirs between railway jobs. Navvies worked together and lived together in lineside encampments. They had prodigious appetites and drank to excess, usually a gallon of beer a day.

Their dress was distinctive: moleskin trousers, double canvas shirts, velveteen square-tailed coats, hobnail boots, white felt hats with upturned brims and gaudy handkerchiefs.

They were known mostly only by their nicknames.

They were paid once a month, usually in a pub; and with money in their pockets they remained in the pub, often for days after pay-day, leaving only when they had drunk until they had nothing left. Drinking was not confined to after work hours. They often worked when they were drunk and on some contracts a navvy would not be given work unless he took part of his pay in beer.

Frequently a farm worker, attracted to railway construction work by the comparatively high wages it paid, became a navvy only to find that the work was far more exhausting than he had expected it to be. It took about a year to turn an agricultural labourer into a navvy for usually the farm worker was an indifferent worker who, unable to stand the pace, would be too exhausted to carry on beyond mid-afternoon. To begin with he would be worth no more than two shillings a day. But, as he gradually got better and could buy better food he would become much stronger and be able to earn better wages.

Navvies working on the Rowrah to Cleator Moor line and beyond were employed by the Whitehaven, Cleator and Egremont Railway which, like the other lines in west Cumbria, was built to carry iron ore.

The length between Rowrah and Cleator Moor was part of the W.C.E. main line which ran from a junction with the Whitehaven and Furness Junction Railway at Mirehouse Junction, two miles south of Workington to the L.N.W.R. Cockermouth and Workington line at Marron Junction, some 16 miles away.

Because it was built across an ore field, the W.C.E. line from Moor Row to Rowrah quickly ran into trouble. The Company experienced that sinking feeling in a big way. Within six year of opening there were fears that subsidence near Cleator Moor could have an adverse effect on traffic over a long period.

On June 8th 1863, powers were obtained for a loop, 1¼ miles long and including a new station for Cleator Moor, to be built to the north of the existing line from Moor Row to Birks Bridge Junction. It was almost ready for use by August 1864, but because of an extended dispute with the Board of Trade over signalling, no passenger trains were diverted to the loop until 19th April 1866. It became known locally as the Bowthorn line.

The original line, which passed through Cleator Moor's first station, remained open for freight and mineral traffic only, and with the station becoming a goods depot. It became known as the Crossfield loop.

Again because of fear of subsidence, a ¾ mile long diversion had to be built as Eskett some two miles up the line from Cleator Moor. So alarming was the situation that in the interest of speed, sanction for the building was given under a Board of Trade certificate rather than through normal Parliamentary channels which would have taken much longer. Yeathouse, a new station, was built on the new line. Eskett station, on the old line, became a goods depot. The old line was truncated as a through route but retained to serve various mines. The deviation was opened in April 1874, for mineral traffic only. Not until 10th June of that year did the Board of Trade allow it to be used by passenger traffic.

Powers were obtained on 2nd August 1875, for a half mile deviation at Frizington following a subsidence at that place.

So the struggle continued. It was part of an almost continuous battle against sinking ground that threatened the permanence of the way itself. Yet despite the Company's fight against subsidence it was decided that the line between Mirehouse and Marron Junction should be doubled to accommodate the steadily increasing traffic. It was a shrewd move because for several years the volume of traffic was enormous.

Of the two bridges that cross the disused line at Rowrah, one does so just to the east of the railway station which is now a private dwelling. You will find the other at the western edge of the hamlet and this makes a good place to begin the walk.

Throughout its length the W.C.E. kept to the narrow band of iron ore lying between the Skiddaw slates of lower Ennerdale to the east and the west Cumbrian coalfields to the west.

It was among the western fells, Ennerdale, Eskdale, Dunnerdale and High Furness that iron ore was first discovered. Then, in the Middle Ages the industry expanded considerably on the coastal plain in the Egremont and Cleator Moor area. But it was not until the middle of the 19th century that the modern haematite pig-iron industry began in Cumberland. In 1841 blast furnaces were opened at Cleator Moor, followed because of expanding trade in the 1880s and '90s, by others at Distington, Maryport and Workington in west Cumberland, Millom to the south and Ulverston and Askam in Furness.

A major factor in the industry's development was its close proximity to the west Cumberland coalfield. So close, in fact, that at one of the Cleator Moor mines coal and iron ore were both raised from the same shaft. Largely because of the development of the iron mines on the coastal plain Workington developed into an industrial town. Other, smaller towns became heavily dependent upon iron mining which, down the years, formed the backbone of west Cumbrian society. The

W.C.E. received a huge percentage of its mineral revenue from hauling iron ore.

Today very few Cumbrians depend upon the production of iron ore for a living; and today the W.C.E. which once so proudly carried it has ceased to exist.

Rowrah, Winder and Frizington station houses are private dwellings, Cleator Moor station is a housing estate and Yeathouse is reduced to platforms and coal drops. But enough evidence remains to link this once busy line to an industry that has left an indelible imprint on the very character of west Cumbrians.

The colour of the evidence is red: becks draining red soil run red: wind blown red dust wedges in cracks in wooden fences, darkening them: red slag heaps are sported by those mines still working. Most are closed and Mother Nature is doing her best with their tips, greening them with coarse grasses. It is an uphill struggle and they still look artificial.

Roughly midway along the walk, where the trackbed curves sharply before leaving a cutting for an embankment, it runs parallel to and less than a quarter of a mile from the River Ehen, which once contained great quantities of horse mussels.

The freshwater horse mussel, *Urio Margaritifera*, used to be plentiful in many rivers - but only in certain ones did it bear pearls. The Ehen, which flows out of Ennerdale and past Egremont to the sea was one such river. It is not known when Ehen's pearl fishing started but in 1692-3 Thomas Patrickson was granted a charter incorporating 'the Company of Pearl Fishers' in the Ehen and the Irt.

Pearls were found in the Ehen at Wath Brow, near Cleator Moor, in 1898 and in 1913 five pearls taken from the river at Wath Brow were displayed in a shop window in Cleator Moor. However, because many of the pearl fishers' operations carried out in the latter part of the 19th century and the first quarter of the 20th century were enveloped in secrecy the number and quality of the pearls taken from the Ehen will never be known. Men who knew a good thing when they saw it had no desire to be prosecuted for trespass by riparian landowners so they kept their mouths shut. Yet despite these walls of silence the Ehen achieved prominence for its pearls during the immediate post World War I period, the pearl fishing boom in the river Ehen was at its height during the General Strike of 1926.

Today there is no mussel fishing in the Ehen; or so the locals would have you believe.

The track crosses the A5086 and continues in a westerly direction to the north of Cleator Moor to where a secondary road crosses it. This road marks the end of the walk. Turn left along it and it will take you into Cleator Moor.

30. ROWRAH AND KELTON FELL (MINERAL) RAILWAY

Length : 3½ miles
Opened : January, 1877
Closed : 1933
O/S   : Sheet No.89; Series 1:50,000

> *Bit furst I'd wish for peace of mind,*
> *Wi conscience free frae owt 'at's wrang,*
> *An' than, whativver comes amiss,*
> *I cudden't be unhappy lang.*
> *John Richardson.*

The view from near the top end of the Kelton Fell mineral line stirs the soul. From close to where it bends northwards to face Murton Fell the eye is caught by Ennerdale Water, cradled to the north by Herdus and the High Stile ridge and to the south by Ennerdale Fell, guarded by that magnificent trio of mountains Great Gable, Pillar and Steeple.

Certainly the line, in its day, had been a scenic one; but the splendid views had played no part in its *raison d'être*. It had been built to carry iron ore from the mines on Kelton Fell and Knock Murton to Rowrah for onward transportation to where they could be converted into iron.

Iron ore was being mined in the Lakeland fells long before the industry was developed along the coastal plain. The workings were mostly small and did not scarify their surroundings to any appreciable degree. By the middle of the 19th century a lot of explorative work, though little development, was taking place on Knock Murton and mines were being worked on nearby Kelton Fell.

On 4th November 1854, the mines of Kelton Fell became the scene of a cold-blooded murder. Isaac Turner, an employee of S. and J. Lindow, who were working the Kelton Fell mines, was taking the wages up to them when he was set upon by Thomas Munroe, an 18 year old miner from Kirkland, and killed. Munroe was subsequently charged with the crime, tried, found guilty, sentenced to death and executed.

During the second half of the 19th century attempts were made to mine iron ore throughout the whole of the Ennerdale and Lamplugh area. This expansion attracted more and more agricultural labourers

205

who were leaving the land to better their lot. In 1862 the lowest wages paid by J. Lindow at his Woodend and Gutterby pits were 4/- per day but 'an energetic, clever man' could earn as much as 7/- per day. The average weekly wage was 24/- for an eight hour day. Agriculture could not compete with that. In many of the households in the Lamplugh parish and in the expanding hamlet of Kirkland the chief wage earner was connected with mining for iron ore in one way or another.

One disadvantage to fellside mining was that not only had the veins of ore to be found and mined, they had to be carted along unmetalled and often well nigh impassable roads to their destinations.

For many years William Baird & Co. the Glasgow ironmasters, had shown an interest in opening up haematite veins in the Skiddaw Slates around Knock Murton and the extension in 1862 of the Whitehaven, Cleator and Egremont line through Rowrah, a mere 3½ miles west of the area they were now working, intensified that interest. However, high rates at first discouraged the construction of a connecting line. Then, in 1874, William Baird & Co., and other mining interests sought the necessary Parliamentary approval for the building of a line from the mines to Rowrah. There was some opposition to this proposal by local landowners fearing that the line would interfere with the workings of their estates, but most of the inhabitants of Kelton township were in favour of it. Thirty-nine local householders and farmers petitioned Parliament saying that 'the public highway from Rowrah station to the village of Kirkland and to Kelton Fell is totally unfit and inadequate for the heavy mineral traffic which has for some time passed over it rendering it dangerous, and in wet weather almost impassable for foot passengers, cattle and vehicles'. They added that the proposed new line 'was generally and substantially supported by the community of the district.'

The necessary powers were obtained on 16th July 1874 and in 1877 the Rowrah and Kelton Fell (Mineral) Railway was built at a cost of £25,000. It climbed steeply out of Rowrah on a ruling gradient of 1 in 40 and terminated at Knock Murton mine 900 feet above sea level, having climbed more than 300 feet in 3½ miles. The Barrow Haematite Steel Co., supplied 'slightly defective steel rails' for the line which also served several limestone quarries as well as a small coal depot at Kirkland. Baird's provided the locomotives and the rolling stock.

The opening date should have been 11th November 1876, but because of disagreements regarding the junction with the Whitehaven, Cleator and Egremont at Rowrah the opening was postponed until the middle of January 1877.

As a direct result of the continued disagreement between the R. and

K.F. and the W.C.E., the R and K.F. turned to the Cleator and Workington Junction railway which on 5th May 1977, agreed to build a 6½ miles long connecting branch from Distington to an end-on junction with the mineral railway at Rowrah. The line was authorised on 4th July 1878, and opened on 1st May 1882. It became known as 'Baird's line' and was noted for its severe gradients. Because it offered more competitive rates than the W.C.E. it was soon taking most of the R. and K.F. traffic.

The arrival of the R. and K.F. line gave a much needed impetus to Kelton's iron ore industry which for some years prior to the line's opening had been working at a disadvantage, since the only means of moving the ore was by carting. The mineral agents' reports tell the story: 1872 - 14,000 tons: 1873 - 22,000 tons: 1877, with the line in operation - 30,000 tons: 1888 - 46,000 tons.

Baird and Co's., workings at Knock Murton and Kelton became the tenth largest mines in the country, raising, in 1882, 61,153 tons. They couldn't have done that without the R. and K.F. which played a large part in bringing prosperity to the area.

Sadly it was short-lived. By the turn of the century the iron ore industry was in decline. Miners were leaving the workings in droves to seek a better life in the Transvaal. In 1900 the output of iron ore from the mines in the Kirkland area had dropped to 14,400 tons and Rowrah limestone became the mainstay of the R. and K.F. line. The situation improved somewhat just before World War I when, in 1913, 15,257 tons were produced.

At that time an ambitious attempt was made to increase iron ore production by cutting a 1,000 yards long, 540 feet deep cross-cut from Kelton C vein towards Kirkland village. Workable quantities of ore were found near the village but lack of capital prevented its exploitation and Kirkland missed out on the boom generated by the demands of war production which was of great benefit to many of the other west Cumberland iron ore mines.

On 9th April 1914, the Kelton Fell mines were abandoned.

Baird and Co. having lost interest in the line tried to sell it and finally managed to do so in 1921. The selling price was a mere £750 and the purchasers were the Whitehaven Haematite Iron Co. of Cleator Moor and the Salter Quarry Co.

By 1927 traffic had dwindled to almost nothing. It closed in 1933 and was dismantled in 1934.

Today with most of the underbridges removed, the deep cutting on the outskirts of Kirkland somewhat tangled with undergrowth and quite a bit of it incorporated into farmland, it looks a bit like the conditions that made it what it is. But don't let that put you off: the whole route is walkable and, if need be, the cutting at Kirkland can be avoided simply by going along its edge where the views are good to begin with and keep getting better.

A few tomorrows hence important improvements are likely to be carried out along the old line because the local council, no doubt aware of its potential as a nature trail with strong mining associations, is seriously thinking of having it developed as such.

Apart from its association with iron ore mining, the R. and K.F. has another and, in some way, more important claim to fame in the shape of some very special hayfields close to Rowrah. No other hayfield in west Cumbria is as fine as these; and for this important reason. Artificial additives have never been used on them and consequently they contain a range of neutral grassland species typical of the haymeadows of old. In them are to be found yellow rattle, ox-eye daisy, eye-bright, the common spotted orchid and some rarities. These grasses have spilled over onto the trackbed which is now similar to its adjacent hayfields. Here, near Rowrah, are the last remnants of the old hay meadows of west Cumbria. All the others have changed out of all recognition because of present day farming techniques. They are a rare and important part of our heritage, these sweet, old fashioned meadows, and oh! what an attraction they could become to future walkers along the R. and K.F. line! For they evoke a more gentle age when life was less complicated and the environment in many ways was more exciting, more romantic, more pleasing than it is today.

Evergreens growing in serried profusion on the eastern and northern sides of Knockmurton Fell and adjoining Lamplugh Fell overwhelm the thin cluster of deciduous trees marking the top end of the R. and K.F. line. The buildings they once sheltered have long since gone and little remains of the line's nameless terminus. It is a remote and lonely railhead, haunted by the ghosts of long dead miners who worked the haematite levels and the railwaymen who served them.

31. HARRINGTON AND LOWCA LIGHT RAILWAY

Length : 4½ miles
Opened : for goods traffic - unknown
          for passenger traffic - 2nd June, 1913
Closed : for passenger traffic - 31st May, 1926
          for goods traffic - 23rd May, 1973
O/S   : Sheet No. 89; Series 1:50,000

208

> *In our black stable by the sea,*
> *Five and twenty stall you see--*
> *Five and twenty strong are we:*
> Robert Louis Stevenson.

The Harrington and Lowca Light Railway has two claims to fame. The passenger service it provided was one of the most obscure in the country and its 1 in 17 gradient was the steepest in Britain to have carried adhesion - worked passenger trains.

Throughout its life its fortunes were inextricably tied to west Cumberland's iron and steel industry in general and to Harrington in particular. Harrington, along with many other west Cumberland industrial towns like Workington, Frizington and Parton, is an Anglican town. In the 7th century, when the ancient Kingdom of Strathclyde began to crumble, two small Anglican Kingdoms, Deira and Bernicia, became established along the north-east coast. Settlers from Bernicia infiltrated along the Eden Valley and became established along the west Cumberland coast. Being primarily an agricultural people, they kept to the coastal regions and left the fells and mountains of the Lakeland to the Norse.

The narrow coastal strip remained predominantly agricultural until the middle of the 19th century when the haematite pig iron industry arrived. Blast furnaces were opened at Cleator Moor in 1841 and during the next decade more were set up, including one at Harrington.

With the development of the west Cumberland iron and steel trade the population of the region increased dramatically. But the new found prosperity did not last long. The slow decline began towards the end of the 1880s, brought about by the perfection of the Gilchrist process of steel making which broke the monopoly enjoyed by haematite and enabled the use of cheaper Spanish ores.

Circa 1877 the Cleator and Workington Junction Railway opened a new branch running south-west from Harrington Junction for about 1½ miles to Rose Hill where it joined an existing mineral railway that climbed from Harrington Harbour on a gradient of 1 in 15. From Rose Hill the gradient eased slightly to 1 in 17. Its destination was Lowca colliery, sited high above the cliffs, overlooking the sea. The mineral line the C. and W.J. joined at Rose Hill was operated by the Workington Iron and Steel Co.

In 1909 the Workington Iron and Steel Co. incorporated Derwent, Harrington, Lowther, Moss Bay and Solway ironworks, Harrington Harbour, a part interest in Workington's dock and harbour and

Lowca colliery. Straight away the new company commissioned a coke and by-product plant at Lowca and expanded the colliery. Then on 7th June 1911, it reached an agreement whereby its own locomotives could run to Lowca colliery from Derwent Iron Works using the C. and W.J. and Harrington branches to reach the existing mineral line from Harrington Harbour at Rose Hill.

Workmen's trains operating from Workington to Lowca colliery were so successful it was decided to make the line public by transforming the private line from Rose Hill Junction into the Harrington and Lowca Light Railway.

On 2nd June 1913, the passenger service commenced with four trains each way providing the service. The Furness Railway provided the locomotives and one coach for the general public. The miners rode in coaches provided by their own company.

Frequently a Furness Railway 0-6-0 S.T. would tackle the 1 in 17 incline, heading a train which was banked by another locomotive which at the same time was pulling its own train which, in turn, was banked. What a terrifying sight it must have made, clattering noisily up the steep gradient, belching smoke and steam and showering sparks high in the air!

The line closed for passenger traffic on 31st May 1926.

Mineral traffic continued to climb the 1 in 17 gradient, known as Copperas Hill, until 23rd May 1973, when closure was forced upon it because that part of the Parton to Distington line giving access to Lowca also closed.

Harrington is larger than I had expected. Formerly a small fishing port with a harbour that was built in 1760, the old village is surrounded by modern housing estates. Today, slag heaps give it a down at heel appearance. Even the church, overlooking the old village, looks forbidding.

Harrington Junction lies a little to the north of High Harrington, at Map Reference 002257, and it was from there that I set off along a firm trackbed to Lowca where my back-up vehicle would be waiting.

At first the way was westerly, towards the sea; but after passing under two bridges in quick succession, crossing the B5296 and going under another bridge, the track took a southerly course, above and roughly parallel to the Whitehaven Junction line, the cliffs and the Irish Sea; and kept to it.

Rose Hill station has gone now but the trackbed down to Harrington Harbour remains and is walkable. However, the bridge over the Whitehaven Junction line has been removed. The remaining stations, Copperas Hill, Micklam and Lowca have not a lot to offer. But don't let that put you off. The line is well worth walking, if only for the fine views over the sea.

Lowca is dingy. Its slag heaps, showing strong mining associations, give it a fairy tale look - Grimm. The church at its southern end is the only nice building I saw there; and it belongs to neighbouring Moresby.

The village's mining links are very intersting but it is the restless, ever changing sea that pulls this track out of the ordinary and makes walking it a pleasure.

32. DISTINGTON - WORKINGTON

Length	2 miles
Opened	for goods traffic - 1st October, 1879:
	Cleator Moor to Harrington Rose Hill
	for passenger traffic - 1st October, 1879:
	Cleator Moor to Workington Central
Closed	for passenger traffic - 13th April, 1931
	Cleator Moor to Siddick
	for goods traffic - 15th June, 1964:
	Cleator Moor to Calva Junction
O/S	Sheet No.89; Series 1:50,000

> *Behold it comes, loud panting from afar,*
> *As if it lived, and of its own fierce will*
> *Ran a free race with wild winds blowing shrill!*
> *Charles MacKay.*

This is the track of the ironmasters, this line that came to be built in an area already close to saturation point with railway lines. Behind it lies a tale of avarice in high places. This is the story of the track of the ironmasters and of how it played an important part in the romance of the railways.

Thinking that its huge share of the west Cumberland iron ore traffic was secure, the directors of the London and North Western Railway adopted a policy aimed at getting as much revenue as they could with as little effort as possible. Passengers were charged exhorbitant fares for the privilege of travelling in carriages so old that the L.N.W.R. had condemned their use on the main line. Weak management prevailed and unpunctuality became an accepted part of the system. It was an intolerable way to run a railway because the travelling public resented being fleeced and treated like dirt. Furthermore, while passengers were soaked, freight charges hit the roof.

The L.N.W.R. was not the only culprit. The Whitehaven, Cleator and Egremont and the Furness Railways were just as ruthless, making equally excessive charges.

In 1873 the bubble burst with the W.C.E. bringing out another round of price increases. It was the last straw. The leading west Cumberland ironmasters decided that Euston's tyranny must stop. That autumn a meeting was called by the West Cumberland Iron and Steel Co., the Moss Bay Haematite Iron Co. and James Bain and Co. of Harrington Ironworks, at which a Bill was promoted for a railway from a junction with the W.C.E. at Cleator Moor to a junction with the L.N.W.R. Whitehaven Junction Railway at Siddick north of Workington, with branches at Harrington and Workington.

The L.N.W.R. opposed the Bill but without success and the Cleator and Workington Junction Railway Company was incorporated in 1876. On 6th April 1877, an agreement with the Furness Railway, that it would undertake to work the C. and W.J. from its opening for a third of the receipts, was signed. It was confirmed by an Act of Parliament the following June.

A provisional committee was appointed whose job it was to find the best route for this new line. It was chaired by the 3rd Earl of Lonsdale with Henry Frazer Curwen of Workington as vice-chairman. Since the L.N.W.R. already held the most obvious coastal route they chose a high-level one diverging from the W.C.E. just north of Cleator Moor. The line climbed steeply to a summit 460 feet above sea level near Moresby Parks before descending along 1 in 70 gradients through Distington to join the L.N.W.R. at Siddick. Opened in October 1879, it was double track with stations at Cleator Moor, Moresby Parks, Distington, High Harrington and Workington Central.

Built at a cost of £150,000, this 11½ miles long line came to be known as 'the track of the ironmasters' because most of the capital was raised by parties associated with the iron industry.

The passenger service, which in 1880 was extended to Siddick, ran four trains each way, weekdays only. There was no Sunday passenger service. The journey for the 11½ miles took half an hour to cover which was reasonable because of the hilly terrain through which the line passed.

At the Siddick end of the line a footbridge gave direct access to the beach from where local shellfish called covens were taken home, boiled, winkled out with a pin and eaten.

Year by year the line's passenger traffic grew, despite its slow and infrequent timetable, until in 1911 a total of 200,000 passengers were carried on it. This very gratifying state of affairs was matched by the line's mineral traffic which by 1911 had reach two million tons per annum.

The freight trains themselves were colourful, diverse affairs for the individual wagons, being privately owned by various collieries and ironworks, came in all shapes and sizes. This situation was not peculiar to the C. and W.Jn.R.: privately owned wagons were used throughout the whole of the railway system. Not until the outbreak of World War II was the use of privately owned mineral wagons ended.

With the west Cumberland ironworks working at almost full capacity mineral traffic on the C. and W.Jn.R. was very busy through-out World War I and this continued into the 1920s. Then, because of changed economic conditions, this area, so far removed from an industrial hinterland and heavily dependent on iron ore and coal had a major disaster on its hands. Much of the iron ore traffic which had been carried over the track of the ironmaster's lines from the Cleator area was re-routed via Whitehaven.

In 1923 all the lines in west Cumberland apart from the Port Carlisle and Silloth branches came under the umbrella of the L.M.S. So the C. and W.Jn.R. 95% of whose shares were held by the United Steel Co. lost its independence and the track of the ironmasters its identity.

The trackbed from Cleator Moor to Distington is in private owner-ship and much overgrown. But from Distington to Workington, this walk, the trackbed is first class for both walking and cycling.

Where once five lines met at Distington the A595(T) crosses the old trackbed on an overbridge that marks the southern end of the walk. Take the track running north-west from the bridge along an embank-ment, ignoring the one that curves south-west into a cutting almost at the start of the walk or you could end up in Lowca. The going is easy and, since the line was double track, along a broad trackbed. After about two thirds of a mile, just beyond the first of two overbridges, the track enters a cutting as it curves towards the north and its destina-tion, Workington. It emerges from this cutting close to the second bridge to the east of High Harrington. Just beyond High Harrington the old trackbed of the Harrington branch cuts in obliquely from the west. Another half mile and you are in Workington.

33. COCKERMOUTH AND WORKINGTON RAILWAY

Length :   8½ miles, of which only a short length at Workington

		is worth walking
Opened	:	28th April, 1847
Closed	:	for goods traffic - 1st June, 1964
		for passenger traffic - 18th April, 1966
O/S	:	Sheet No.89; Series 1:50,000

> *Smoke trails from an engine.*
> *Before a traveller's eye*
> *Blue against the dark earth*
> *Brown in blue sky:*
> > *Witter Bynner.*

West Cumbria is a place apart, cut off from the rest of England by the mountains of Lakeland. Saddled with this geographical handicap it might have remained isolated but for its rich mineral resources and the ingenuity of its people.

Coal was being mined around Whitehaven as early as the 13th century, but it was not until the 17th century, when the Lowthers came into possession of the area, that its systematic development began. By the early 18th century Whitehaven had over 2,000 inhabitants making it the third largest town in the north of England after Newcastle and York.

Further north, Maryport's prosperity under the guidance of the Senhouse family had increased to such a degree that by the late 1830s almost 100,000 tons of coal were being exported annually through the harbour. Railway fever had by now gripped the nation and Humphrey Senhouse, realising its potential, took steps to have a line built from Maryport to Carlisle. This coincided with attempts by the rival Lowthers for a larger scheme that would give Whitehaven a rail link with Carlisle and beyond. The Whitehaven proposal came to nothing; the Maryport one worked and the Maryport and Carlisle Railway was formed with George Stephenson as engineer.

The line's early years were troubled ones, due largely to the incompetence of its officials. Then John Addison was appointed the Company's secretary, general manager and engineer, a position he was to hold for twenty-seven years. Under his direction the Maryport and Carlisle gained a stability which was to provide the base for the Company's amazing prosperity in the 1870s and 80s.

As the railways continued to expand it became increasingly obvious that an extension from Maryport to Whitehaven could not be long delayed. In a report commissioned by Lord Lowther, George Stephenson and F.Foster strongly advocated that the extension should

214

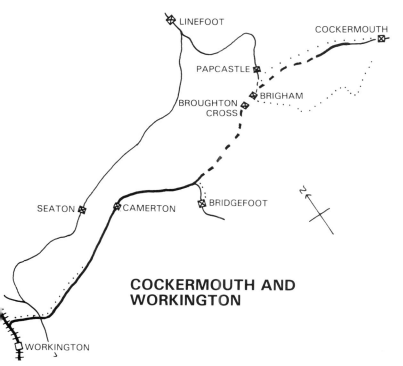

be made. The cost would be £80,000 and failure to construct the line would lead to Maryport harbour being improved to such an extent that trade from Whitehaven would suffer. Lord Lowther was quick to act on the report's finding and the line was built. Now the only large town in west Cumberland without any railway link was Cockermouth, an agricultural town of some 5,000 inhabitants.

The Cockermouth and Workington Railway Company was incorporated on 21st July 1845, with a capital of £80,000 and the line was opened in 1847. It was 8½ miles long and followed the valley of the Derwent, crossing the river five times before connecting with the coast line at Derwent Junction. Because the double track line kept to the flat floor of the Derwent Valley, no heavy engineering was required. There were wayside stations at Brigham, Broughton Cross, Camerton and Workington Bridge.

At Brigham the line's constructors hit a major problem in the person of John Wordsworth, son of William, the greatest of the Lakeland poets. John was the vicar of Brigham and the planned route was through the vicarage garden, between the house and the river. This was abhorrent to him and he angrily demanded compensation in the form of a new vicarage to be built within a quarter of a mile of the original complete with a stable, other outbuildings and a garden of not less than ½ an acre. On top of this he demanded, and got, £5 for every month between the beginning of the building of the railway and the completion of the new vicarage, together with £50 removal expenses. John Wordsworth, a true chip off the old block, might have had his head in heaven but his feet were firmly planted on earth.

Besides providing a passenger service, the line's main function was the transportation of agricultural produce from all points along it and coal from a colliery near Camerton. Indeed the Camerton coalfield which the Cockermouth and Workington had opened up provided it with some three quarters of its traffic.

The line opened as a purely local concern until, in 1865, the Cockermouth, Keswick and Penrith Railway was opened. Then it became the first link in a line built to connect west Cumberland with Penrith and County Durham.

Like the Maryport and Carlisle, the Cockermouth and Workington got off to a bad start. Its secretary and general manager, John Dodds, was so lackadaisical that under his slipshod direction both the permanent way and the rolling stock fell into serious disrepair. As a direct consequence of this the C. and W. Board was obliged to spend large sums of money simply to rectify matters.

The coal used in the Company's five locomotives caused them to belch black smoke onto the passengers, leaving them, at the end of a journey, with dirt impregnated clothes and smutty features that matched their dark thoughts. Coke, they vehemently declared, not coal, should have fuelled the locomotives and they called the directors skinflints for not using the cleaner method of propulsion.

The same year that saw the opening of the C.K. and P. Railway saw an attempt by the Furness Railway to gain control of the full length of the line between Carnforth and Carlisle along the coast. Only the Whitehaven Junction section separated it from the Maryport and Carlisle line at Maryport. To stop any attempt by the Furness Railway to gain control of the Whitehaven Junction the rival L.N.W.R. presented Bills for the absorption of the Cockermouth and Workington Railway and the Whitehaven Junction. As a direct consequence of this both lines were amalgamated with the L.N.W.R. in 1866. Thus the ambition of the F.R. Board to control the entire coastal route was thwarted.

We arrived in Cockermouth and parked on the site of Cockermouth station, now a car park, and went to explore this pleasant Cumbrian town, which was once the eastern terminus of the Cockermouth and Workington line.

Cockermouth is the birthplace of William Wordsworth, undisputed King of the Lakeland poets. He came into the world in a house on Main Street in 1770. Wordsworth House, as it has come to be known, was built in 1745. It is a pleasant building which still contains its original staircase, fireplaces, plaster ceilings and panelling. It houses some china collections and a Turner painting. The garden at the rear of the house is mentioned in Wordsworth's 'Prelude'.

Although the old line from just west of Cockermouth to within half a mile of Marrow Junction has now become part of the A66(T), the car park which was once the town's railway station deserves attention. For it makes a good start for a pleasant circular walk, some six miles long; a diversion that is particularly well worth walking because of its interesting associations.

On leaving the car park take the A5086 south, south-westwards for 1½ miles to where, on the right, a farm road leads north-west for a quarter of a mile, past Moorland Close where, in 1764, Fletcher Christian was born. It was he who, on 28th April 1789, led the mutiny on *H.M.S. Bounty.*

Just beyond Moorland Close the way is left E.S.E. for ¾ mile to Eaglesfield village, birthplace of Robert Eaglesfield who became confessor to Edward III's Queen Philippa. He founded Queen's College, Oxford and was buried there in 1349.

In 1766 John Dalton, Eaglesfield's most famous son was born. He was educated at the village school, became a school teacher and then taught maths and physical science at New College, Manchester. He was a member of the Royal Society and other learned societies and lectured at the Royal Institution. He published his *New System of Chemical Philosophy* in 1808-10. Besides achieving real fame as the first developer of the atomic theory he is remembered for his law that the total pressure exerted by a mixture of gases is equal to the sum of the pressures which each gas would alone exert in the same space. Colour blind himself, he investigated colour blindness and made a prolonged series of meteorological observations over 57 years. He died in 1844; and the village church, which stands away from the village, close to the A5086 is called the John Dalton Memorial Church. It was erected by the Royal Society to commemorate this highly talented man.

We took the road leading from the western edge of the village to a T junction and turned right along a country road to Brigham, 'the meadow by the bridge', just over a mile away.

Our way back to Cockermouth was along another country road to our right as we entered the village. But first we continued northwards to have a look at its church.

We covered the two miles or so back to Cockermouth using another minor road in preference to the A66(T) and so completed a most interesting and informative walk: a walk we would probably have missed had the disused line westwards from Cockermouth not become part of the A66(T).

There being not a lot of railway memorabilia to see at Cockermouth, we took the A66(T) westwards and drove to Nepgill, from where we walked along the Whitehaven, Cleator and Egremont, northwards to its triangular junction with the C. & W.R.

A plate girder bridge spans the River Marron, west of which the trackbed is walkable for about a mile. Then the Derwent gets in the way. The railway bridges, all five of them, have been removed. Only the abutments remain. So it was back to the car and on - to Workington, where the trackbed has been landscaped, making a pleasant riverside walk.

34. KESWICK - THRELKELD - LATRIGG CIRCULAR

Length :   9½ miles of which 3½ miles are along the trackbed of
              the C.K. and P.
Opened :   Cockermouth to Penrith: all traffic - 2nd January, 1865
Closed :   Workington to Penrith: for goods traffic - 1st June, 1964
              Keswick to Penrith: for passenger traffic -
              6th March, 1972
O/S   :   Sheet Lake District Tourist Map

> *Far beyond shine grassy uplands;*
> *Dense the mist lies deep below;*
> *Touching heaven are rugged hill-tops.*
> *Streaked with fire and capped with snow.*
> *Francis Bennock.*

Keswick today is a Lakeland honeypot: yet up to the coming of the railway it was an acquiescent township still heavily dependent on its

KESWICK, THRELKELD & LATRIGG CIRCULAR

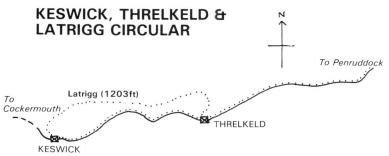

stage-coach traffic for its links with the outside world. When, in 1865, the railway arrived its directors, fully aware of the town's superb setting, ringed by lakes and mountains, were quick to promote its tourist trade. But when, in 1866, the number of passengers carried on excursion trains doubled those of the previous year the railway's directors became concerned for Keswick's rather staid image and decided against promoting special excursion trains in the future. This aspect of the Board's policy remained throughout the life of the Company and largely because of it Keswick's middle class image was retained.

Since discerning visitors demand good hotels, the railway's Board decided to build a first class hotel next to the station with private access to it. Built at a cost of about £11,000, the Keswick Hotel, as it is called, was completed in 1869 and leased to the Keswick Hotel Company. With seventy-six guest rooms, portraits of famous artists on the stained glass doors and windows of the conservatory and more, this time of the Lakeland poets, on the dining room windows, the Keswick Hotel rivalled the Royal Oak, which for many years had been the smartest place in town. Today the Keswick Hotel continues in business but both station and railway are no more.

A model shop and a model railway are housed in that part of the station still remaining. The way to them, and to what remains of the rest of the station, is through the main entrance. If this is closed, retrace your steps to where, near the station end of the access road, a path leads past a goods shed, over a derelict platform to a broad, flattened area where once stood platforms and associated buildings. It is here that this very exciting and most unusual railway walk begins.

The excitement begins right from the word 'go' when the River Greta is crossed for the first of eight times as the course of the old C. K. and P. line is followed along the full length of a beautiful, arboreal

219

Tunnel near Threlkeld

ravine. This gorge, through which the river loops and twists, is so thickly wooded that when viewed from above few traces of the old line, apart from its bow-string, girder bridges, can be seen. It is an ornithologist's delight, with blackbirds, thrushes, wood pigeons, chaffinches, pied-wagtails, dippers and blue tits being among the more common species to nest there.

Three friends and I walked the route one winter's day. With the river, an access road and some houses below us, on our left, we continued along an embankment and came to a wayside halt which looked as though time had passed it by. We did likewise, went under a bridge and were immediately confronted with an unexpected sight: the trackbed suddenly shot up at an angle so acute that no engine could possibly have mounted it. This puzzled us somewhat, but soon all became clear. The A66 Keswick bypass sweeps across the valley just beyond this point and the abrupt change in the height of the old trackbed is a direct result of associated landscaping.

Now the way is over a stile and under the bridge carrying the A66, beyond which the path climbs to road level before descending to the erstwhile trackbed, joining it close to where the original track entered a tunnel.

On the approach to this tunnel the track had been constructed on a rocky foundation so close to the river that strengthening buttresses were needed to prevent the line sliding into the dark water some way below. So, what with the line crossing the Greta eight times and with two tunnels, cuttings through rock and a stone buttress having to be built, this section of the C.K. and P. must have cost a great deal of money.

It was the heel of winter with snow lying on those parts of the track the warming sunlight could not reach when we stood on the buttressed section and watched a dipper seeking food. The exposed mid-stream rock on which it stood wore a collar of ice and following four weeks of severe frost, ice-rind clung to the riverside.

The Lake District Special Planning Board maintains the route from Keswick to Threlkeld and has made handrailed footpaths across all the bridges. Further, it has promised to maintain them as long as the bridges remain safe for pedestrians.

Crossing the Greta for the second time since leaving Keswick station, we saw, straight ahead, the bulk of Blencathra which reminded us that despite the trees crowding the trackway we were still deep in Lakeland's fell country.

But always it was the river that held the eye, splashing along its icy, boulder-strewn bed as it had for centuries. Upstream of where we made our third crossing, using a girder bridge built on the slant, the aspect became more open with the river sweeping around a broad piece of level, treeless ground. The overall effect was so pleasing we tarried awhile, letting the harmony of the place flow over us; and felt the better for it.

At the various places along the way nest boxes have been fixed to young trees by the Lake District Planning Board who are to be

Bow Girder bridge on Lonscale Fell. Keswick-Threlkeld section

congratulated on their positive concern for the wildlife of the area.

Two miles upstream from Keswick a tributary, Glenderaterra Beck, flows from the north into the Greta where yet another bow-string bridge spans it. An old pack-horse bridge crosses the feeder just before the confluence and the contrast between the two bridges is very profound.

Anyone who so wishes can leave the trackbed here, cross the pack-horse bridge and return to Keswick through Brundholme Woods. But with more thrills ahead I suspect that few avail themselves of it.

It takes little to fire the imagination and on a walk such as this the stimulants are infinite. This is as it should be because imagination is the highest kite that can fly. When you have nothing but dreams that is all you think about, all that matters, all that takes you away from the humdrummery.

The next crossing, this time where the river makes a particularly light loop, is followed almost at once by the short Wescoe Wood tunnel which, in turn, is very quickly followed by yet another river crossing. Then, some three quarters of a mile further on and after yet one more river crossing, the trackbed is left behind, the clear way ahead being along a path which leads steeply to the A66 Threlkeld bypass.

The way is now left along the bypass to a nearby Threlkeld road sign and left again, gently uphill, into the village. Continue through it, past the school, to Town Head Farm where turn left in front of it and follow a well marked way through a series of fields, using the stiles as guides, to the hamlet of Wescoe.

Threlkeld, 'the spring of the thralls', snuggles nicely into Blencathra, its older buildings steadily losing ground to modern development. Its church, St. Mary's, was built in 1777 to replace a thatched one which replaced an even earlier one. At weddings, in accordance with local custom, the local youngsters tie together the churchyard gates and refuse to open them again until the best man responds by showering them with coins. Bountiful largesse augurs well for the marriage.

Find a church and you have found a pub. Threlkeld has two, The Horse and Farrier and The Salutations.

Wescoe has none; but it has more than its fair share of superb views in all directions and the approach from Threlkeld is a spanker, across a patchwork of irregular pastures fashioned by the crazy traceries of hedges and dry stone walls.

Leave Wescoe along the right-hand lane which climbs past Derwent Folds and descend to Glenderaterra Beck. Magnificent views will accompany you all the way and the wooded gorge down which the old line used to run is seen to advantage.

Cross the beck on a narrow bridge and take the lane ahead that climbs steeply up the wooded beckside to open ground. The surrounding views are absolutely delightful and the way to the top of Latrigg is easily identified.

It was while making this long approach to Latrigg's summit that our attention was drawn towards a buzzard making lazy circles in the blue sky above. I felt privileged to watch this proud bird gliding on a thermal, now clearly seen in the void, now rendered invisible by the sun's brilliance.

When close to the summit of Latrigg the direct ascent of Skiddaw from Keswick is clearly visible to the north as is the Hawell monument which was erected as a memorial to three members of the Hawell family, all of whom were shepherds.

Latrigg is a pastoral David at the foot of Skiddaw, a rough fell Goliath. Yet despite its lack of stature - the summit is 1,203ft. above sea level - the views to the north embracing the bottom end of Bassenthwaite Lake, southwards across Keswick and Derwent Water to the Jaws of Borrowdale and beyond, eastwards beyond Blencathra to

WALKING NORTHERN RAILWAYS — WEST

Cross Fell on the distant horizon and westwards to Whinlatter, are breathtaking. Little wonder that this particular walk is a firm favourite with the locals.

From the broad top of Latrigg we have a bird's eye view of Brundholme Woods through which we had begun the walk and they looked as good from this angle as they had from the trackbed itself.

The ways down from the summit are manifold, some being long, some short. We opted for one of the longer ones; a favourite descent south-westerly from the summit, first down open grassland then through woods to Spooney Green Lane. As the descent was made the bridge over the Keswick bypass was clearly seen and Spooney Green Lane crosses it. At the town end of the lane, at a T junction, we turned left along a tarmac road then shortly before it turns right to go under the defunct railway cut across open ground on the right. This very quickly brought us to Keswick station and the completion of a magic circle of walk.

35. THRELKELD - PENRUDDOCK

Length : 7 miles
Opened : Cockermouth to Penrith: all traffic - 2nd January, 1865
Closed : Workington to Penrith: for goods traffic - 1st June, 1964
           Keswick to Penrith: for passenger traffic -
           6th March, 1972
O/S   : Sheet Lake District Tourist Map

> *Whizzing through the mountains,*
> *Buzzing o'er the vale --*
> *Bless me! this is pleasant,*
> *Riding on the rail.*
>   *John G. Saxe.*

Although not as spectacular as the adjoining Greta gorge, this section of the Cockermouth, Keswick and Penrith railway between Threlkeld and Penruddock is, nevertheless, particularly suited to walkers. The trackbed is airy, crosses some fine open country and offers excellent views of the fells on Lakeland's eastern periphery, those of Blencathra, or Saddleback, to give it its Sunday name, being especially good. From the old line this mountain's distinctive saddle shape is clearly identified. In the distance ahead, walking eastwards, are the Pennines at their highest and most enigmatic. Surrounded by

224

such granduer, the line, when operational, was one of the most scenic routes in England. Yet because the Board of the C.K. and P. had insisted on maintaining Keswick's middle class image this appealing feature of the line was not promoted. Now the track has been lifted and what remains is a trackbed that offers very impresive views of a dramatic and varied landscape.

The C.K. and P. line, the only one to go right through Lakeland, was a late starter, the reason being that the area had little to offer in the way of traffic.

All this changed when, in 1857-8, the Stockton and Darlington Railway (South Durham and Lancashire Union and Eden Valley) route was authorised to Clifton, south of Penrith. For this development offered prospects of considerable freight traffic from the south Durham coalfields to the developing iron industry of west Cumberland.

The C.K. and P Company was incorporated on 1st August 1861, with a capital of £200,000 and construction began in May of the following year. The route was engineered by Thomas Bouche, who had been responsible for the Stainmore line. The contract price of £267,000 was for 31¾ miles of single track, including 135 bridges. In 1863, by a further Act of Parliament, the L.N.W.R. and the S. and D. Railway were given powers to subscribe to the C.K. and P. and enter into traffic and working arrangements.

Also in 1863 the S. and D. was amalgamated with the North Eastern Railway and when, in 1865, the C.K. and P. was opened it was with the N.E.R. that it made contact at Penrith. On 23rd June 1864, the N.E.R. was authorised to build a mile long spur from Eamont Bridge Junction on the London and North Western route one mile south of Penrith to Redhills Junction on the C.K. and P. line, thus eliminating the need for mineral traffic to reverse at Penrith.

From slightly east of Threlkeld the line climbed at 1 in 62½ to its summit at 889ft. just east of Troutbeck, gaining almost 400ft. in 4 miles. At this point the line was only 26ft. lower than the summit of the L.N.W.R. at Shap. For the remaining 9½ miles to Penrith the line dropped to 650ft. at an average gradient of 1 in 70 and made a long horseshoe to pass through Blencow close to where it went through Andrew's Cutting, which was blasted through solid rock.

From the outset mineral traffic was intensive and constant; and summer passenger traffic steadily increased to such a degree that, in 1900, the sections from Threlkeld to Penruddock and from Blencow to Redhills Junction were doubled to accommodate it. Yet despite this improvement the average journey from Penrith to Cockermouth still took 1¼ hours. Moreover, the rolling stock was antiquated, uncomfortable and dirty.

The line's peak year in terms of numbers of passengers carried was 1913 when just over 482,000 people used it. Thereafter the numbers fell steadily. After World War II, largely due to the increase in car ownership, passenger traffic decreased to such a degree that by 1960 less than 20% of Keswick's visitors arrived by train.

The introduction of diesel multiple-units on 3rd January 1955, was greeted with an optimism that was to be short-lived, for by 1960 the line was losing an estimated £50,000 per annum. Through goods workings were withdrawn on 1st June 1964, and the section west of Keswick closed completely on 18th April 1966. Keswick hoteliers and tradesmen protested vociferously and the Minister of Transport decided not to close the Keswick to Penrith section, which reverted to single track. On 1st July 1968, all the remaining stations became unstaffed halts and remained so until the withdrawal of the diesel-unit service on 6th March 1972.

Soon after it is crossed by the A66 near Threlkeld the old line goes over the Greta for the last time just upstream of its confluence with St. John's Beck and follows the broad valley bottom toward Penrith. The scenery is excellent with the ground on the right climbing over Threlkeld Common to Clough Head. Grand exhilarating country to be sure. Yet it is the view over to the left, to the north, that the head keeps turning for there tower Blencathra and Souther Fell.

Part of the Skiddaw group of fells, Blencathra is composed of slate, the oldest rock in the district. Its name is Celtic, the origin of the first syllable being Blaen, meaning 'top' or 'hill'. Seen from the trackbed it appears to be isolated from its neighbours. It describes a three miles long arc with its south face eroded into four combes, divided by three ridges. Each ridge is given a distinctive name: Gategill Fell, the most westerly, then Hall's Fell and Doddick Fell, all of which face directly south towards the old line and Scales Fell, which faces east. North of Scales Fell is another ridge, Sharp Edge, the south side of which drops to Scales Tarn, lying cold and dark 800ft. below. Sharp Edge is to be avoided by nervous walkers for it is much steeper than either Striding Edge or Swirrel Edge and its ridge is much sharper. No one walks along the top of Sharp Edge but there is a path of sorts just below it. The views of Blencathra from the trackbed are very impressive indeed. Yet as good as they are they cannot compare with those enjoyed for more than a mile by anyone walking along the slight hollow between Foule Crags and the main summit, 2,847ft., which gives the mountain its other name, Saddleback.

226

Souther, pronounced Sow'ter Fell, next door to Saddleback, is a long, humped ridge on the very edge of Lakeland's mountain area. It is the first of the Northern fells to be reached from Penrith; and it is almost an island. The River Glenderamackin flows north along its western side to the hamlet of Mungrisdale where it curves and flows south along the full eastern edge of the fell to bend around its southern limit into the vale of Threlkeld. There a feeder flows from the north to meet it, leaving only a narrow col joining it to Saddleback.

You can walk all day on Souther Fell and never see a soul. Yet one incredible day in 1745, when there were fears of an invasion by Bonnie Prince Charlie's forces, several people saw a host of soldiers marching across its summit. Of course no one believed them, the more charitable calling it a mirage. The following Midsummer's Eve a party of at least twenty-six people gathered on Souther to see if this army would make another appearance although not one of them really expected anything unusual to happen. Yet, amazingly, it did. For hours on end a long column of foot soldiers, horsemen and coaches crossed the top of the fell and vanished at one end as quickly as more appeared at the other. At the end of the day twenty-six witnesses testified soberly to the validity of this strange encounter. Maybe, one day it will happen again; and perhaps you or I will be walking along the trackbed -watching. Wouldn't that be something?

Both Saddleback and Souther Fell are lovely to look at, especially from Mosedale viaduct. Mosedale viaduct, over Mosedale Beck, is 404ft. long, 100ft. high and has twelve 30ft. arches. There is a brick parapet on its northern side but the other side sports a simple open-working iron railing. I wonder why? Perhaps the method of construction was altered when the track was doubled. The beck it crosses is a little one, out of all proportion to the viaduct.

Troutbeck station, two miles east of Mosedale viaduct, is now a private residence, but it is easily skirted. Apart from the station building, the signal-box and a stone shed remain. A stone overbridge carrying the road to Ullswater offers a good view of the station's layout.

How exhilarating it is to walk through this most pleasant open country. The mountains are at our backs and to the south-east the twin cones of Great Mell Fell and Little Mell Fell dominate and add character to this delightful neighbourhood.

Between Troutbeck and Penruddock station all the underbridges and embankments have been removed at the road junctions but this tends to enhance rather than impair the walk.

Penruddock station is derelict and the nearby village it served is a rather uninteresting scatter of houses along the A66. But the surrounding countryside has many fine views to offer and the walk itself is a cracker.

36. THE BLENCOW HORSESHOE: (circular with extensions)

Length : 2½ miles: 1½ miles along the trackbed: 1 mile along country roads
Opened : Cockermouth to Penrith: all traffic - 2nd January, 1865
Closed : Workington to Penrith: for goods traffic - 1st June, 1964
Keswick to Penrith: for passenger traffic - 6th March, 1972
O/S : Sheet No.90; Series 1:50,000

> *When I am lying awake at night*
> *With weary limbs and aching brain*
> *Sometimes I hear the clanking wheels*
> *And whistle of a distant train.*
> *Vivian de Sola Pinto.*

This wonderful little circular could have been purpose built for the alleviation of the stresses of modern living. It lies close to the A66(T) yet far enough removed from it to avoid all traces of the traffic flowing to and from Keswick and other Lakeland honey pots. Blencow station, now a well cared for private dwelling is sited some three miles west of Penrith as the crow flies, deep in the rich Cumbrian countryside. It sits on the eastern side of a long horseshoe, part of which includes Andrew's Cutting which was blasted through solid rock.

On leaving Blencow the trackbed became increasingly overgrown but the encroaching saplings never impeded our progress, which was along a well worn track. In next to no time the ground on either side began to rise and we were in Andrew's Cutting. To our fore was what looked like the escape across Watership Down. There were rabbits everywhere, scurrying into the enveloping undergrowth as though their lives depended on it.

Now the trackbed cut a curving swath through a wonderous landscape dominated to the west by the distant fells of Bowscale, Souther and Saddleback.

Much closer, above a large rookery in a copse of tall, mature trees, rooks circled, twisted, soared and dived, drowning the morning stillness in hoarse cawing. Here we met a local out for a walk and fell into conversation.

Inevitably the conversation swung round to the C.K. and P. line, the remains of which we were walking, and our new found friend regaled us with reminiscences of distant days when he often watched the Lake's expresses haul their heavy carriages along the 9½ miles long climb from Penrith to where, just east of Troutbeck a summit was reached at 885ft., only 26ft. lower than Shap summit. The first four miles out of Penrith were the steepest, the gradient being 1 in 70.

All the passenger trains and the local goods trains were operated by the L.N.W.R. but the N.E.R. worked the mineral trains to and from County Durham to Workington.

The first locomotives used on the line were Ramsbottom DX 0-6-6s. Then in 1880, Webb 0-6-0 Cauliflowers were introduced and eventually became the line's principal means of locomotion. They remained in constant use on the line for over 70 years. During the line's lifetime other L.N.W.R. locomotives worked it, chiefly 2-4-2 and 0-6-2 tank engines. Later, when some of the line's iron bridges had been strengthened, Class 5 Jubilee and Royal Scot 4-6-0s were used on through services. Then, towards the last days of steam power, Class 2 2-6-0s were most frequently used.

For many years the N.E.R. mineral trains were pulled by Worsdell 0-6-0s.

On January 3rd 1955, steam gave way to diesel-units on the line and this, despite an initial surge of optimism, marked the beginning of the end for the C.K. and P. The introduction of the diesels led to the re-introduction of Sunday services and the re-opening of Blencow station which had been closed since 8th March 1950. But the euphoria was short-lived. The sight of steam locomotives struggling up the long haul westwards from Redhills Junction, pouring swift showers of sparks and clouds of smoke became progressively rarer. Their days were numbered.

By 1960 the line was losing an estimated £50,000 per annum, a situation which could not be allowed to continue. Through goods workings were withdrawn on 1st June 1964, and the section west of Keswick closed completely on 18th April 1966. Strong objections by Keswick tradesmen and hoteliers led to the Minister of Transport refusing to confirm the closure of the remainder of the line which continued in use as a single track branch along which all the stations were reduced to unstaffed halts. In this truncated form the line remained open until 6th March 1972, when the diesel-unit shuttle service was withdrawn. For a further few months, until 19th June 1972, mineral trains continued to operate from Penrith to Flusco quarry, west of Blencow.

We were not surprised to see, on emerging from the second and shallower of the two cuttings on the horseshoe, that the trackbed curve was so prounounced. Assiduous study of horseshoes had prepared us.

What did surprise us, however, was the height of the trackbed above the fields to our right: fields which fell and rolled away, past Greystoke village and Greystoke forest to the Lakeland fells.

As Ron and I stood by the side of the old line admiring the gently undulating countryside I though back to the days before the Cockermouth, Keswick and Penrith line was built. What, I pondered, would this lovely area have looked like in pre-C.K. and P. days and to what degree had the railway changed it?

Curiously, despite the stupendous scale of the building of the line, it slipped easily into the landscape, harmonising well with the spiders' web of tracks, drove roads and turnpike roads that laced the villages, hamlets and isolated farms to the west of Penrith. Its wayside stations - each with its neat station house, sidings and railway men's cottages - viaducts, bridges, embankments and cuttings consorted very well with the tidy pattern of fields, hedgerows and dry stone walls. In fact the landscape, not only west of Penrith but throughout 'Britain, was not ruined by the railways. Today's motorways have assaulted the landscape in a far more brutal and land hungry way than the railway ever did.

Few people cared that natural beauties or amenities were in danger of being destroyed by the builders of the line; and although many landowners used this argument to get more money from the Company, once this had been paid most were quite happy to continue living on their ravaged estates.

Radical changes swept the whole country during the 19th century and the railways were central to this change. Not only were the changes environmental: almost every aspect of people's lives was invaded. Cheap goods could now be conveyed throughout the country and this enabled local builders to replace local building materials with ubiquitous red brick. Factory workers used the trains to take them to the coastal resorts and so were sown the seeds of the tourist industry. People in rural areas, who had never before moved more than a few miles from their villages could now visit distant places which had been too remote for their parents to see. The railways brought the penny post and brought about the decline in the coaching business. The country shrank as distance ceased to be measured in miles and became defined in miles per hour.

An important consequence of this revolutionary mode of travel was the breaking of the time barrier. This came about when the railways imposed their own time on Britain. The means they used was called Railway Time and for the first time throughout the country people set their clocks in unison, using Greenwich mean time. Yet this conformity did not happen right away. The first railway timetable had to make allowances to conform to local opinion on the matter. A Great Western Railway timetable of 30th July 1841, states: 'London time is about four minutes earlier than Reading time, 7½ minutes before Cirencester, and 14 minutes before Bridgewater'. With Railway Time all these places and every other in Britain had the same time, G.M.T.

From where we stood one mile distant Greystoke could clearly be seen. It has a castle which stands impressively on the edge of a large, wooded park. The original castle was medieval but what can be seen today was built in the 19th century by the Howard family and is Elizabethan in style. Hardly any of its medieval origins remain. Its stone entrance overlooks the village green but you can't go in: it is privately owned and not open to the public.

On the other side of the village green stands a building that is most definitely open to the public. It stands in front of some attractive 17th century cottages with dates carved above their doors and cobbled forecourts. It is the Boot and Shoe Inn.

The village church, St. Andrew's was built at the same time as the original castle and a few traces of that period survive. The building was considerably altered in the 15th century. The medieval stained glass in the east window shows incidents in the life of St. Andrew.

On the east side of Greystoke there are three 18th century farmhouses. They were built by the 11th Duke of Norfolk to enhance the landscape and are follies. Fort Putnam and Bunkers Hill are shaped like forts and Spire House resembles a church.

The village is easily reached from the horseshoe either by a footpath-cum-bridlepath route or by pleasant roads.

Soon after leaving the second cutting an escarpment carries the trackbed to more level ground. And there, among cowslips, bluebells, lanky rosebay willow herb and tiny violets we met two friends of ours. Chatting like magpies, the four of us walked to where once a bridge had carried the line over a country road. The bridge had gone, long since, and the land to each side of where it had been gently sloped to eliminate landslip. This, for us, was the western end of Blencow horseshoe.

From now on the way was eastwards, uphill, along a straight and very quiet country road for three quarters of a mile to a T junction to the north of Newbiggin village, then left for a further quarter of a mile to Blencow station and the completion of a most pleasant circular.

From Blencow the line is walkable eastwards for almost two miles as far as the A66(T) and, on the west side of the horseshoe, from the country road where you leave the trackbed on the circular near Flusco quarry to Penruddock, but with the underbridges removed both ways. There is a stone viaduct of five, forty foot high arches at Penruddock, east of its derelict station, and this makes a good starting point for anyone doing the walk from the western extension. Both extensions are interesting to walk but it is the quality of the horseshoe itself that lifts it from the ordinary to the special.

It is all enjoyable, but the horseshoe circular holds the magic.

Near Warcop, Kirkby Stephen - Penrith Line

Bibliography

Banks, F.R.	The Peak District	Robert Hale	1975
Bellamy, R.	The Peak District Companion	David & Charles	1981
Bethell, D.	Portrait of Cheshire	Robert Hale	1979
Earnshaw, A.	The Peak District	Discovery Guides	1984
Earnshaw, A.	The Eden Valley	Discovery Guides	1984
Goddarth, F.	Foothills of the Fells	Robert Hale	1981
Jones, E.	The Penguin Guide to the Railways of Britain	Penguin Books	1981
Joy, D.	A Regional History of the Railways of Great Britain: Vol.14: The Lake District	David & Charles	1983
Holt, G.	A Regional History of the Railways of Great Britain: Vol.10: The North West	David & Charles	1978
Lefebure, M.	Cumbrian Discovery	Victor Gollancz	1977
Lofthouse, J.	Lancashire's Fair Face	Robert Hale	1952
Lofthouse, J.	Lancashire Villages	Robert Hale	1973
Mitchell, W.R.	Wild Cumbria	Robert Hale	1978
Perkin, H.	The Age of the Old Railway	David & Charles	1970
Rollinson, W.	Life and Tradition in The Lake District	J.M.Dent	1974
Tuplin, W.A.	Midland Steam	David & Charles	1973
B.R. Regrouping	Atlas and Gazetteer	Ian Allan Publications	1972

NOTES

NOTES

OTHER RAILWAY BOOKS
by CICERONE PRESS

WALKING NORTHERN RAILWAYS
Volume 1: East
Charlie Emett

In this companion volume to Vol. 2: West, the author describes 37 defunct lines from the Humber to Northumberland. Full of historical detail, practical advice and intriguing anecdotes.
ISBN 0 902363 76 X   160pp

SCOTTISH RAILWAY WALKS
M.H.Ellison

Thirty nine defunct lines from Galloway to the Highlands are described, with details of their history.

ISBN 1 85284 007 2   192pp

CICERONE PRESS publish a wide range of books for the outdoor enthusiast. Subjects include walking and climbing guides to many places in Britain and Europe; books on canoeing, birdwatching, ski-touring - and more general books on Cumbria

Available from bookshops and outdoor equipment shops or send for latest catalogue and price list to:
CICERONE PRESS, 2 Police Square, Milnthorpe, Cumbria.

Printed by Carnmor Print & Design,
95/97, London Road, Preston, Lancashire.